SOCIAL MOVEMENTS, 1768–2004

SOCIAL MOVEMENTS, 1768–2004

Charles Tilly

Paradigm Publishers
Boulder • London

Copyright © 2004 by Paradigm Publishers, LLC

Published in the United States by Paradigm Publishers, 3124 Noble Court, Boulder, Colorado 80301 USA.

Paradigm Publishers is the trade name of Birkenkamp & Company, LLC, Dean Birkenkamp, President and Publisher.

Library of Congress Cataloging-in-Publication Data

Tilly, Charles.
Social movements, 1768–2004 / Charles Tilly.
p. cm.
Includes bibliographical references and index.
ISBN 1-59451-042-3 (cloth : alk. paper) — ISBN 1-59451-043-1 (pbk. : alk. paper)
1. Social movements. I. Title.
HM881.T55 2004
303.48'4—dc22

2003025659

Printed and bound in the United States of America on acid-free paper that meets the standards of the American National Standard for Permanence of Paper for Printed Library Materials.

Designed and Typeset by Straight Creek Bookmakers.

09 08 07 06 05 04 03
5 4 3 2 1

To Lionel Grossbard MD, Joseph G. Sweeting MD, Michael H. Wechsler MD, and their collaborators at New York Presbyterian Hospital, who sustained my life as I wrote this book

CONTENTS

PREFACE

In June 2003, when the good people at New York Presbyterian Hospital began what an optimistic view projected as four or five months of chemotherapy and related treatments for lymphoma, they faced me with an interesting choice: mope as an invalid, or invent a special project that would lend coherence to a difficult interlude. With vivid inspiration from friends who have borne hardship resolutely, the second course looked more attractive. Having long thought that someone else should write the book you see before you, I started writing it to calm my nerves during my first chemotherapy session, with the fantasy of finishing it precisely as the last drop of chemicals entered my veins on the final day of treatment. Like most fantasies, this one did not quite work out. But it did discipline my efforts during months of chemo, and it did lead to the book's completion during what we all hope will be the treatment's final, successful phase.

Although I did not speak much of "contenders" before the 1970s, did not explicitly define my subject as "contention" until the 1980s, and did not start theorizing about "contentious politics" until the 1990s, for half a century a major stream of my work has concerned how, when, where, and why ordinary people make collective claims on public authorities, other holders of power, competitors, enemies, and objects of popular disapproval. For many years I generally avoided the term "social movement" because it sponged up so many different meanings and therefore obscured more than it clarified. Preparing detailed catalogs of contentious events for periods from the seventeenth to twentieth centuries in Western Europe and North America changed my mind. The catalogs made clear that major shifts in the array of means by which ordinary people made collective claims on others—their contentious repertoires— occurred in those regions between 1750 and 1850; that despite considerable differences in timing from regime to regime, in each regime the shifts clustered together; and that within the cluster emerged a distinctive combination of campaigns, performances, and displays. Participants and observers alike eventually began calling that new form of politics a "movement." Why not pin down that change?

Despite the current tendency to call everything from fads to established interest groups "movements," the emergence, transformation, and survival of that new, distinctive political form deserved historical attention. With some trembling about likely turf wars and definitional disputes, I decided to use the standard term "social movement" instead of inventing some substitute such as "full-fledged social movement" or "the type of social movement that first emerged in Western Europe and North America at the end of the eighteenth century." It certainly simplified the text.

Fortunately for friendship and future collaboration, in the book that most resembles this one with respect to argument and content, my friend and collaborator Sidney Tarrow explicitly disavows undertaking the social movement's history (Tarrow 1998: 3). This book therefore picks up where Tarrow's splendid survey of social movements leaves off. *Social Movements, 1768–2004* provides a historical survey of social movements from their eighteenth-century origins into the twenty-first century, ending with speculations about possible futures for social movements.

In order to avoid encumbering the text with references to my own previous publications, I have borrowed evidence freely from my earlier work, mostly without citing it. I have adapted a few passages from *Stories, Identities, and Political Change* (Rowman & Littlefield, 2002), *The Politics of Collective Violence* (Cambridge University Press, 2003), and *Contention and Democracy in Europe, 1650–2000* (Cambridge University Press, 2004), but at least 95 percent of the text is quite new.

For information, citations, criticism, and editorial advice, I am grateful to Lance Bennett, Vince Boudreau, Pamela Burke, Dana Fisher, Elisabeth Jay Friedman, William Ivey, Vina Lanzona, Daniel Menchik, Vicente Rafael, Sidney Tarrow, Cecelia Walsh-Russo, Lesley Wood, and Viviana Zelizer. I hope they will be pleasantly surprised by what they helped create.

1

SOCIAL MOVEMENTS AS POLITICS

"Building a strong pro-democracy social movement," editorialized Zimbabwe's *Harare Daily News* on 5 December 2002,

> is always the task of civil society when operating under an oppressive political environment. . . . A starting point would be to be able to define a social movement. As the name suggests, social movements are inclusive organisations comprised of various interest groups. Social movements will contain the significant strata of society such as workers, women's groups, students, youth and the intellectual component. These various interest sectors of society will be bound together by one common grievance which in most cases will be the commonly perceived lack of democracy in a specific political setting. This has been particularly the case within the last two decades of the South African antiapartheid struggle and more relevantly in the last four years in Zimbabwe. The only significant difference between the Zimbabwean situation and the antiapartheid social movement in South Africa is that the former tends to be less defined and less focused. In fact, in Zimbabwe people can sometimes be forgiven for thinking that the social movement has been split. (*Harare Daily News* 2002: 1)

Leaders of the opposition to Robert Mugabe's violent, vindictive regime in the Zimbabwe of 2002 deplored the splits that the regime's twinning of repression with co-optation had produced among their beleaguered country's suffering citizens. They looked to South Africa's earlier and more successful mass mobilization against apartheid as a model. They called for a larger, more effective social movement in opposition to tyranny and in favor of democracy. For the newspaper's presumption in giving the opposition voice, Mugabe's regime closed down the *Harare Daily News* in September 2003. On 17 September, regime forces arrested about one hundred people who dared to march through Harare protesting the newspaper's closing and calling for a new constitution (*Economist* 2003b: 46).

1

As the Zimbabwean opposition sought to solve a political problem by calling for a social movement, it had plenty of company elsewhere. In 1997, the Manchester-based socialist journal *International Viewpoint* called for a "European social movement" to back workers' rights as the European Commission moved toward cuts in social spending (*International Viewpoint* 1997). Through the following years, European activists—socialist and otherwise—continued to call for a genuine movement at a continental scale. A Europe-centered but worldwide network called Jubilee 2000 campaigned for eradication of Third World debt. According to one of its organizers:

> **A global social movement was built, united around this one issue.** By 2000, after just four years of campaigning, there were Jubilee 2000 campaigns, of varying strengths and character, in 68 countries. The national campaigns were autonomous but shared overall goals, symbols, and information—and a tremendous sense of solidarity. The campaigns were based in countries as diverse as Angola and Japan, Colombia and Sweden, Honduras and Israel, Togo and the United States. The ability to cooperate and coordinate our campaigning was greatly enhanced by use of the Internet. (Pettifor 2001: 62; emphasis in original)

By 2004, many Europeans were looking hopefully at mobilization against global capital as the movement that would redeem the dashed hopes of European workers and the troubles of Third World countries as well.

Latin America and Asia chimed in as well: In March 2002, the website of the Costa Rica–based antidiarrhea group Rehydration Project posted an article by Sabir Mustafa, associate editor of the Dhaka *Financial Express*. Mustafa titled his article "Diarrhoea Control Becomes a Social Movement in Bangladesh" (Mustafa 2002). The article reported that great numbers of Bangladeshi "schoolteachers, religious leaders, voluntary organizations, village doctors, rural groups and even local auxiliary police forces" are actively promoting antidisease measures (especially oral rehydration therapy) to save children's lives.

The hopeful appeal to social movements also rises across North America. In 1999, Canadian activist Murray Dobbin called for "building a social movement in Canada" to make sure that where the left-leaning New Democratic Party actually took office it did not abandon its constituency:

> The most basic understanding of state theory tells us that when a social democratic party wins "power" in an election it really does no such thing. Senior bureaucrats, virtually all of whom are now schooled in neo-liberal ideology, operate as a fifth column to sabotage progressive policies. As well, when transnational corporations threaten a capital strike, as they did in Ontario and carried out in BC [British Columbia], NDP governments don't have the "power" to stop them.
>
> That is where social movements come in. And if we can't get thousands of people into the streets (without having to spend hundreds of thousands of dol-

lars and do months of organizing) we can expect NDP governments to cave in to the very real power of corporations, exerted with breathtaking ferocity and on a daily basis. When it comes to social movements effectively confronting corporate power we have failed almost as badly as the NDP. (Dobbin 1999: 2)

By the turn of the twenty-first century, people all over the world recognized the term "social movement" as a trumpet call, as a counterweight to oppressive power, as a summons to popular action against a wide range of scourges.

It was not always so. Although popular risings of one kind or another have occurred across the world for thousands of years, what the *Harare Daily News* described as "inclusive organisations comprised of various interest groups" existed nowhere in the world three centuries ago. Then, during the later eighteenth century, people in Western Europe and North America began the fateful creation of a new political phenomenon. They began to create social movements. This book traces the history of that invented political form. It treats social movements as a distinctive form of contentious politics—contentious in the sense that social movements involve collective making of claims that, if realized, would conflict with someone else's interests, politics in the sense that governments of one sort or another figure somehow in the claim making, whether as claimants, objects of claims, allies of the objects, or monitors of the contention (McAdam, Tarrow, & Tilly 2001).

Social Movements, 1768–2004 shows that this particular version of contentious politics requires historical understanding. History helps because it explains why social movements incorporated some crucial features (for example, the disciplined street march) that separated the social movement from other sorts of politics. History also helps because it identifies significant *changes* in the operation of social movements (for example, the emergence of well-financed professional staffs and organizations specializing in the pursuit of social movement programs) and thus alerts us to the possibility of new changes in the future. History helps, finally, because it calls attention to the shifting political conditions that made social movements possible. If social movements begin to disappear, their disappearance will tell us that a major vehicle for ordinary people's participation in public politics is waning. The rise and fall of social movements mark the expansion and contraction of democratic opportunities.

As it developed in the West after 1750, the social movement emerged from an innovative, consequential synthesis of three elements:

1. a sustained, organized public effort making collective claims on target authorities (let us call it a *campaign*);
2. employment of combinations from among the following forms of political action: creation of special-purpose associations and coalitions, public meetings, solemn processions, vigils, rallies, demonstrations, petition drives, statements to and in public media, and pamphleteering (call the variable ensemble of performances the *social movement repertoire*); and

3. participants' concerted public representations of WUNC: worthiness, unity, numbers, and commitment on the part of themselves and/or their constituencies (call them *WUNC displays*).

Unlike a one-time petition, declaration, or mass meeting, a *campaign* extends beyond any single event—although social movements often include petitions, declarations, and mass meetings. A campaign always links at least three parties: a group of self-designated claimants, some object(s) of claims, and a public of some kind. The claims may target governmental officials, but the "authorities" in question can also include owners of property, religious functionaries, and others whose actions (or failures to act) significantly affect the welfare of many people. Not the solo actions of claimants, object(s), or public, but interactions among the three, constitute a social movement. Even if a few zealots commit themselves to the movement night and day, furthermore, the bulk of participants move back and forth between public claim making and other activities, including the day-to-day organizing that sustains a campaign.

The social movement *repertoire* overlaps with the repertoires of other political phenomena such as trade union activity and electoral campaigns. During the twentieth century, special-purpose associations and crosscutting coalitions in particular began to do an enormous variety of political work across the world. But the integration of most or all of these performances into sustained campaigns marks off social movements from other varieties of politics.

The term WUNC sounds odd, but it represents something quite familiar. WUNC displays can take the form of statements, slogans, or labels that imply worthiness, unity, numbers, and commitment: Citizens United for Justice, Signers of the Pledge, Supporters of the Constitution, and so on. Yet collective self-representations often act them out in idioms that local audiences will recognize, for example:

- *worthiness:* sober demeanor; neat clothing; presence of clergy, dignitaries, and mothers with children;
- *unity:* matching badges, headbands, banners, or costumes; marching in ranks; singing and chanting;
- *numbers:* headcounts, signatures on petitions, messages from constituents, filling streets;
- *commitment:* braving bad weather; visible participation by the old and handicapped; resistance to repression; ostentatious sacrifice, subscription, and/or benefaction.

Particular idioms vary enormously from one setting to another, but the general communication of WUNC connects those idioms.

Of course all three elements and their subdivisions had historical precedents. Well before 1750, to take an obvious case in point, Europe's Protestants had repeatedly mounted sustained public campaigns against Catholic authorities on behalf of the right to practice their heretical faith. Europeans engaged in two centuries of civil wars and rebellions in which Protestant/Catholic divisions figured centrally (te Brake 1998). As for the repertoires, versions of special-purpose associations, public meetings, marches, and the other forms of political action existed individually long before their combination within social movements. We will soon see how social movement pioneers adapted, extended, and connected these forms of action. Displays of WUNC had long occurred in religious martyrdom, civic sacrifice, and resistance to conquest; only their regularization and their integration with the standard repertoire marked off social movement displays from their predecessors. No single element, but the *combination* of repertoire and WUNC displays within campaigns, created the social movement's distinctiveness.

Some overlapping political phenomena also emerged in the time of social movements. As later chapters will show in detail, political campaigns with their parties and electoral contests interacted extensively with social movements at times yet developed their own bodies of rights, obligations, personnel, and practices. At various times in the nineteenth century, workers in capitalist countries generally acquired rights to organize, assemble, strike, and speak collectively, sometimes winning those rights by means of social movement campaigns, performances, and WUNC displays. Organized interest groups such as manufacturers and medical professionals similarly achieved special political rights to speak and act collectively, although rarely by social movement means. Mostly, groups that already commanded substantial resources, connections, and prestige acquired rights through direct negotiation with governments.

During the nineteenth and twentieth centuries, most states that had established churches conceded to new religious sects at least the rights to assemble and speak if not to enforce their doctrines or practices on members. Separatist communities—religious, political, or lifestyle—have sometimes emerged from social movements, although most regimes have either repressed or contained such communities energetically. Organizations participating in social movements, furthermore, sometimes moved into these other political spheres: conducting political campaigns, establishing labor unions, creating durable interest groups, becoming religious sects, or forming separatist communities. These overlaps should not keep us from recognizing that after 1750 a distinctive body of law and practice grew up around social movements as such.

Interpretations of Social Movements

In a book titled *History of the French Social Movement from 1789 to the Present* (1850), German sociologist Lorenz von Stein introduced the term "social movement" into scholarly discussions of popular political striving (von Stein 1959). At first it conveyed the idea of a continuous, unitary process by which the whole working class gained self-consciousness and power. When von Stein wrote, Marx and Engels's *Communist Manifesto* (1848) had recently adopted just such a meaning in its declaration that "All previous historical movements were movements of minorities, or in the interest of minorities. The proletarian movement is the self-conscious, independent movement of the immense majority, in the interests of the immense majority" (Marx & Engels 1958: I, 44).

Nevertheless, political analysts also spoke of social movements in the plural; in 1848, the German journal *Die Gegenwart* [The Present] declared that "social movements are in general nothing other than a first search for a valid historical outcome" (Wirtz 1981: 20). Most nineteenth-century analysts of social movements differentiated them by program, organization, and setting. Engels himself adopted the plural in his preface to the *Manifesto*'s English edition of 1888, remarking that "Wherever independent proletarian movements continued to show signs of life, they were ruthlessly hunted down" (Marx & Engels 1958: I, 26). From the later nineteenth century, political analysts not only regularly pluralized social movements but also extended them beyond organized proletarians to farmers, women, and a wide variety of other claimants (Heberle 1951: 2–11).

Names for political episodes gain weight when they carry widely recognized evaluations and when clear consequences follow from an episode's acquisition of—or failure to acquire—the name. To call an event a riot, a brawl, or a case of genocide stigmatizes its participants. To tag an event as a landslide election, a military victory, or a peace settlement generally polishes the reputations of its organizers. When either happens widely, critics or supporters of disputed actions regularly try to make the labels stick: to label an enemy's encounter with police a riot, to interpret a stalemate as a military victory, and so on. As our reports from Zimbabwe, the European Union, Bangladesh, and Canada suggest, the term "social movement" has acquired attractive overtones across the world. Consequently, participants, observers, and analysts who approve of an episode of popular collective action these days frequently call it a social movement, whether or not it involves the combination of campaign, repertoire, and WUNC displays.

In the cases of episodes of which parts clearly do meet the standards, furthermore, three confusions often arise.

1. Analysts and activists often extend the term "social movement" loosely to all relevant popular collective action, or at least all relevant popular collective action of which they approve. Feminists, for example, retroactively incorporate heroic women of the centuries before 1750 into the women's movement, while for environmental activists any popular initiative anywhere on behalf of the environment becomes part of the worldwide environmental movement.

2. Analysts often confuse a movement's collective action with the organizations and networks that support the action, or even consider the organizations and networks to *constitute* the movement, for example by identifying the environmental movement with the people, interpersonal networks, and advocacy organizations that favor environmental protection rather than the campaigns in which they engage.

3. Analysts often treat "the movement" as a single unitary actor, thus obscuring both a) the incessant jockeying and realignment that always go on within social movements and b) the interaction among activists, constituents, targets, authorities, allies, rivals, enemies, and audiences that makes up the changing texture of social movements.

Inflation of the term to include all sorts of popular collective action past and present, conflation of the movement with its supporting population, networks, or organizations, and treatment of movements as unitary actors do little harm in casual political discussion. In fact, within social movements they often aid recruitment, mobilization, and morale. But they badly handicap any effort to describe and explain how social movements actually work—especially when the point is to place social movements in history. That is the task at hand.

Let me make my own claims crystal clear. No one owns the term "social movement"; analysts, activists, and critics remain free to use the phrase as they want. But a distinctive way of pursuing public politics began to take shape in Western countries during the later eighteenth century, acquired widespread recognition in Western Europe and North America by the early nineteenth century, consolidated into a durable ensemble of elements by the middle of the same century, altered more slowly and incrementally after that point, spread widely through the Western world, and came to be called a social movement. That political complex combined three elements: 1) campaigns of collective claims on target authorities; 2) an array of claim-making performances including special-purpose associations, public meetings, media statements, and demonstrations; 3) public representations of the cause's worthiness, unity, numbers, and commitment. I am calling that historically specific complex a social movement. This book traces the history of that complex.

Despite incessant small-scale innovation and variation from one political setting to another, the social movement's elements evolved and diffused as a connected whole. In that sense, the social movement has a history. The social movement's history distinguishes it from the history of other political forms such as electoral campaigns, patriotic celebrations, displays of military force, investitures of public officials, and collective mourning. When this book refers to social movements, then, it does not mean all popular action, all the actions people ever take on behalf of a cause, all the people and organizations that back the same causes, or heroic actors that stand astride history. It means a particular, connected, evolving, historical set of political interactions and practices. It means the distinctive combination of campaign, repertoire, and WUNC displays.

By these exacting standards, do the Zimbabwean, European, Bangladeshi, and Canadian mobilizations with which we began qualify as social movements? Yes, mostly. In 2002 and 2003, Zimbabwe's opposition was using such procedures of social movement claim making as demonstrations, meetings, and press releases in the face of a regime that treated any such claims as subversive. The Bangladeshi rehydration campaign straddled the boundary between routine governmental public health measures and popular mobilization through associations, marches, and meetings. Confronted with an increasingly powerful European Union and the internationalization of capital, European workers were conducting difficult experiments in the extension of familiar national social movement routines to an international scale, as European organizers involved themselves energetically in coordinating worldwide campaigns concerning Third World debt, AIDS, and hundreds of other issues. By the turn of the twenty-first century, Canadian activists—including wary supporters of the New Democratic Party—could look back on almost two hundred years of associating, demonstrating, meeting, and making WUNC-style claims. Across important parts of the world, the social movement has become a familiar, generally reliable vehicle of popular politics (Buechler 2000, Edelman 2001, Ibarra & Tejerina 1998, Mamdani & Wamba-dia-Wamba 1996, Ray & Korteweg 1999, Tarrow 1998, Wignaraja 1993).

Partly because of the social movement's unquestioned contemporary prevalence, students of particular social movements have shown little interest in the locations of those movements within the larger history of the social movement as a form of politics. On the whole, analysts of social movements treat them as expressions of current attitudes, interests, or social conditions rather than as elements of longer-run histories. True, students of such nineteenth-century movements as antislavery, temperance, and suffrage have had to place them in their historical contexts and follow their historical developments (see, for example, d'Anjou 1996, Buechler 1990, Drescher 1986, 1994, Eltis 1993, Gusfield 1966, McCammon and Campbell 2002, Young 2002). Self-styled histories of regional, national, or international labor movements often reach back well before the nineteenth century's glory days for precedents and frequently sweep in a wider range of social movements than those focusing specifically on workers' welfare (see Bogolyubov, R'izhkova, Popov, & Dubinskii 1962, Dolléans & Crozier 1950, Kuczynski 1967a, 1967b, Zaleski 1956).

Broad surveys of protest, violence, and political conflict likewise regularly transect the zone of social movement activity (see Ackerman & DuVall 2000, Botz 1976, 1987, Brown 1975, Gilje 1987, 1996, Grimsted 1998, Lindenberger 1995, McKivigan & Harrold 1999, Mikkelsen 1986, Tilly, Tilly, & Tilly 1975, R. Tilly 1980, Walton & Seddon 1994, Williams 2003). Nearby, the reflecting mirrors of an abundant historical literature on policing, surveillance, and repression often capture social movements at unusual angles (see Balbus 1973, Broeker 1970, Bruneteaux 1993, Earl, Soule, & McCarthy 2003, Emsley 1983, Emsley & Weinberger 1991, Fillieule 1997b, Goldstein 1983, 2000, 2001, Gurr 2000, Huggins 1985, 1998, Husung 1983, Jessen 1994, Liang 1992, Lüdtke 1989, 1992, Monjardet 1996, Munger 1979, 1981, Palmer 1988, Storch 1976, Wilson 1969).

Some particular social movement performances—notably French and Irish marches and demonstrations—have attracted first-rate histories (Blackstock 2000, Farrell 2000, Favre 1990, Fillieule 1997a, Jarman 1997, Mirala 2000, Pigenet & Tartakowsky 2003, Robert 1996, Tartakowsky 1997, 1999). Broader social and political histories, furthermore, commonly pay attention to social movements as they trace their overall historical trends (e.g., Anderson & Anderson 1967, Cronin and Schneer 1982, González Calleja 1998, 1999, Hobsbawm 1975, 1988, 1994, Montgomery 1993). All these kinds of historical study will serve us well in later chapters. Even taken together, however, they do not provide a coherent history of the social movement as a political phenomenon parallel to, say, the histories of legislative elections, political parties, revolutions, or coups d'état.

For particular countries and periods, some general historical surveys of social movements as such do exist (see, for example, Ash 1972, Bright and Harding 1984, Burke 1988, Castells 1983, Clark 1959, Clark, Grayson, & Grayson 1975, Duyvendak, van der Heijden, Koopmans, & Wijmans 1992, Fredrickson 1997, Gamson 1990, Kaplan 1992, Klausen & Mikkelsen 1988, Kriesi, Koopmans, Duyvendak, & Giugni 1995, Lundqvist 1977, Nicolas 1985, Tarrow 1996, Wirtz 1981). In one of the sharpest available statements on the subject, John Markoff sets the explanatory problem deftly:

> Social movements as we know them today were beginning to flourish in England by the late eighteenth century and during the nineteenth century took root in Europe, North America, and elsewhere. To understand why, we need to consider many linked changes: a strengthened government but a weakened king; a people organizing themselves to assert claims on that government; a political elite prone to claim that it ruled in the name of the people; transportation improvements and commercial relations linking distant people; the beginnings of widespread literacy and new communication media leading people separated in space to feel themselves moving to a common rhythm. (Markoff 1996b: 45)

In general, however, such surveys subordinate the history to some other line of analysis, such as S. D. Clark's demonstration of divergence in the paths of Canadian and U.S. movements after the 1830s and William Gamson's investigation of whether American political opportunities narrowed during the twentieth century. Markoff himself subordinates his analysis of the formation and transformation of social movements to the spread of democracy. I draw on these surveys repeatedly, as well as on historical studies of particular movements. I give special attention to chronologies and catalogs such as Gamson's because they provide material for comparison and systematic evidence of change (Tilly 2002b). Still, the following historical analysis has required a good deal of interpolating, synthesizing, and borrowing from my own historical research.

Social movement history poses an acute version of a characteristic problem in political analysis. Social movements unquestionably have a distinctive, connected history. This book pursues just that history. The pursuit brings on two strong—and quite opposite—temptations. From one side beckons the seductive temptation to treat the social movement as a phenomenon sui generis, and to search for general laws of its operation. Similar temptations beset students of revolutions, strike waves, and election campaigns. The search for grand laws in human affairs comparable to the laws of Newtonian mechanics has, however, utterly failed.

Some such laws might conceivably exist (in the form, let us say, of evolutionary and/or genetic universals), but they surely do not operate at the levels of particular structures or processes such as churches, corporations, revolutions, or social movements. Anyone who wants to explain political structures and processes in the present state of knowledge does much better sorting out the more limited causal mechanisms that produce change, variation, and salient features of those structures and processes. The effort necessarily depends on turning away from "laws" of social movements toward causal analogies and connections between distinctive aspects of social movements and other varieties of politics (Goldstone 2003, Tilly 2001a, 2001b). Explanations of social movements and their history must mesh with explanations of other sorts of contentious politics.

That effort, however, calls up the opposite temptation: having noticed smaller-scale regularities in social movements, one may see social movements everywhere. Considered separately, campaigns, performances such as public meetings or petitions, and WUNC displays such as badge wearing and ostentatious sacrifice often occur outside of social movements: within churches, schools, corporations, intellectual communities, and elsewhere (Binder 2002, Davis, McAdam, Scott, & Zald 2004, Davis & Thompson 1994). Sometimes, by analogy, they even attract the label "movement." Take the so-called militia movement in the United States of the 1990s. Across the United States, hundreds of small, loosely connected groups wore military garb, conducted war games, distributed apocalyptic texts, declared their independence from U.S. jurisdiction including the obligation to pay taxes, and prepared for the Armageddon their leaders predicted for the year 2000. The Southern Poverty Law Center, which keeps tabs on such groups, counted 858 militias across the country at their peak in 1996, a number that shrank to 143 by 2003 (*Economist* 2003a: 22).

If such groups took up the full combination of campaigns, social movement performances, and WUNC displays, then they would enter the terrain of social movements properly speaking. If, on the other hand, some of them organized as the Militia Party, began running candidates in local or state elections, and started buying time on local television stations, they would have opted for yet another available form of public politics: the electoral campaign. In the absence of such unlikely shifts in strategy, instead of declaring that the activities of militias "really are" social movements, it forwards the work of explanation more effectively to recognize them as constituting another form of contentious politics. That recognition allows us to study their similarities to social movements but also to see what distinctive explanatory problems they pose.

The respectable worlds of science and medicine similarly generate analogies to social movements from time to time, but mostly without forming full-fledged social movements. Take just one example: recent disputes over water in the Klamath River Basin, near the California-Oregon border. The headwaters of the Klamath, including the desert-surrounded Upper Klamath Lake, supply irrigation for many dry-earth farmers in the uplands. But they also drain into the lowland region where salmon breed and where the Klamath Tribes insist on treaty rights to fishing established by an 1864 settlement with the United States. In 2002, a report of the National Academy of Sciences concluded that there was "no sound scientific basis" for terminating irrigation flows in favor of sending more water to downstream fisheries. The scientists' statement satisfied neither side, including the biologists lined up with one group of water users or the other. "The report's conclusion," remarked *Science* magazine's reporter from Klamath Falls, Oregon,

> sparked an outcry in this small farming community that federal agencies are supporting "junk science," and it bolstered calls for reforming or scrapping the Endangered Species Act (ESA). But over the past year, it has also sparked another, more muted outcry, this one among fisheries biologists. They contend that the report's analyses were simplistic, its conclusions overdrawn, and—perhaps worst of all—that the report has undermined the credibility of much of the science being done in the region if not fueled an outright antiscience sentiment. (Service 2003: 36)

Opposing groups of advocates are clearly conducting campaigns and occasionally employing such performances as press conferences to publicize their claims. If the farmers, the biologists, or members of the Klamath Tribes started to combine public campaigns, social movement performances, and WUNC displays in sustained claims on federal authorities or the National Academy of Sciences, they would move their struggles onto the terrain of full-fledged social movements. They, too, could conceivably take up the public politics of electoral campaigns—or, for that matter, move in the direction of regularly constituted interest groups by creating lobbyists, Washington offices, and newsletters broadcasting their causes. In the meantime, however, we will understand their actions better if we recognize analogies and differences without simply treating the Klamath Basin controversy as one more variety of social movement. The same goes for analogous struggles within corporations, churches, schools, intellectual disciplines, art worlds, and neighborhoods (Davis, McAdam, Scott, & Zald 2004). In exactly that sense, the historical project of tracing the social movement's distinctive politics forms part of the larger program of explaining contentious politics at large.

Toward Historical Explanations

This project, therefore, has four interdependent aspects. First, we must trace the origins and transformations of the social movement's major elements: campaigns, repertoires, and WUNC displays. How, for example, did the now-familiar street demonstration take shape and even acquire an uneasy legal standing in most democratic countries? Second, we must uncover the social processes that encourage or inhibit proliferation of social movements. Given the significant but still incomplete correspondence of democratization and social movements, for instance, what causal connections explain that correspondence? Third, we must examine how the elements of social movements interacted with other forms of politics. To what extent and how, for example, did industrial strikes, electoral campaigns, and social movements intersect and influence each other? Finally, we must show what causes important aspects of change and variation in social movements. Does the emergence of professional political brokers, for instance, help explain the formation of a specialized, connected sector of social movement organizations in leading capitalist democracies (Ibarra 2003, Meyer & Tarrow 1998)? Close historical analysis helps answer all four sorts of questions.

Following that line of inquiry, here are the book's main arguments.

From their eighteenth-century origins onward, social movements have proceeded not as solo performances, but as interactive campaigns. Like electoral campaigns, popular rebellions, and religious mobilizations, they consist of interactions between temporarily connected (and often shifting) groups of claimants and the objects of their claims, with third parties such as constituents, allies, rival claimants, enemies, authorities, and various publics often playing significant parts in the campaigns' unfolding. We will never explain social movements' variation and change without paying close attention to political actors other than the central claimants, for example the police with whom demonstrators struggled, collaborated, and codeveloped their strategies.

Social movements combine three kinds of claims: program, identity, and standing. Program claims involve stated support for or opposition to actual or proposed actions by the objects of movement claims. Identity claims consist of assertions that "we"—the claimants—constitute a unified force to be reckoned with. WUNC (worthiness, unity, numbers, and commitment) performances back up identity claims. Standing claims assert ties and similarities to other political actors, for example excluded minorities, properly constituted citizens' groups, or loyal supporters of the regime. They sometimes concern the standing of *other* political actors, for example in calls for expulsion of immigrants or their exclusion from citizenship. Program, identity, and standing claims conform to partly separate codes built up from a regime's particular political history; Zimbabweans and Canadians do not—and cannot—signal collective worthiness in exactly the same way.

The relative salience of program, identity, and standing claims varies significantly among social movements, among claimants within movements, and among phases of movements. A good deal of negotiation within social movements, indeed, centers on the relative prominence the different claims will receive: do we, for example, present ourselves as a durable alliance of rights-deprived people who are currently lining up against this governmental program (but tomorrow might line up in support of another), or as a diverse cross section of the general population whose main connection consists of the harm that all of us will receive from this particular program and who therefore may never again join in making claims?

Democratization promotes the formation of social movements. By democratization, let us mean development of regimes featuring relatively broad and equal citizenship, binding consultation of citizens with respect to governmental policy, personnel, and resources, and at least some protection of citizens from arbitrary actions by governmental agents (Tilly 2004). Democratization actually limits the range of feasible and effective popular collective action. Democratic institutions, for example, generally inhibit violent popular rebellions (Tilly 2003: chap. 3). But empowerment of citizens through contested elections and other forms of consultation combines with protections of civil liberties such as association and assembly to channel popular claim making into social-movement forms.

Social movements assert popular sovereignty. Although particular movements differ fiercely over who counts as "the people," the whole apparatus of campaign, repertoire, and WUNC displays embodies the more general claim that public affairs depend, and should depend, on the consent of the governed. The claim is not necessarily democratic, since ethnic, religious, and nationalist movements sometimes invest their powers in charismatic leaders rather than democratic deliberation yet still insist that those leaders embody the will of the people at large. Such movements, furthermore, often reject whole categories of the local population as unworthy of belonging to "the people." But the stress on popular consent fundamentally challenges divine right to kingship, traditional inheritance of rule, warlord control, and aristocratic predominance. Even in systems of representative government, as we will soon see, social movements pose a crucial question: do sovereignty and its accumulated wisdom lie in the legislature or in the people it claims to represent?

As compared with locally grounded forms of popular politics, social movements depend heavily on political entrepreneurs for their scale, durability, and effectiveness. The local routines of retaliation, rebellion, and resistance that prevailed across most of the world before the era of social movements drew on widely available local knowledge and existing interpersonal networks. The social movement combination of campaigns, WUNC displays, and coordinated performances, in contrast, always results at least in part from prior planning, coalition building, and muting of local differences. As we will soon see, smart political entrepreneurs figured in campaigns, social movement performances, and WUNC displays from the very birth of social movements. During the twentieth and twenty-first centuries, however, professional political organizers, brokers, and partly autonomous nongovernmental organizations took on increasingly prominent parts in promotion of social movements—to the dismay of populist critics. Ironically, a good deal of twentieth- and twenty-first-century social movement work therefore went into disguising the entrepreneurial effort in favor of images portraying the spontaneous emergence of WUNC.

Once social movements establish themselves in one political setting, modeling, communication, and collaboration facilitate their adoption in other connected settings. Transfers often occur within the same regime from the initial foci of social movements—more often than not claims on national governments—to other objects of demand or support such as local leaders, landlords, capitalists, or religious figures. Social movement strategies also transfer *among* regimes as political organizers, exiles, and members of international religious groups collaborate across national boundaries and as rulers of authoritarian regimes (especially those that claim to rule on behalf of a coherent, united people) find themselves under pressure from other countries to concede something to their critics. Colonies of countries that already have established social movements provide inviting environments for infusion of social movement activity.

The forms, personnel, and claims of social movements vary and evolve historically. Three distinguishable but interacting sources of change and variation in social movements produce variation in time and space. First, overall political environments (including democratization and dedemocratization) alter in partial independence of social movement activity and affect its character. Second, within the interactions that occur in the course of social movements (for example, interactions between demonstrators and police), change occurs incrementally as a consequence of constant innovation, negotiation, and conflict. Third, participants in social movements—including not only activists but also authorities and other objects of claims—communicate with each other, borrowing and adapting each other's ideas, personnel, assistance, rhetorics, and models of action. They also borrow, adapt, and innovate as they compete with each other for advantages or constituencies. Sometimes the borrowing and adaptation take place over great distances and between quite disparate social movements (Chabot 2000, Chabot & Duyvendak 2002, Scalmer 2002b). Changes in political environments, incremental changes within the social movement sphere, and transfers among movements interact to produce substantial change and variation in the character of social movements.

The social movement, as an invented institution, could disappear or mutate into some quite different form of politics. Just as many forms of popular justice and rebellion that once prevailed have quite vanished, we have no guarantee that the social movement as it has prevailed for two centuries will continue forever. Since the social movement spread with the growth of centralized, relatively democratic states, for example, either governmental decentralization, extensive privatization of governmental activities, eclipse of the state by transnational powers, or widespread dedemocratization could all put the social movement as we know it out of business. Indeed, with the set of changes that people loosely call "globalization" occurring, citizens who count on social movements to make their voices heard must look very hard at the future.

This book follows these arguments through a straightforward historical analysis. Chapter 2 looks at the eighteenth-century invention of the social movement, concentrating on North America and England but looking briefly at other parts of Western Europe as well. Chapter 3 surveys the nineteenth century, during which extensive national and international movements grew up in the West and some also formed in European colonies. Chapter 4 moves up to the twentieth century, a time of worldwide proliferation in social movement activity. Chapter 5 follows up with the twenty-first century, focusing on the expansion of international communication and coordination among social movement activists.

At that point, the book's broadly chronological analysis ends in favor of pressing questions raised by the history. Chapter 6 analyzes what the previous chapters tell us about mutual influences of democratization and social movements: when, how, and why democratization promotes social movements, but also under what conditions and how social movements advance democratization or dedemocratization. Finally, chapter 7 draws together conclusions in the form of possible futures for the social movement. Between here and there we will see that social movements have a dramatic history all their own, one that today's participants in social movements almost never recognize and will gain handsomely from recognizing.

2

INVENTIONS OF THE SOCIAL MOVEMENT

Imagine an eighteenth-century voyage investigating variations in contention. You sail from London to Boston to Charleston during the turbulent year of 1768. Instead of a tourist guide—the great guide-making pioneer Karl Baedeker, after all, was not born until 1801!—you carry an atlas of contentious gatherings (CGs). In a contentious gathering, a number of people (let us say ten or more) gather in a publicly accessible place and collectively make claims on others outside their number, claims that if realized would affect those others' interests (Tilly 1995: chap. 2 and appendix). The claims can run from physical attacks to pleas for mercy to expressions of political support.

As of the 1760s, most CGs in London, Boston, and Charleston do not resemble the marches, meetings, and delegations of social movements. Much more often, they involve direct applications of force or threat to parties who have offended group standards or interests. Yet the 1760s also bring important signs of change in popular contention. An inventory of CGs for London during April 1768 includes these events:

2 April: Near suburban Brentford, a crowd stops a passing carriage and forces the occupants to shout "Wilkes and Liberty!" on behalf of parliamentary candidate John Wilkes.
14 April: In the house of a master weaver behind the Shoreditch church, journeymen weavers cut cloth from six looms.
14 April: At the houses and shops of journeymen weavers in Spitalfields, other journeymen cut cloth from another six looms belonging to blacklisted masters.
15 April: During a battle between striking and nonstriking coal heavers in Wapping, participants sack nearby houses.
15 April: On the Brentford road, Wilkes's supporters stop a carriage and demand declarations on behalf of Wilkes and liberty.
16 April: Coal heavers of Shadwell attack a coal merchant whose servant tore down their strike handbill.

18 April: At Sutton Common, part of the audience at an execution seizes the corpses of the victims and buries them, shouting against the surgeons whom they accuse (plausibly) of planning to carry off the bodies for dissection.

20 April: In the Roundabout Tavern of Shadwell, coal heavers attack a publican–coal merchant who also serves as a hiring agent.

21 April: In Goodman's Fields, brothel workers attack a man who is trying to retrieve his daughter from prostitution, whereupon a crowd sacks the house of ill repute.

21 April: Spitalfields journeymen weavers cut cloth from looms.

26 April: Coal heavers board coal boats in Wapping and rough up their captains.

27 April: Supporters of Wilkes accompany him up the Strand and across Westminster Bridge on his way to prison, then free him from his captors, but Wilkes escapes and commits himself to prison.

28 April: Around the King's Bench Prison (Southwark) where Wilkes has incarcerated himself, Wilkes's supporters call for lighting up of houses as well as ritually burning a boot and a bonnet.

The vivid chronology identifies abundant, colorful contention in the London of April 1768.

Three main conflicts dominate the month's CGs. First, coal handlers in Shadwell and Wapping (near London's major port) are backing their demands for higher piece rates by blocking the sale and shipment of coal. Second, silk weavers of London's East End (especially Spitalfields) are putting pressure on wage-cutting masters and the journeymen who persist in producing for them at the lower wage by cutting cloth from the incriminated parties' working looms. Third, a political hurricane roars around the controversial figure of John Wilkes. In the first two conflicts, we see routines of pressure and vengeance that English workers have been employing for centuries. But in the third we witness an innovation that foreshadows the social movement repertoire: conversion of a parliamentary election campaign into an occasion for display of popular solidarity and determination. In a time of narrow voting rights, disciplined mass participation of nonvoters breaks with customary electoral decorum.

Wilkes was an agitator, but certainly no plebeian. Using his own money and his position as a member of the lesser gentry, he had entered Parliament in 1757. While in Parliament, he started to edit an opposition newspaper, *The North Briton,* in 1762. Wilkes named his polemical paper in response to *The Briton,* a pro-administration paper that Scots-born novelist and pamphleteer Tobias Smollett had started earlier the same year, in part to defend the regime against Wilkes's attacks. Wilkes's title referred slightingly to Scots in the royal administration, especially the king's favorite, Lord Bute. (The boot and Scots bonnet burned on 28 April 1768 punned on the name and Scottish origins of minister Bute.)

The North Briton's issue number 45 (1763) criticized a royal speech, written by the minister, in which the king praised the Treaty of Paris that had just ended the Seven Years War:

The *Minister's speech* of last Tuesday is not to be paralleled in the annals of this country. I am in doubt whether the imposition is greater on the Sovereign, or on the nation. Every friend of this country must lament that a prince of so many great and admirable qualities, whom England truly reveres, can be brought to give the sanction of his sacred name to the most odious measures and the most unjustifiable public declarations from a throne ever renowned for truth, honour, and unsullied virtue. (Rudé 1962: 22)

For this statement, the crown's attorneys charged Wilkes with seditious libel. In the legal environment of the time, not even a Member of Parliament could publicly imply that the king had lied. For that offense, Wilkes spent time in the Tower of London. In his subsequent court appearances, Wilkes challenged the general warrant on which the king's officers had arrested him and seized his papers. He also explicitly identified his personal wrong with a general cause. In the Court of Common Pleas (May 1763), Wilkes declared that:

The LIBERTY of all peers and gentlemen, and, what touches me more sensibly, of all the middling and inferior class of the people, which stands most in need of protection, is in my case this day to be finally decided upon: a question of such importance as to determine at once, whether ENGLISH LIBERTY be a reality or a shadow. (Brewer 1976: 168)

He eventually won his case, receiving compensation from the government for his illegal arrest and for seizure of his papers. He also appealed to freedom of speech, which won him cheers in the courtroom and the streets. His courtroom speeches launched the cry "Wilkes and Liberty!" as a fateful slogan for resistance to arbitrary power.

Wilkes's victory did not convert him to smug conformity. Later in 1763, he not only reprinted issue number 45 but also produced a pornographic pamphlet called *Essay on Woman*. When government agents seized the proofs, began new proceedings against Wilkes, and assigned the London sheriff and the hangman to burn no. 45 publicly in Cheapside, an assembled crowd assaulted the sheriff and hangman, rescuing the sacred text from their hands. Wilkes himself soon fled across the Channel into France to escape prosecution. Parliament expelled him, and the courts declared him an outlaw.

In 1768, however, Wilkes secretly returned to England, stood again for Parliament, won the poll, entered jail to be tried for his earlier offenses, and saw Parliament refuse to seat him. The Wilkite events of April 1768 inventoried earlier sprang from Wilkes's parliamentary campaign. During 1769, Parliament formally expelled Wilkes again, then rejected three elections that he won from his prison cell. While Wilkes served his term as a popular hero, he received ample press attention, distinguished visitors, and gifts from all over the country; supporters in the town of Stockton, for example, sent him forty-five hams, forty-five tongues, and forty-five dozen bottles of ale (Brewer 1976: 177). By that time, the number forty-five was becoming a popular icon not only for Wilkes but also for liberty in general.

Wilkes went on to a distinguished career as public official and dissenting voice. In 1769, he managed election as a London alderman while still serving his prison term. He only went free (to great popular acclaim, fireworks, illuminations, and salvos of forty-five artillery shells) in 1770. He became London's sheriff in 1771 and soon began campaigning for the supreme municipal post of Lord Mayor. He actually won the City of London poll for the office in 1772, but the aldermen chose his less-tainted competitor, James Townsend. At that point, three thousand people entered the yard of Guildhall (the Lord Mayor's residence), shouting "Damn my Lord Mayor for a scoundrel, he has got Wilkes's right, and we will have him out" (Rudé 1971: 125).

After one more failed attempt, Wilkes gained election as Lord Mayor in 1774 and finally reentered the House of Commons that same year. He became a major speaker for the American cause during the bitter years of the Revolutionary War. Despite his time in prison, his court cases definitively established the legal rights of British periodicals to report and criticize governmental actions, including those of the Crown. He not only commanded widespread popular support (including bands of activists from among the Spitalfields silk weavers) but also found allies among London merchants and officials who sought a counterweight to arbitrary royal power. An elite association that began as Friends of Mr. Wilkes and the Constitution soon became the Society of Supporters of the Bill of Rights, an important force for parliamentary reform. Although no one then used the term social movement, the association laid some of the foundations for the social movement as a new form of public politics in Great Britain.

In the very process of supporting Wilkes for Parliament, Wilkes's plebeian backers innovated. Almost no workers could vote in parliamentary elections of the 1760s, but workers came out in droves to accompany Wilkes to the polls. After Wilkes won the first round at Brentford on 28 March 1768, his followers began the attacks on opponents and the demands for cheers that continued through the election. The conservative *Annual Register* (founded by Edmund Burke in 1758, and still going strong in the twenty-first century) tut-tutted:

> The mob behaved in a very outrageous manner at Hyde-park-corner, where they pelted Mr. Cooke, son of the city marshal, and knocked him from his horse, took off the wheels of one of the carriages, cut the harness, and broke the glasses to pieces; several other carriages were greatly damaged. The reason assigned for their proceedings is, that a flag was carried before the procession of Mr. Wilkes' antagonists, on which was painted, "No Blasphemer." (*Annual Register* 1768: 86)

Over the long run, Wilkites pushed out the boundaries of previously permissible public assemblies. They not only expanded electoral processions and public meetings into mass declarations of support for their hero but also converted delegations and petition marches into opportunities to fill the streets instead of simply sending a few dignified representatives to speak humbly on behalf of their constituents. They pioneered the synthesis of crowd action with formal appeals to supporters and authorities. Although Wilkites remained stronger on unity, numbers, and commitment than on public displays of worthiness, they helped fashion the connection between the social movement repertoire and displays of WUNC.

Long before the 1760s, ordinary English and American people had made public claims of one kind or another. Authorized public assemblies such as holidays, funerals, and parish assemblies had, for example, long provided opportunities for people to voice complaints and to express support for popular leaders. Within limits, organized artisans and militia companies exercised the right to parade on their own holidays, and they sometimes used that right to state their opposition to powerful figures or oppressive programs. With proper shows of respect, they could also send humble delegations to petition for redress of collective wrongs. Within their own communities, workers, consumers, and householders repeatedly mounted resistance or vengeance against offenders of local rights or morality (Tilly 1983). The custom of Rough Music, for instance, involved an assembly outside the house of a moral offender, such as a widower who proposed to marry a young woman; a racket made by the striking of pots and pans, calling of insults, and/or singing of obscene songs; reparations, such as payment for the avengers to go off for drinks; and dispersal of the crowd (Thompson 1972, 1991). Retaliatory rituals of this sort varied dramatically in detail from place to place. They had nothing like the transferability across settings—the modularity—of later social movement performances such as the demonstration and the formation of special-purpose associations.

Seen from the authorities' perspective, the implicit British theory of popular public politics during the earlier eighteenth century ran something like this.

- British subjects group into legally recognized bodies, such as guilds, communities, and religious sects, which exercise some specifiable collective rights, for example the right to meet regularly in designated places of assembly.
- The law protects such collective rights.
- Local authorities have an obligation to enforce and respect the law.
- Chosen representatives of such recognized bodies have the right—indeed, the obligation—to make public presentations of collective demands and grievances.
- Authorities have an obligation to consider those demands and grievances, and to act on them when they are just.
- Outside this framework, no one who has not been convoked by established authorities has a clear right to assemble, to state demands or grievances, or to act collectively.
- Anyone who presumes to speak for the people at large outside these limits infringes illegally on the prerogatives of Parliament; in fact, even electors have no right to instruct their parliamentary representatives once they have gained election.

Local and national authorities often looked the other way when local people violated these principles by activating customary routines of vengeance, approbation, and control. But authorities commonly invoked the principles—as represented, for example, in the Riot Act—when popular action threatened ruling class property, targeted influential members of the ruling classes, or banded together across local boundaries. During major episodes of rebellion and civil war like those that beset the British Isles between 1640 and 1692, to be sure, ordinary people frequently voiced radical claims in the names of religion and political tradition. They even violated the final principle in the list above by staging deliberative assemblies without governmental authorization or even in straightforward competition with Parliament (see, e.g., Mendle 2001). But before the later eighteenth century, postrebellion repression always shut down those dangerous forms of popular expression.

On both sides of the Atlantic, members of the ruling classes had less risky ways of making claims. Authorities tolerated their clubs, dinners, pamphlets, and sometimes boisterous legislative assemblies. Elections to assemblies, especially to Parliament, provided splendid opportunities for license, as candidates treated electors, paid them off, and made extravagant public shows of their patronage. (Despite a highly restricted franchise, Wilkes's 1757 election to Parliament cost him 7 thousand pounds, at a time when a farm laborer in London's hinterland was lucky to earn 30 pounds in a year [Armstrong 1989: 693–98, Rudé 1962: 19].) Social movements innovated not by inventing any one of these elements but by converting, expanding, standardizing, and combining them into disciplined vehicles for expression of popular demands. Equally important, social movement efforts created a contested but genuine legal space within which their combination of campaigns, claim-making performances, and WUNC displays acquired political standing.

War and the Elements of Social Movements

The Seven Years War (1756–1763) gave this sort of political innovation a major impetus. For half a century before the 1750s, France and Great Britain had fought each other intermittently in Europe, on the high seas, in Asia, and across the Americas. France, which had earlier conquered Louisiana and what eventually became eastern Canada, found itself under attack in North America from both British colonists and British armies. Since colonists and armies alike were pushing back Amerindian settlements, the French recruited ready allies within the major Indian federations. For residents of North American colonies, the Seven Years War therefore became the French and Indian War.

Although the British side won dramatically—seizing Canada from the French, for example—momentous military efforts in Europe, India, and the Americas left the British treasury depleted and the government heavily in debt. In the North American colonies, British authorities tried to recoup some of their financial losses and to spread the cost of their greatly expanded military establishment. They tightened customs surveillance and imposed expensive duty stamps on a wide range of commercial and legal transactions. Resistance against customs and the Stamp Act united colonists as never before. It stimulated boycotts of British imports and the formation of extensive communication among cities of the thirteen colonies as well as some of their Canadian counterparts. Chapters of the Sons of Liberty organized and enforced boycotts throughout the colonies. The Stamp Act's repeal (1766) only came after merchants, artisans, and other city-dwellers had created an elaborate resistance network.

Boston and Massachusetts led the early effort, but other colonies soon joined them. Boston merchants had formed a Society for the Encouragement of Trade during the early 1760s; that society became a nucleus of dignified opposition to excessive taxation and regulation. It coordinated elite resistance to the Stamp Act, for example, in 1765 and 1766. At the same time, a group of smaller businessmen with substantial ties to workers began speaking out as Boston's Sons of Liberty, thus linking the mercantile community with the street activists who burned effigies, sacked houses, and assailed tax collectors. Radical members of the mercantile elite, such as Samuel Adams, served as brokers between the two groups.

In December 1766, Adams wrote to Christopher Gadsden, leader of the Charleston, South Carolina, Sons of Liberty, proposing regular communication among patriotic merchants from all the colonies (Alexander 2002: 45). In response to the 1767 Townshend Acts, which imposed a wide range of levies on the colonies, Adams drafted a circular letter of protest in hopes of collecting endorsements from Massachusetts and the other colonies. Late that year, a meeting of Boston inhabitants organized by the expanding web of patriotic associations resolved to encourage American manufacturing and reduce reliance on British imports. In January 1768, the Massachusetts legislature itself submitted a humble petition to the king stating provincial objections to taxation in muted, respectful terms. After initial rejection, in February the same legislature endorsed a strong version of the Adams-initiated circular letter to the other colonies. By this time Massachusetts patriots were insisting that Parliament had no right to pass bills solely for the purpose of raising revenue from the colonies.

"These resolutions," reported the *Annual Register,* distancing itself prudently from the American claims,

> were adopted, or similar ones entered into, by all the old Colonies on the continent. In some time after, a circular letter was sent by the Assembly of Massachuset's Bay, signed by the Speaker, to all the other Assemblies in North America. The design of this letter was to shew the evil tendency of the late Acts of Parliament, to represent them as unconstitutional, and to propose a common union between the Colonies, in the pursuit of all legal measures to prevent their effect, and a harmony in their applications to Government for a repeal of them. It also expatiated largely on their natural rights as men, and their constitutional

ones as English subjects; all of which, it was pretended, were infringed by these laws. (*Annual Register* 1768: 68)

Despite an explicit demand from King George, the Massachusetts legislature voted 92 to 17 not to rescind its assent to the circular letter. To rescind would, the majority declared, "have left us but a vain Semblance of Liberty" (Alexander 2002: 55).

While leading merchants pursued their program by means of deliberate legal action, Boston sailors and artisans frequently took the law into their own hands. They forcefully resisted press gangs, blocked the quartering of soldiers, attacked customs agents, and hung effigies of British officials or their collaborators on the so-called Liberty Tree near the common that had been a flashpoint of action during the Stamp Act crisis of 1765–1766. They often doubled mercantile and official resistance with direct action.

When negotiations with the governor (representative of the Crown in Massachusetts) and with the British government grew rancorous, for example, the populace of Boston joined in. In May 1768, British customs officers seized Boston merchant (and smuggler) John Hancock's ship *Liberty* for its failure to pay duties, whereupon Bostonians manned another ship, cut loose the sequestered vessel, and took it away.

> The populace having assembled in great crowds upon this occasion, they pelted the Commissioners of the Customs with stones, broke one of their swords, and treated them in every respect with the greatest outrage; after which, they attacked their houses, broke the windows, and hauled the Collector's boat to the common, where they burnt it to ashes. (*Annual Register* 1768: 71; for details, see Hoerder 1977: 166–68)

The customs officers fled first to a royal warship and then to Castle William in Boston Harbor. Town meetings of protest convened without official authorization throughout the Boston area. When word reached Boston (12 September) that two regiments were coming from Ireland and another body of military was assembling in Halifax (Nova Scotia) to restore order in Boston, members of the Massachusetts Bay assembly began organizing resistance committees throughout the colony.

Massachusetts patriots quickly gathered allies throughout the other colonies. Mostly the allies began by using the established forms of elite public politics: resolutions, petitions, and solemn meetings. Innovative forms of contentious gatherings elsewhere in America, furthermore, regularly adapted the forms of previously tolerated assemblies. Consider this account of the king's birthday celebration of Charleston (Charles Town), South Carolina, in June 1768.

> The same was celebrated here, with every demonstration of joy, affection and gratitude, that the most loyal subjects could give. The morning was ushered in

with ringing of bells: At sun-rise, the forts and shipping displayed all their colours. Before noon, the detachment of his Majesty's troops posted here, under the command of Capt. Lewis Valentine Fyser; the Artillery company in a new and very genteel uniform, commanded by Capt. Owen Roberts; the Light-Infantry company, in their uniform; and the other companies of the Charles Town regiment of Militia, commanded by the honourable Colonel Bexie, were drawn up in different places, and marched to the Parade, where they made a handsome appearance, and were reviewed by his honour the Lieutenant-Governor, attended by his Council, the public Officers, &c. At noon, the cannon, &c. were fired as usual, and his Honour gave a most elegant entertainment at Mr. Dillon's, to a very numerous company, consisting of the Members of his Majesty's Council, and of the Assembly, the public officers, civil and military, the Clergy, &c., &c. The afternoon was spent in drinking the usual, with many other loyal and patriotic toasts, and the evening concluded with illuminations, &c. (*South Carolina Gazette* 6 June 1768: 3; for toasting as political claim making, see Epstein 1994: chap. 3)

Note the parallels with the fall's elections to the colonial assembly, when "mechanicks and other inhabitants of Charles Town" met at Liberty Point to choose candidates:

This matter being settled, without the least animosity or irregularity, the company partook of a plain and hearty entertainment, that had been provided by some on which this assembly will reflect lasting honour. About 5 o'clock, they all removed to a most noble LIVE-OAK tree, in Mr. Mazyck's pasture, which they formally dedicated to LIBERTY, where many loyal, patriotic, and constitutional toasts were drank, beginning with the glorious *NINETY-TWO Anti-Rescinders of Massachusetts Bay,* and ending with, *Unanimity among the Members of our ensuing Assembly not to rescind from the said resolutions,* each succeeded by three huzzas. In the evening, the tree was decorated with 45 lights, and 45 skyrockets were fired. About 8 o'clock, the whole company, preceded by 45 of their number, carrying as many lights, marched in regular procession to town, down King Street and Broad Street, to Mr. Robert Dillon's tavern; where the 45 lights being placed upon the table, with 45 bowls of punch, 45 bottles of wine, and 92 glasses, they spent a few hours in a new round of toasts, among which, scarce a celebrated Patriot of Britain or America was omitted; and preserving the same good order and regularity as had been observed throughout the day, at 10 they retired. (*South Carolina Gazette* 3 October 1768: 2)

In addition to its impressive capacity for alcohol, the Charleston electoral assembly's blend of political ingredients boggles the mind. In general form, it resembles the king's birthday, except for the notable absence of military and royal officials. But Charleston's Liberty Tree directly emulated its Boston model. The toast to ninety-two antirescinders (those members of the Massachusetts assembly who voted against withdrawing Samuel Adams's circular letter) identified the South

Carolinians with Massachusetts patriots. The number forty-five, obviously, signaled the relevance of John Wilkes. Lighting up (in this case the procession rather than the city's windows) likewise enacted a public declaration of allegiance and solidarity.

As of 1768, opponents of arbitrary rule in London, Boston, and Charleston had not yet invented social movements. Nevertheless, their innovations moved popular public politics toward social movement forms. They enlisted ordinary citizens such as artisans and sailors in campaigns of sustained opposition to royal policies (in contrast to Boston's small merchants, Charleston's Sons of Liberty expanded from a volunteer fire company composed largely of artisans [Maier 1972: 85]). They combined special-purpose associations, public meetings, marches, petitions, pamphleteering, and statements widely reported in the public media. To some extent, they even adopted displays of WUNC: worthiness, unity, numbers, and commitment. The *South Carolina Gazette* remarked on "the same good order and regularity as had been observed throughout the day."

Although the "mechanicks and other inhabitants" of Charleston remained quite capable of attacking royal officials, resisting customs agents, and sacking the houses of their designated enemies, at least on ceremonial occasions they abandoned direct action in favor of program, identity, and standing claims: we are upright people, we deserve a voice, and we oppose arbitrary rule with determination. In fact, Charleston's artisans "spearheaded" the city's anti-importation agreements in alliance with merchant-patriot Christopher Gadsden (Maier 1972: 116). Integration of popular forces into elite opposition campaigns split the ruling classes but took an important step toward the creation of the social movement as a distinct form of public politics.

Political and Economic Contexts

The social movement emerged in England and America against the background of profound political and economic changes. Four catchwords tag the essential changes: war, parliamentarization, capitalization, and proletarianization. As the influence of the Seven Years War has already suggested, war did not simply mobilize national populations; it also expanded state structures, inflated governmental expenditures, increased extraction of resources from the government's subject population, created new debt, and at least temporarily fortified the state's repressive apparatus. On the British side, the wars of American independence dwarfed the Seven Years War in all these regards, only to seem puny themselves by comparison with the gigantic wars of the French Revolution and Napoleon (Brewer 1989, Mann 1988: 106).

In North America, the aftermath of the Seven Years War weighed heavily, as the British stationed a peacetime army of ten thousand men, tightened control over customs, and imposed a series of revenue measures such as the Stamp Act of 1765. The Revolutionary War (as the struggle of 1775 onward came to be known across the thirteen rebellious colonies) cost the Americans incomparably more in personal services, money, and debt than had British impositions after the Seven Years War. The war effort created the thin national state structure that prevailed for decades. During the European wars of the French Revolution and Napoleon, the new United States first evaded, then abrogated, its treaty obligations to France, which had provided crucial aid to the American cause during the American Revolution.

The next major American involvement in Europe's war came with the Jefferson administration's 80-million-franc purchase of Louisiana from Napoleon's France (1803), which doubled the territory of the United States. With minor exceptions, the United States then kept its distance from the European war until 1812, fighting mainly with Indians on its western and southern frontiers. But in 1812 the Americans ended five years of uneasy negotiation by declaring war on Great Britain, invading Canada, battling Indians deemed to be allied with Britain, and conducting a series of maritime battles in the Great Lakes, the Atlantic, and the Gulf of Mexico. They also suffered the torching of Washington and the invasion of Maine before the European war ground to a halt in 1814.

Parliamentarization occurred more subtly than making war, but with no less effect on public politics. It had two related components: a general expansion of Parliament's power and a shift of national political struggles from the king and his clients toward Parliament (Tilly 1997, Tilly & Wood 2003). War-driven taxation and debt increased parliamentary power; each governmental request for new funds initiated a struggle in which Parliament extracted new concessions. (Parliamentary consent to taxes also reduced open rebellion against taxation, in contrast to eighteenth-century France and the American colonies [Brewer 1989: 132].) As parliamentary power increased, royal patronage became less crucial to political success, Parliament intervened more broadly in public affairs, and the stakes of parliamentary actions for national constituencies (whether enfranchised or not) greatly increased. The Americans replaced the king with weak executives, investing heavily in parliamentary power at the national and, especially, state levels.

Capitalization occurred on both sides of the Atlantic, as agrarian, commercial, and industrial capital all greatly increased in scope. Great Britain was becoming the world's greatest center of manufacturing and trade while its agricultural production increased dramatically in scale. The older American colonies and their successor United States served chiefly as tributaries to the British economy, but they too experienced momentous agrarian, commercial, and industrial expansions after 1750. Although landlords certainly did well and manufacturers were beginning to make their marks, merchant capitalists in particular gained heft within the British and American economies.

By proletarianization, let us understand not just the growth of routinized factory labor (although that did occur to an unprecedented extent) but more generally an increase in the proportion of the population depending on wage labor for survival (Tilly 1984). In British agriculture, the concentration of landholding and leaseholding greatly increased the share of wage-laborers among all cultivators. Proletarianization occurred even more rapidly in manufacturing, where self-employed artisans lost ground to wage-dependent workers in shops, factories, and their own households. The picture differed significantly in North America, where slaves performed an increasing proportion of all labor in southern agriculture, proletarianization resembling its British counterpart occurred in the coastal zones of commerce and manufacturing, but the expanding frontier provided abundant opportunities for smallholders and petty traders.

What connects war, parliamentarization, capitalization, and proletarianization, on one side, with the growth of social movements, on the other? To put complex matters very schematically:

- Mobilization and payment for war simultaneously increased the influence of governmental activity on ordinary people's welfare and engaged governmental agents in negotiation over the terms under which landlords, merchants, workers, soldiers, sailors, and others would contribute to the collective effort.
- Despite a narrow franchise, the shift of power toward Parliament meant that the impact of legislative actions on everyone's welfare greatly increased and that, because of parliamentary representation's geographic organization, everyone in Great Britain and the colonies acquired a more direct connection to the men—the elected legislators—who were taking consequential political actions.
- Although great landlords continued to dominate national politics, capitalization expanded the independent influence of merchants and financiers in London and elsewhere who increasingly became the government's creditors and managers of capital.
- As many a social commentator feared, proletarianization reduced dependence of workers on particular landlords, masters, and other patrons, and thereby freed workers to enter political life on their own.
- In combination, these changes promoted contingent alliances between dissident aristocrats and bourgeois (who lacked the numbers for independent action against the bulk of ruling classes) and dissatisfied workers (who lacked the legal and social protection supplied by patrons).
- Such alliances, in their turn, facilitated appropriation and expansion of special-purpose associations, public meetings, petition campaigns, disciplined marches, and related forms of claim making by working-class and petit bourgeois activists while making it more difficult for authorities to maintain legal prohibitions of those activities when ordinary people engaged in them.
- Such alliances turned the same working-class and petit bourgeois activists away from direct, destructive action as a means of making claims.
- Joint actions of dissident aristocrats, radical bourgeois, indignant petit bourgeois, and workers thus created precedents and legal spaces for social movement actions, even when current campaigns and alliances ended.

Of course, these changes did not occur in an instant. Between the turbulent events of 1768 and the clear availability of social movement politics to a wide variety of actors on either side of the Atlantic, another half century of struggle and evolution elapsed.

On the British side, London provided the first major setting for social movement innovation. Growing from about 675 thousand to 865 thousand inhabitants between 1750 and 1800, London competed with Istanbul for the rank of largest European city and, thus, of earth's second-biggest metropolis (after Beijing). By that time, London had become Europe's greatest port, a vastly influential center of trade, and the world center of banking, housing the preeminent Bank of England. As Adam Smith put it in 1776:

> The stability of the Bank of England is equal to that of the British government. All that it has advanced to the public must be lost before its creditors can sustain any loss. No other banking company in England can be established by act of parliament, or can consist of more than six members. It acts, not only as an ordinary bank, but as a great engine of state. It receives and pays the greater part of the annuities which are due to the creditors of the public, it circulates exchequer bills, and it advances to government the annual amount of the land and malt taxes, which are frequently not paid up till some years thereafter. (Smith 1910: I, 284–85)

London's financiers had their fingers on the pulse (or their hands on the throat) of the entire British Empire.

Within London, however, financiers did not become radicals. On the contrary: the bourgeois who supported Wilkes and his radical successors concentrated disproportionately among middling tradesmen (Rudé 1971: 172–77). They aligned themselves against both the Court and great capitalists, whom they portrayed as coconspirators against the public good. Their popular backers, in turn, came especially from workers in London's better organized trades: the sailors, coal heavers, and silk weavers we have already seen in action, but also a host of other artisans and clerks.

Not that all London workers supported radical causes; the thousands mobilized by Lord George Gordon's anti-Catholic Protestant Association in 1780, for example, also seem to have come chiefly from the London working classes. Members of the Protestant Association first marched with Lord Gordon to Parliament for presentation of a petition for repeal of a 1778 act that had made minor concessions to Catholic rights, then (on parliamentary refusal to negotiate under pressure) broke into groups, some of which went on to sack Catholic chapels, houses of prominent Catholics, and houses of officials reputed to be protecting Catholics. Of those apprehended and prosecuted for participating in attacks on Catholic properties, "two in every three of those tried were wage-earners, journeymen, apprentices, waiters, domestic servants and labourers; a smaller number were petty employers, craftsmen and tradesmen" (Rudé 1971: 226). Broadly speaking, nevertheless, London's major mobilizations of the later eighteenth century pitted worker-bourgeois alliances against coalitions of finance and Court, with a dissident segment of Parliament typically aligned against the Court.

As the Protestant Association's temporary prominence suggests, mass-membership associations figured ever more centrally in British popular mobilizations. The eighteenth century's greatest surge of associational activity occurred during the early years of the French Revolution. During those years, elite demands for parliamentary reform that had been active for two decades coupled with popular demands for democratization in the French style, both based in clubs, societies, and popular associations as well as religious congregations. Revolution societies, constitutional societies, and corresponding societies took the French Revolution, the American Revolution, and Britain's own Glorious Revolution of 1689 as their points of reference. Defenders of church and king likewise mobilized against secular democrats by means of specialized associations. From 1794 to the end of the Napoleonic Wars, governmental repression damped down associational activity, especially on the part of workers. Associations returned in a great burst after war's end. By that time, with the prominent exception of still-illegal workers' "combinations," associations and their public meetings had become standard means of popular expression.

Crystallization of the British Social Movement

At what point, then, can we reasonably say that the social movement had become a distinctive, connected, recognized, and widely available form of public politics? We are looking for times and places in which people making collective claims on authorities frequently form special-purpose associations or named coalitions, hold public meetings, communicate their programs to available media, stage processions, rallies, or demonstrations, and through all these activities make concerted public displays of worthiness, unity, numbers, and commitment. If the complex occurs together regularly outside of electoral campaigns and management-labor struggles, we will be more confident that the social movement has arrived on its own terms. We recognize all the individual elements in British public politics of the later eighteenth century. But by these standards British politics did not institutionalize social movements until late in the Napoleonic Wars.

In Britain, those late war years proved crucial. From about 1812, nationwide campaigns arose for parliamentary reform: broadened franchise, more equal representation of electors, annual meetings of Parliament, and often further refinements such as secret ballots and MP stipends that would make officeholding possible for poorer men. At the same time, and in overlapping efforts, unprecedented energy went into organizing workers to demand parliamentary action on their behalf. They coupled with demands for peace after a long, costly, disruptive war. In a Bristol by-election of 1812, radical Henry Hunt lost badly because most of his support came from disfranchised workers

who marched in huge crowds to the cry 'Hunt and Peace' behind a loaf of bread on a pole and Cap of Liberty, cheered his stentorian harangues, assailed anyone wearing blue with a volley of mud, stones and dead cats, and attacked the White Lion (headquarters of the Loyal and Constitutional Club) and Council House. Troops were called to restore order. (Prothero 1979: 82)

By 1812 the Liberty Cap, derived from the headgear that Romans placed on the head of an emancipated slave, had a long iconic history in Great Britain. Borrowed from the Dutch as William of Orange became the English king in the Glorious Revolution of 1688–1689, it had represented Dutch liberation from Spain. In Britain, it came to signify liberty in the Wilkite sense (Epstein 1994: 78–80). In fact, during the Wilkite agitation of the 1760s, William Hogarth produced a famous, savage drawing of the ugly Wilkes holding a pole topped by a Liberty Cap.

In the nineteenth century's early decades, marches with Liberty Caps did not get radicals elected. But they did dramatize popular support for radical programs. Since officials often refused authorization for popular reformers to meet in public buildings, assemblies repeatedly took place on the streets or in open fields. They thus became half meetings, half demonstrations. What is more, delegations frequently marched to the place of assembly, thus linking the twinned forms of the demonstration: the street march and the disciplined assembly in a public space. Although London continued to play a significant role, greater innovations occurred in England's northern industrial districts, where workers organized and acted energetically during the postwar years.

In the cotton manufacturing center of Stockport, the formation of the Stockport Union for the Promotion of Human Happiness in October 1818 helped mobilize people of the industrial North on behalf of relief for political prisoners as well as on behalf of parliamentary reform. The Seditious Meetings Act of 1817 had forbidden closed meetings that planned direct efforts to influence the government. But it tolerated open public meetings to express support for parliamentary reform. The Stockport Union pioneered popular political organizers' response to the new repressive context, becoming the model for political unions all over the country, including London.

The Stockport Union sponsored repeated reform meetings, organized petitions for political prisoners, issued remonstrances, and staged demonstrations. The union sent a delegation of some 1,400 men and 40 women marching in ranks with banners to the famous reform meeting of 16 August 1819 at St. Peter's Fields, Manchester, a meeting attacked by the Manchester and Salford Yeomanry (the incident was thenceforth infamous as Peterloo). Of the delegation's march, Manchester merchant Francis Philips reported:

> On the 16th August I went on the Stockport Road about eleven or a little after, and I met a great number of persons advancing toward Manchester with all the regularity of a regiment, only they had no uniform. They were all marching in file, principally three abreast. They had two banners with them. There were persons by the side, acting as officers and regulating the files. The order was beautiful indeed. (Glen 1984: 245)

Particular organizations such as the Stockport Union rose and fell with the times and continued to face governmental surveillance or outright repression. Threatened governments tried repeatedly to squelch organizational activity through such acts as the Coercion and Seditious Meetings Acts of 1817, the broadly repressive Six Acts of 1819, and the Malicious Trespass Act of 1820. But dissident organizations and their parliamentary allies fought back. Sometimes they actually won. In 1824, for example, Parliament conceded ground by repealing the Combination Laws that it had enacted in 1799 to suppress workers' associations; it thereby partially legalized public activity by trade unions. The relaxation of repression promoted social movement activity. By the later 1820s, all the essential elements of social movements—campaigns, repertoires, and public WUNC displays—had cohered and become widely available to organized interests in Great Britain.

Vast, effective mobilizations of the 1820s and 1830s for workers' rights, Catholic emancipation, and parliamentary reform locked those elements in place (Belchem 1990: 73–144, Tilly 1995: 240–339). In the process, the social movement repertoire separated increasingly from older forms of signaling support or opposition such as forced illuminations, Rough Music, serenades, and the sacking of houses. By the 1830s, furthermore, social movement strategies had become available not only to reformers and radicals but also to conservative activists. Conservative users of social movement tactics included the widely influential, if ultimately unsuccessful, English opponents of Catholic emancipation (Hinde 1992, O'Ferrall 1985, Tilly 2004: 149–56).

Social Movements Nevertheless?

In 1925, leading American historian J. Franklin Jameson devoted an influential lecture series to "The American Revolution Considered as a Social Movement." As celebrations of the 150th anniversary of the revolution were beginning, Jameson called for students of the American Revolution to emulate specialists in the French Revolution by expanding from political and military to social history. "The stream of revolution," he argued,

> could not be confined within narrow banks, but spread abroad upon the land. Many economic desires, many social aspirations were set free by the political struggle, many aspects of colonial society profoundly altered by the forces thus let loose. The relations of social classes to each other, the institution of slavery, the system of land-holding, the course of business, the forms and spirit of the intellectual and religious life, all felt the transforming hand of revolution, all emerged from under it in shapes advanced many degrees nearer to those we know. (Jameson 1956: 9)

He closed his lectures with his major claim: "that all the varied activities of men in the same country and period have intimate relations with each other, and that one cannot obtain a satisfactory view of any one of them by considering it apart from the others" (Jameson 1956: 100). For Jameson, it turns out, "social movement" equaled large-scale social transformation rather than a specific form of politics. As our earlier looks at Boston and Charleston might lead us to expect, Jameson drew attention away from the heroic leaders and dramatic moments of revolutionary action to the broad participation of colonists in the struggles of 1765 to 1783. But he did not make the case for the revolution as a social movement in the narrower historical meaning of the term.

Might we nevertheless claim the American Revolution as a social movement or a series of social movements? Considering the same period we have examined in London and Boston, Sidney Tarrow points to innovations in political actions: amid the burning of effigies and sacking of houses, the organization of boycotts and nonimportation agreements signaled the creation of "modular" forms of politics that could easily migrate from place to place, group to group, issue to issue:

> Thenceforth, nonimportation and boycotting became the modular weapons of the American rebellion, employed most clamorously in the controversy over tea in Boston harbor. The effectiveness of the tactic was not lost on Britain: in 1791, the English antislavery association used a boycott on the importation of sugar from the West Indies to put pressure on Parliament to abolish the slave trade. From a parochial response to new taxes from the periphery of the British Empire, the boycott had migrated to its core. (Tarrow 1998: 38)

Tarrow rightly identifies the invention of quick-moving modular tactics as a hallmark of social movement activity and as a significant contrast with the more parochial attachments to local settings involved in Rough Music, effigy burning, and house sacking. But does the emergence of modular tactics qualify the American Revolution as a social movement?

We are still looking for times and places in which people making collective claims on authorities frequently form special-purpose associations or named coalitions, hold public meetings, communicate their programs to available media, stage processions, rallies, or demonstrations, and through all these activities make concerted displays of worthiness, unity, numbers, and commitment. As in Great Britain during the same period, the answer is clear: all the individual elements existed in the new United States of 1783, but they had not yet congealed into a distinctive, widely available form of popular politics. As in Great Britain, the proliferation of interconnected associations from 1765 onward transformed popular politics and laid the basis for emergence of full-fledged social movements. But it still took decades before the full social movement apparatus became widely available to popular claimants.

Might antislavery mobilization, as Tarrow hints, constitute a crucial exception? During the 1770s and 1780s, jurists in both Great Britain and North America began to deliver rulings that challenged the legality of slavery. The Vermont constitution of 1777 banned slavery, while between 1780 and 1784 Pennsylvania, Massachusetts, Rhode Island, and Connecticut took legal steps toward general emancipation. (New York did not join the move toward general emancipation until 1799, however, and blanket freeing of slaves did not occur there until 1827.) In both Great Britain and the American colonies, organized Quakers were creating antislavery associations during the 1770s. In fact, Friends congregations on both sides of Atlantic were then expelling members who refused to free their own slaves.

In 1783, English Quakers sent Parliament its first (but by no means its last) petition for abolition of the slave trade. Britain's nationwide campaigns against the slave trade began, however, in 1787, with mass petitioning and formation of the Society for the Abolition of the Slave Trade. At that point, antislavery organizers worked chiefly within Quaker and Evangelical congregations; church services therefore overlapped with petition-generating meetings (Davis 1987, Drescher 1982, 1986, Temperley 1981, Walvin 1980, 1981). The initiative did not come from London but from the industrial North, especially Manchester. The eleven thousand signatures on the Manchester petition of December 1787 represented something like two-thirds of all the city's men who were eligible to sign (Drescher 1986: 70). As Tarrow says, furthermore, antislavery activists introduced another weighty innovation: a general boycott of sugar grown with the labor of slaves, with perhaps 300 thousand families participating in 1791 and 1792 (Drescher 1986: 79).

New petition drives surged from 1806 to 1808, in the midst of which both Great Britain (or, rather, the United Kingdom, which had formally joined Ireland with England, Wales, and Scotland in 1801) and the United States outlawed the slave trade. In 1833, after multiple mobilizations, Parliament finally passed an emancipation act applicable throughout its colonies. The United States remained fiercely divided on the issue of slavery and eventually fought a civil war over it. Yet by the 1830s abolition had become the crux of a vast American social movement as well. Where in this sequence might we reasonably say that full-fledged social movements were flying?

We face a classic half full–half empty question. Somewhere between the Manchester petition of 1787 and the 1833 parliamentary banning of slavery in the British Empire, the full panoply of campaign, repertoire, and WUNC displays came together. When did it happen? Let us split the question into two parts: When did antislavery meet all the tests for a genuine social movement? When did the political form represented by antislavery become widely available for other sorts of claims? To the first part, we may reply that sometime between 1791 (the sugar boycott) and 1806 (the second great petition drive) British abolitionists assembled campaign, repertoire, and WUNC displays into a single political package; they thus have some claim to constitute the world's first social movement.

For the second part, however, we must allow another decade to elapse; on models drawn quite directly from antislavery, we then find workers, reformers, Catholics, and others regularly forming special-purpose associations, holding public meetings indoors and outdoors, adopting slogans and badges, staging marches, producing pamphlets, and projecting claims with regard to programs, identities, and political relations. For such a complex and momentous change, the quarter century from 1791 to 1816 looks like a very rapid transition indeed.

Might Francophiles then make a case for French priority? As the Revolution of 1789 proceeded, French activists certainly formed politically oriented associations at a feverish pace, made concerted claims by means of those associations, held public meetings, marched through the streets, adopted slogans and badges, produced pamphlets, and implemented local revolutions through most of the country (Hunt 1978, 1984, Jones 2003, Markoff 1996a, McPhee 1988, Woloch 1970, 1994). If such mobilizations had continued past 1795 *and* if they had become available for a wide variety of claims thereafter, we would probably hail the French as inventors of the social movement—or at least coinventors with their British counterparts. As it happened, however, the full array of social movement claim making did not acquire durable political standing in France for another half century, around the Revolution of 1848 (Tilly 1986: chap. 9). Even then, repression under Louis Napoleon's Second Empire delayed the full implementation of social movement politics through much of the country for another two decades.

More unexpectedly, Dutch eighteenth-century activists might also have some claim to have institutionalized social movements, at least temporarily. In what Dutch historians call the Fourth English War (1780–1784), Dutch forces joined indirectly in the wars of the American Revolution, taking a severe beating from superior British naval power. As the disastrous naval engagements continued, a sort of pamphlet war broke out within the Netherlands. Supporters of the Prince of Orange attacked the leaders of Amsterdam and its province Holland as the opposing patriots (based especially in Holland) replied in kind; each blamed the other for the country's parlous condition. Drawing explicitly on the American example, patriots called for a (preferably peaceful) revolution. Earlier claim making in the Low Countries conformed to local variants of the older repertoire we have already seen operating in England and America (Dekker 1982, 1987, van Honacker 1994, 2000). But during the 1780s petition campaigns began in earnest: first demanding recognition of John Adams as a legal representative of that contested entity, the United States of America, then proposing remedies to a whole series of domestic political problems.

Citizens' committees (possibly modeled on American committees of correspondence) soon began to form along with citizens' militias across Holland's towns. In a highly segmented political system, their incessant pressure on local and regional authorities actually worked. Between 1784 and 1787, patriot factions managed to install new, less-aristocratic constitutions in a number of Dutch cities and even in a whole province, Overijssel. The Prince of Orange and his followers, however, still disposed of two crucial advantages: British financial support and military backing from the prince's brother-in-law, King Frederick William of Prussia. Late in 1787, a Prussian invasion broke the Netherlands' Patriot Revolution (te Brake 1989, 1990, Schama 1977).

As the French Revolution began nearby, those Dutch patriots who had not fled their country hoped, conspired, and even (late in 1794) made a poorly coordinated attempt at a coup. The next invading army arrived in January 1795, when French revolutionary forces established a Batavian Republic with active support from revived patriots. (Liberty Trees went up in Leiden and Amsterdam [Schama 1977: 194].) Despite governmental alterations on a French model, the new republic soon deadlocked between advocates of centralizing reforms in the French style and the customary federalism of the Netherlands. From 1798 to 1805, a quartet of faction-backed coups—unaccompanied by widespread popular mobilization—produced the major political changes. The republic gave way to a French satellite Kingdom of Holland (1806), then to direct incorporation into France (1810–1813).

The post-Napoleonic settlement created a bifurcated kingdom that until 1839 nominally included both the Netherlands and what became Belgium. From the French takeover onward, the Dutch state assumed a much more centralized administrative structure than had prevailed in the heyday of autonomous provinces. With the Batavian Republic of 1795, committees, militias, and patriots returned temporarily to power, only to be integrated rapidly into the new sort of regime, with French overseers never far away. Recognizable social movements did not start occurring widely in the Netherlands until after Napoleon's fall. Thus counterrevolution, reaction, and conquest wiped out another possible candidate for the social movement's inventor. Great Britain retains priority, in close interaction with its American colonies.

Arguments Revisited

With some solid history in hand, we can now revisit this book's organizing arguments to see where they are taking us. Here they are:

From their eighteenth-century origins onward, social movements have proceeded not as solo performances but as interactive campaigns. The tales of Britain and America we have reviewed leave little doubt that social movements emerged out of struggle engaging many parties, with each campaign centering on the repeated efforts of a shifting coalition to achieve a relatively well-defined set of political changes. At least in the early stages of social movements, coalitions between elite political figures (who enjoyed a degree of protection for their claims) and relatively organized segments of the working classes (who had the benefits of numbers, internal connections, and local grounding) played an exceptional part.

Social movements combine three kinds of claims: program, identity, and standing. The struggles we have witnessed always featured programs of political change, but they also included claims that the proponents of those programs enjoyed the capacity for autonomous, effective action and that participants had the political standing to speak publicly on the issues at hand. (So far we have not yet encountered claims that others be *excluded* from political standing, but we will.) In the transition from the eighteenth to the nineteenth century, we see emerging a durable combination of the three sorts of claims in public meetings, petition drives, public declarations, demonstrations, and shared symbols of membership.

The relative salience of program, identity, and standing claims varies significantly among social movements, among claimants within movements, and among phases of movements. We have not yet examined enough variation among social movements to establish this argument conclusively. Yet we have already glimpsed the alternation between 1) supporting relief or parliamentary reform in British workers' movements after the Napoleonic Wars, 2) asserting that organized workers constitute a formidable, worthy force, and 3) complaining that they occupy an unduly marginal position within the regime.

Democratization promotes the formation of social movements. This part of our analysis has barely begun. Still, the American and British experiences, plus the aborted experiments of France and the Netherlands, establish a plausible correspondence between democratization and proliferation of social movements. These histories identify, moreover, significant connections of social movement operation with parliamentarization of public politics and with the rise of consequential, contested elections. The finer causal connections in both directions, however, remain open for exploration.

Social movements assert popular sovereignty. All four of our cases illustrate emerging assertions of popular sovereignty. They also show how such assertions raise acute political issues: Who has the right to speak for the people? Does the right to speak include the right to attack the governing regime? When does the interest of public order override that right? Far more so than retaliatory rituals, popular rebellions, or even contested elections, social movements place these questions of right at the center of popular politics. Through their often grudging toleration of the new synthesis among campaigns, repertoires, and WUNC displays, British and American authorities made themselves vulnerable to the claim that their critics, rather than they, genuinely spoke for the people.

As compared with locally grounded forms of popular politics, social movements depend heavily on political entrepreneurs for their scale, durability, and effectiveness. Rough Music or riding someone out of town on a rail could begin with little more than street corner encounters of local youths. Abolitionism, in contrast, could have gone nowhere without the religious officials, congregational leaders, and legislators who kept the issue in the press, constructed links between local groups of activists, planned public meetings, organized petition drives, and injected the issue of slavery into electoral campaigns. During the 1760s, London's John Wilkes and his lieutenants (as well as Boston's Samuel Adams and his confederates) pioneered major components of social movement claim making. But they still lacked the knowledge of campaigns, performances, and WUNC displays that British (and American) political entrepreneurs took for granted fifty or sixty years later.

Once social movements establish themselves in one political setting, modeling, communication, and collaboration facilitate their adoption in other connected settings. We have already noticed the generalization of social movement strategies across sectors in North America and, especially, the British Isles. We have also seen some precursors of international facilitation and collaboration in America, Britain, the Netherlands, and France; each borrowed some social movement innovations from at least one of the others. Antislavery in particular soon became an international undertaking. But the nineteenth century would bring far more extensive international facilitation of social movements, for example in the support lent to Ireland's anti-British activists by emigrants and sympathizers in England and America (Hanagan 1998).

The forms, personnel, and claims of social movements vary and evolve historically. This is perhaps the main conclusion our preliminary review of European and North American histories authorizes. Whatever else we see in struggles between 1765 and the 1830s, it certainly includes substantial variation and continuous evolution. As we have yet to see in detail, social movement claim making originated in challenges to national authorities, but it soon came into use not only in expressions of support for such authorities but also in claims on other authorities such as local elites, religious leaders, and capitalists. We are dealing with a political phenomenon deeply embedded in regional and national histories.

The social movement, as an invented institution, could disappear or mutate into some quite different form of politics. The point follows in principle from the previous arguments. We might even stretch our observations of reversals in France and the Netherlands into evidence that the elements of social movements need not endure forever and, indeed, prove vulnerable to authoritarian repression. As we will see abundantly later, furthermore, the recent proliferation of international connections among activists may be creating new forms of bottom-up politics only vaguely resembling those we have encountered during the social movement's first half century. Still, we need a good deal more analysis before deciding what conditions are crucial, and what conditions fatal, for the survival of social movements. The next chapter's survey of the nineteenth century will advance that inquiry.

3

NINETEENTH-CENTURY ADVENTURES

On 25 February 1848, news of yet another French revolution, started in Paris on the previous day, reached Lyon—Lyons for English-speakers. Several hundred weavers marched down into the city center from the silk-producing quarter of Croix-Rousse. Singing "La Marseillaise," they proceeded along the Rhône River, then crossed the city's central island to the Place des Terreaux and the Lyon city hall. Overwhelmed by the crowd, the military on hand asked the acting mayor to declare the Republic from a city hall balcony. After he did so, members of the gathering entered the hall and chose an executive committee consisting of weavers plus a minority of bourgeois republicans. During the preceding July Monarchy (1830–1848), organized silk weavers had missed few opportunities to show their strength by marching in funerals and on authorized holidays. During insurrections of 1831 and 1834, they had also marched. But outside of crises and authorized public assemblies they had until then generally avoided anything like the self-initiated parade of February 1848, if only because royal officials could take the very fact of their organized assembly as evidence that they were visibly violating the legal ban on workers' *coalitions.*

As the revolutionary regime settled into place, popular militias emerged from the organizations of workers and revolutionaries that had lurked in Lyon's political shadows. Political associations likewise multiplied, some of them new and some of them simply transforming clandestine cells or informal drinking clubs into legal entities. They often staged patriotic ceremonies that included the planting of Liberty Trees. Despite efforts of an increasingly conservative national government to restrain Lyon's radicals, militias and clubs assembled and marched through the city streets repeatedly between the February revolution of 1848 and Louis Napoleon's coup d'état of December 1851. In its issue of 14 March 1848, for example, Lyon's left-wing newspaper *Tribun du peuple* reported that:

> With four men carrying the liberty cap, a numerous troop of citizens crossed the city on the 12th. Following that holy emblem of our deliverance, the cor-

tege marched in two files. Toward the middle, an equally significant emblem attracted great attention. It was a man bound with rough ropes held by citizens forming a square around him. He carried a pathetic faded flag hung with black crepe; it was the white flag, carried almost horizontally and poorly attached to its pole, resembling the coffin of a miserable criminal on his way out, to everyone's great satisfaction. (Robert 1996: 86)

The red cap stood for revolution, the white flag for legitimacy, the claim of the elder Bourbon branch (which had returned to power after Napoleon's defeat, but lost out in the revolution of 1830) to rule France. Within two weeks of the Parisian revolution, Lyon's citizens were regularly mounting or watching street demonstrations. Using widely recognized national symbols, furthermore, demonstrators enacted the worthiness, unity, numbers, and commitment—the WUNC—of their cause.

As of March 1848, then, had Lyon and France installed the social movement as a regular vehicle of popular politics? The question turns out to be both interesting and controversial. We must look closely at 1848 to determine whether the combination of campaign, repertoire, and WUNC displays had become readily available to a wide range of claimants. The best answer is: yes, but only temporarily.

Speaking specifically of the demonstration rather than of the entire social movement apparatus, Lyon's historian Vincent Robert argues that despite a flurry of demonstrations under the Second Republic (1848–1851), demonstrations did not really become readily available ways of pressing collective claims until the great May Day mobilizations of the 1890s put them on the map. (Warning: the word *manifestation,* which Robert employs and which I am translating as "demonstration," did not actually displace such words as *cortège, défilé, démonstration,* and *rassemblement* in common French usage until after World War II [Pigenet & Tartakowsky 2003: 84].) Authorities themselves did not publicly recognize demonstrations as valid forms of political action, according to Robert, until just before World War I. At that point, Lyon's authorities began assigning police to protect and channel demonstrations instead of routinely breaking them up as illegal assemblies.

Yet Robert recognizes protodemonstrations in Lyon as early as 1831. On 19 January of that year, some 1,400 workers assembled across the Saône River from Lyon's center and marched to shouts of "work or bread"; the authorities eventually arrested 15 participants (Rude 1969: 198–202). Further demonstrations occurred on 12 February (this time with a black flag of insurrection) and on 25 October (with about six thousand participants) before the full-scale insurrection that began with a massive demonstration then took over the city from 21 to 24 November (Rude 1969: 208, 316, 357–596). In partial collaboration with Parisian rebels, Lyon's silk workers mounted another major insurrection in 1834. At least among Lyon's silk workers, demonstrations had already laid down a significant political history before the revolution of 1848. From that point forward, they occurred more frequently in times of relaxed repression or democratization, but still receded when governmental repression tightened again.

At least eight demonstrations crossed Lyon during the first month of the 1848 revolution. During March and April the Central Democratic Club organized major demonstrations on behalf of radical democracy (Robert 1996: 94–100). Soon women's groups, political clubs, veterans of Napoleonic armies, school children, workers from the national workshops set up to combat unemployment, and strikers who actually had jobs were demonstrating in Lyon. Most of them demonstrated in displays of solidarity with the new regime combined with statements of particular demands. They made program, identity, and standing claims, insisting that their participants and the people they represented had the right to public voice.

Soon, however, popular street marches and assemblies ceased under the weight of repression; for about fifteen years, demonstrations disappeared. During the later years of Louis Napoleon's Second Empire, a time of rapid industrialization in France, the regime began to relax some of its controls over workers' organizations and actions. In 1864, the empire granted a limited right to strike. In 1868, it became legal for workers to hold public meetings without prior authorization from the government. Later the same year an imperial edict permitted trade unions to organize, so long as they had their rules approved by authorities, deposited minutes of their meetings with the authorities, and allowed police observers to attend.

Thus backed by partial legality, Lyon's workers' demonstrations reappeared in abundance during the Second Empire's crisis year, 1870. As the police agent in charge of the Jardin des Plantes station reported on 30 April:

> Yesterday evening a band of about two hundred people came down from the Croix-Rousse into my quarter, led by an improvised master of ceremonies who carried a stave and who preceded four torch-bearers with a sixteen-year-old carrying a red flag. . . . Of these individuals, who seemed to range from fourteen to twenty five years of age, two-thirds were carrying staves. They sang the Marseillaise, the song of the Girondins, and then to the melody of the Lampions "Down with the Emperor! Long live the Republic!" On each side of the sidewalk, the band was followed by about thirty individuals thirty to forty-five years old who appeared to be workers and who seemed to be serving as protection. (Robert 1996: 168–69; the Lampion, literally a torch, comes from the name of an older revolutionary song including a three-beat chant on a single note)

Between then and the new revolution of 4 September 1870, authorities and demonstrators played cat and mouse in Lyon.

A red flag of revolution flew at the Lyon city hall from September into the spring. The city established its own version of a radical, autonomous commune, which government forces crushed brutally in April 1871 (Aminzade 1993, Gaillard 1971, Greenberg 1971). Demonstrations reappeared during the new revolutionary interval, although at a slower pace than in 1848. Once the Third Republic's authorities restored top-down order, nevertheless, for two more decades Lyon's demonstrations consisted chiefly of adaptations within other sorts of events: anti-clerical funerals, local celebrations of Bastille Day, official ceremonies, religious processions, and workers' delegations to municipal or state authorities. Legalization of trade unions (1884) did not change the situation fundamentally. Only with the expansion of voluntary associations during the later 1880s did demonstrations again assume prominence in Lyon's public life.

As it did elsewhere in France (Tilly 1986: 313–19), May Day 1890 inaugurated a great series of annual workers' demonstrations in Lyon; perhaps fifteen thousand workers came out for that first great international display of workers' solidarity (Robert 1996: 270). During the next two decades, many more groups in addition to workers demonstrated in Lyon: Catholics, anti-Catholics, anti-Semites, and many more, increasingly in cadence and coordination with national social movements. As Robert puts it, by World War I:

> the demonstration had become a normal form of urban political life, and a significant element in political life at large; even though the organization of a march depended on official permission, by then the authorities knew that it would be more dangerous to forbid than to authorize and that barring accidents it would occur peacefully. (Robert 1996: 373)

Robert chooses to state his conclusion as a challenge to my own dating of repertoire changes in France. But in fact we agree: around the 1848 revolution, many of the older forms of public claim making began a rapid decline across the country, while for a privileged year or so the demonstration became a standard way of supporting programs, projecting identities, and claiming political standing in France.

After the revolution of 1848, it took another half century of alternation between relatively repressive and relatively permissive regimes for the demonstration to acquire the widespread availability it retained until the German conquest of 1940 and then regained with a vengeance after the Liberation of 1944–1945 (Duyvendak 1994, Fillieule 1997a, Tartakowsky 1997, Tilly 2003: 207–13). But that was also true for other components of social movements: formation of special-purpose associations and coalitions, organization of claim-making public meetings, multiplication of WUNC displays, packaging of these and other elements into sustained public campaigns. With these qualifications, we can date France's establishment of social movements as widely available forms of popular politics during the nineteenth century's final decades.

Meetings and Demonstrations in Belgium

What about France's neighbor, Belgium? Belgian historian Gita Deneckere has assembled a catalog of "collective actions" in Antwerp, Brussels, Ghent, and Liège spanning 1831 to 1918 from a wide range of archives, official publications, periodicals, and historical works. Her catalog includes about 440 occasions on which people gathered and made collective demands "in the socio-economic field of conflict," which means largely workers' actions and actions concerning work (Deneckere 1997: 10). Deneckere's narratives actually overflow the definition, however, since they include such events as patriotic resistance to the creation of a separate Grand Duchy of Luxemburg as part of Belgium's independence settlement of 1838–1839 (Deneckere 1997: 66–68).

Deneckere's selection principle still excludes widespread violence surrounding the Netherlands' separation of church and state in 1834, just as the uneasy union of north and south was breaking up. Similarly, it omits extensive struggles over relations between church and state between 1879 and 1884. Intense competition between organized French- and Dutch-speakers over language rights and political power likewise casts only faint shadows over Deneckere's chronology of collective actions (Carter 2003, Zolberg 1978). Within Deneckere's chosen field, nevertheless, her evidence demonstrates a great increase in performances attached to the social movement repertoire.

Deneckere's evidence reveals significant alterations in Belgian forms of contention between 1830 and 1900. Before the semirevolutionary mobilizations of 1847–1848, Deneckere's contentious events feature workers' assemblies and marches to present petitions, attacks on the goods or persons of high-priced food merchants, and work stoppages by people in multiple shops of the same craft. During the earlier nineteenth century, few junctions formed between ardent democrats and workers. As Deneckere puts it:

> The case for a new collective action repertoire had little appeal to workers before 1848. Concerted [radical] efforts to create a workers' movement that matched the structure of the young Belgian state had no effect whatsoever. Radical democrats received little or no response from workers. Nowhere did genuine labor leaders break with the organizational templates they already had in their hands. (Deneckere 1997: 68)

Workers' actions then frequently took the form of turnouts: occasions on which a small number of initiators from a local craft went from shop to shop demanding that fellow craft workers leave their employment to join the swelling crowd. The round completed, turnout participants assembled in some safe place (often a field at the edge of town), aired their grievances, formulated demands, and presented those demands to masters in the trade (often through a meeting of delegations from both sides), staying away from work until the masters had replied satisfactorily or forced them to return. Before 1848, we see little of the social movement repertoire in play.

Immediately after the outbreak of the 1848 revolution in France, Belgian republicans and radicals began calling for a fraternal revolution in their own country. But the government reacted quickly, expelling Karl Marx from the country on 4

Table 3.1. Meetings, Demonstrations, and Petitions in Belgium, 1831–1900

Decade	Meetings	Demonstrations	Petitions
1831–1840	4	2	7
1841–1850	0	1	3
1851–1860	2	0	0
1861–1870	1	3	0
1871–1880	1	11	0
1881–1890	0	59	0
1891–1900	2	57	0

Compiled from Deneckere 1997: 403–11.

March, among other measures. By the time of Marx's hasty exit, the liberal-dominated Belgian government had already taken steps to forestall revolutionary mobilization in Belgium. It did so chiefly by reducing wealth requirements for voting and officeholding, nearly doubling the Belgian franchise. The split between French- and Dutch-speakers worked to the government's advantage, since republicans and advocates of the French model came disproportionately from among the Francophones, a fact that raised doubts about democratic programs on the Flemish side, ever wary of plots to incorporate Belgium into France (Dumont 2002: chap. 3).

Between the political reforms of 1848 and the 1890s, the character of Belgian contention, as registered in Deneckere's catalog, altered considerably. Turnouts practically disappeared, for example, as demonstrations and large-firm strikes became much more frequent and prominent. In the 1890s, regionally and nationally coordinated general strikes emerged as major forms of contentious action. Deneckere's catalog also reveals a significant shift during the later decades of the nineteenth century toward the demonstration as a site of public claim making. Crude counts from the catalog of Belgian public meetings, demonstrations, and petitions by decade indicate the extent of change. Table 3.1 presents the counts.

Working-class organizations lay behind a great many of the meetings, demonstrations, and petitions. Petition delegations soon disappeared as ways of making public claims, in favor of autonomously organized meetings and, especially, demonstrations. (The decline of public meetings results in part from an illusion: Belgian demonstrations often started from or included public meetings, but this tabulation accepts Deneckere's designation of a gathering as mainly meeting or mainly demonstration.) Organized workers increasingly made international connections: we first encounter the International Workingmen's Association in action, for example, during a Ghent demonstration of 1876.

Many of the later demonstrations occurred in the course of attempts to organize general strikes. As Deneckere says, workers and socialist leaders designed general strikes to be large, standard in form, coordinated across multiple localities, and oriented toward national holders of power. Instead of particular localities and trades, participants commonly represented themselves generally as socialists or as workers at large. Belgian workers began making nationwide program claims for socialism at large, identity claims as coherently connected workers, and standing claims that emphasized their improper exclusion from power. These new actions signaled a significant shift of repertoire. To our alerted eyes, they offer evidence that social movements established themselves in Belgian popular politics between 1848 and 1900.

Deneckere sees increasingly tight interdependence between popular contention and national politics. In the 1890s

> the correspondence between successive socialist mass actions and the parliamentary breakthrough to universal suffrage is too striking for anyone to miss the causal connection. On the basis of published and unpublished correspondence from ruling circles one can conclude that the general strike had a genuine impact, in fact more significant than contemporary socialists themselves realized. Time after time socialist workers' protests confronted power-holders with a revolutionary threat that laid the foundation for abrupt expansion of democracy. (Deneckere 1997: 384)

Thus in Belgium, as in France, street politics and parliamentary politics came to depend on each other. Social movements provided a significant portion of the connective tissue.

The history of the demonstration in France and Belgium, then, tracks the more general institutionalization of social movements in French and Belgian public politics. Over the nineteenth century, that happened widely in Western democratizing countries and within a few colonies of those countries as well. With its eighteenth-century head start, Great Britain institutionalized demonstrations and other social movement performances well ahead of France and Belgium (Prothero 1997: 202–29). By early in the nineteenth century, the public holidays, funerals, and other authorized assemblies that continued to attract French and Belgian political critics and claimants well into the century lost much of their appeal for British, Canadian, and U.S. claim makers. Elections were different, however: with an expanding franchise and rising demands on the part of disfranchised citizens, both election campaigns and parliamentary sessions became increasing sites of claim making. In Britain, bills before Parliament frequently became the focus of social movement claim making. Parliamentarization promoted social movements (Tilly 1997, Tilly & Wood 2003).

Demonstrations nicely illustrate the historical origins of specific social movement performances. Despite their later generalization and diffusion across a wide variety of settings, issues, and claimants, demonstrations took shape differently in their places of origin. Initial settings contributed three features to demonstrations: models of interaction, legal precedents for assembly and movement, representations of relations between demonstrators and other political actors, including authorities and objects of claims. We have already seen the British demonstration adapting forms, legal precedents, and representations from delegations, petition marches, public holidays, artisans' parades, electoral assemblies, and authorized meetings. Military parades also provided some of the models, if not the legal precedents.

Where citizens' militias retained legal standing into the eighteenth century—as they did, for example, in the Netherlands, but not in France—the armed militia parade offered a model and a (risky) legal precedent. In Catholic countries such as France and Spain, religious processions made their mark, not only offering occasions for expressions of sentiment that authorities could not easily contain but also providing exceptional opportunities for WUNC displays. In Ireland, the nineteenth-century demonstration drew on a century or so of religious processions, fraternal order outings, artisans' holidays, and militia marches; that earlier history cast a sharp shadow on Irish demonstrations into the twenty-first century (Bryan 2000, Kinealy 2003, Tilly 2003: 111–27). Yes, as compared with tarring and feathering or drinking forty-five toasts, the street demonstration has modular qualities that facilitate its spread across the wide world of social movements. Those qualities, however, do not free it from history.

The same holds for other social movement performances: creation of special-purpose associations and coalitions, public meetings, solemn processions, vigils, rallies, petition drives, statements to and in public media, and pamphleteering. Even though they eventually cohered in a widely available repertoire that distinguished social movements from other forms of politics, each of these performances has a history that stamps itself on meanings and practices, sets limits on permissible and impermissible uses, varies somewhat from setting to setting, and produces internal changes within the performance itself.

Take one small but significant example from the reports on demonstrations we have already examined. The early demonstrations Robert describes for Lyon employed striking symbols such as the Liberty Cap, acted out politically significant tableaux, and featured stirring songs but included little or no printed matter. By century's end, French demonstrators commonly marched under signs and banners broadcasting slogans and identifying the segments of the population they represented in words rather than pictures. Beneath that change lay not only advances in popular literacy but also the relaxation of legal restrictions on political speech. Those shifts in the social and political context likewise affected the activities of special-purpose associations, access to the media, and the whole array of social movement performances.

Chartists

To see more clearly what happened once social movements institutionalized, let us return briefly to Great Britain—or rather to the United Kingdom, which incorporated Ireland with England, Wales, and Scotland in 1801. Once the struggles of the 1820s and early 1830s set social movements firmly on the political map, the United Kingdom, including Ireland, became a major creator of social movements. Antislavery continued, as we have seen, to the abolition of slavery in 1833. Social movements helped bring political rights to Protestant Dissenters in 1828 and to Catholics in 1829. The next three years brought immense social movement mobilization on behalf of parliamentary reform, culminating in the Reform Act of 1832 (Tilly 1995: 284–339). The act did not enfranchise the many workers who joined that mobilization, but did greatly increase the voting of merchants and masters as it moved the system modestly toward representation proportional to the number of electors. Organized workers, too, increasingly employed social movement means—campaigns, repertoire, and WUNC displays—as they demanded relief and equal rights.

Workers and their radical allies complained bitterly, publicly, and rightly that the newly enfranchised bourgeoisie had sold them out by accepting the 1832 Reform Act. The legislation pointedly excluded wage workers and, indeed, raised property qualifications in parliamentary districts that had previously given at least some prosperous workers the vote. They also complained when the newly constituted Parliament enacted its liberal version of political economy by passing a New Poor Law (1834) that authorized parishes to collaborate in Poor Law Unions. Those unions ended outdoor relief for able-bodied workers, sent them to workhouses if they did not find adequate employment, and made conditions within workhouses more punitive. The two issues generated separate social movements during the later 1830s. But they merged in the remarkable mass movement called Chartism.

Published in May 1838, the People's Charter issued from negotiation and compromise between radical and reformist leaders. It dropped, for example, radical demands for female suffrage and a ten-hour limit to the working day. It also omitted demands, popular among liberal reformers, for abolition of the Corn Laws that until 1846 provided U.K. grain producers with sliding-scale protection against competing imports and thereby increased the cost of daily bread. The charter itself took the predictable form of a petition beginning "Unto the Honourable the Commons of the United Kingdom of Great Britain and Ireland in Parliament assembled, the Petition of the undersigned, their suffering countrymen, humbly sheweth . . . ." After a preface dramatizing the misery of workers in the midst of plenty and singling out the Reform Act of 1832 for criticism, the charter went on to make these specific demands:

1. universal [that is, adult male] suffrage;
2. secret ballots [instead of viva voce voting] in parliamentary elections;
3. annual parliaments;
4. salaries for Members of Parliament;
5. abolition of property requirements for membership in Parliament; and
6. equal electoral districts across the country. (Black 1969: 127–31)

The proposal first emerged from the reformist London Workingmen's Association that had formed in 1836. It soon drew support from an extraordinary variety of reformist, radical, and special-purpose associations throughout the United Kingdom.

Many existing workers' organizations attached themselves to the movement. An umbrella National Charter Association (NCA) originated in Manchester (1840) and soon had more than four hundred branches, drawn especially from previously active local workers' groups. The NCA "was able to organize two million signatures to a petition in 1841 for the release of Chartist prisoners, and three million to a second petition for the Charter in 1842" (Prothero 1997: 222). Chartist leaders regularly spoke of their activities as a "movement." They also drew consciously on recognizable symbols; at a London Chartist demonstration of August 1842, for example, the police arrested two men carrying a large Union Jack and "a small blue and white printed silk, having on it the words, 'Reform in Church and State' and surmounted by a Crimson Cap of Liberty" (Goodway 1982: 108).

Chartists held General Conventions of the Industrious Classes more or less annually from 1839 to 1848. Although these conventions followed a two-decade-old radical program of forming a counter-Parliament to dramatize weaknesses of the existing body, to have held elections for a large national assembly would have directly challenged Parliament's legal claim to represent the nation. To evade prosecution, the national meetings therefore typically brought together small numbers of delegates. Those delegates came, however, from voice-vote elections at mass meetings in localities across the country. Around these conventions, furthermore, flowed large demonstrations and multiple public meetings.

In Nottingham, for example, organizers sought to draw shopkeepers into their mass meeting in preparation for the 1839 convention by distributing a handbill declaring that:

> we are far from thinking that the Retailers are a useless portion of society, their interest and our own is the same: unless the working classes are well paid for their labour, the Retailers cannot exist as a respectable body, but that they must share the same fate as the working classes. We therefore call upon you Fellow Countrymen to assist us in this righteous struggle . . . come forward to the assistance of the People's delegates. So shall the working classes form one phalanx which Despotism cannot penetrate. (Church 1966: 131)

Notice the bid to project WUNC: worthiness, unity, numbers, and commitment. We see Chartists combining program claims centered on the Charter itself, identity claims as the connected, worthy working classes, and standing claims protesting their exclusion from political power.

Not all Chartist activity, to be sure, took the form of nonviolent WUNC displays. It ranged from peaceful meetings to open attacks on enemies. (Historians, in fact, often make a rough distinction between "moral force" and "physical force" Chartists on these very grounds.) Several abortive insurrections—summarily repressed and brutally prosecuted—arose within the Chartist movement. With the French Revolution of 1848, many Chartist demonstrations displayed French tricolors and called for revolutionary change. Lawyer-Chartist-poet Ernest Jones preached in 1848:

> I believe that we stand upon the threshold of our rights. One step, were it even with an iron heel, and they are ours. I conscientiously believe the people are prepared to claim the Charter. Then I say—take it; and God defend the right! . . . We'll respect the law, if the law-makers respect us. If they don't—France is a Republic! (Ward 1973: 200)

As in many later-nineteenth-century large-scale social movements, priorities in local demands and strategies varied wildly within Chartism. Yet the center of gravity remained the collective placing of demands to equalize political rights in the United Kingdom.

After a last great burst in 1848, Chartism disintegrated as a national movement. Some activists moved into temperance, cooperatives, local betterment programs, or into educational, land, or property reform, while a minority stuck with local and regional Chartist associations (Price 1986: 56–67). The formal Chartist program as a whole did not become part of U.K. law until the twentieth century, and its more general populist demands failed utterly (Thompson 1984: 335–37). Nevertheless the Chartist movement provided a seedbed and a template for the nineteenth century's major popular mobilizations. Later demands for an expanded franchise, female suffrage, disestablishment of the Anglican Church, and home rule in Ireland all followed some of the patterns set in place by Chartism.

A Glance at the Nineteenth-Century United States

What was happening to North American social movements during the nineteenth century? In a pathbreaking study of American social movements between 1800 and 1945, William Gamson devised a shrewd cataloging strategy for that unruly world of campaigns, social movement performances, and WUNC displays. He and his research team went through about 75 historical reference works tagging any named organization that participated in a wide variety of social movements and/or protest activities. From that listing of nearly 4,500 organizations they drew a random sample of 11 percent—467 organizations—from which they selected the 53 that detailed examination showed to be a) seeking the mobilization of an unmobilized constituency and b) making claims on an antagonist outside that constituency. Of the 53, the 27 organizations listed in table 3.2 began their activity before 1900. Thus they provide a rough calendar of nineteenth-century social movement initiation in the United States.

As I warned earlier, social movement organizations (SMOs) and social movements are by no means identical; movements are interactive campaigns, not organizations. SMOs sometimes outlast campaigns, and campaigns almost always in-

Table 3.2 William Gamson's Nineteenth-Century Challenging Groups and Their Program Claims

Year(s)	Group	Program Claims
1816–1834	North Carolina Manumission Society	promotion of voluntary manumission for slaves
1825–1830	Prison Discipline Society	prison reform
1831–1833	Society for the Promotion of Manual Labor in Literary Institutions	physical fitness
1832–1840	National Female Anti-Slavery Society	abolition of slavery
1833–1836	Union Trade Society of Journeymen Tailors	professional benefits
1833–1840	American Anti-Slavery Society	abolition of slavery
1843–1847	American Republican Party (Native American Party)	Protestant anti-Catholic
1858–1873	United Sons of Vulcan	benefits for ironworkers
1865–1872	Grand Eight Hour Leagues	legislation for eight-hour day
1869–1872	American Free Trade League	tariff repeal
1869–1876	International Workingmen's Association (First International)	socialist politics
1880–1887	Social Revolutionary Clubs (Anarcho-Communists)	economic reorganization
1880–1905	League of American Wheelmen	remove road restrictions on bicycles
1881–1912	United Brotherhood of Carpenters and Joiners of America	professional benefits
1881–1935	American Federation of Labor	legal and political support for labor movement
1882	League of Deliverance	opposition to Chinese labor
1885–1891	National Brotherhood of Baseball Players	professional benefits
1885–1934	Order of Railway Conductors	professional benefits
1886–1888	American Party	anti-immigration
1887	Progressive Labor Party	socialist political candidates
1888–1910	United Hebrew Trades	benefits for Jewish immigrant workers
1888–1935	International Association of Machinists	professional benefits
1892–1915	Brotherhood of the Kingdom	religion and social conditions
1892–1921	Amalgamated Association of Street and Electrical Railway Workers	professional benefits
1892–1933	International Longshoreman's Association (East)	professional benefits
1893–1932	American Proportional Representation League	PR against urban political machines
1896–1914	Brotherhood of the Cooperative Commonwealth	cooperatives and electoral power

Source: Gamson 1990: 277–85.

volve multiple organizations, shifting coalitions, and unnamed informal networks. British Chartism shows us many previously mobilized constituencies (which Gamson's procedure excluded unless a new organization formed to mobilize them) joining in a vast social movement. Like the tracing of demonstrations alone, Gamson's organizational catalog therefore takes just one selective picture of American social movement activity.

Still, the picture flashes some striking highlights.

1. It portrays a remarkable acceleration of social movement initiation during the later nineteenth century. Only seven of the twenty-seven nineteenth-century organizations began acting before 1850, and well over half started up after 1875.
2. The sorts of organizations engaged in social movements shifted markedly. Before 1850 we see the predictable antislavery and social reform associations but only one workers' organization (the Union Trade Society of Journeymen Tailors) and one nascent political party (the nativist American Republican Party). After midcentury, groups trying to organize workers for either their own professional advantages or general political programs, from Chinese exclusion to socialist revolution, loom much larger.
3. Most of the challengers sought benefits or protection for special interests rather than generalization of political rights. In twenty-first-century perspective some of them—notably nativist mobilizations—look downright reactionary (cf. Hoffmann 2003, Kaufman 2002, Skocpol 1999: 72–75).

Across the nineteenth century, social movement claim making clearly became available to a widening variety of American interests. By the luck of the draw, Gamson's sampling procedure bypassed two of the most prominent nineteenth-century social movement issues, temperance and female suffrage. It also passed by most countermovements, for example the widespread mobilization *against* abolitionism before the Civil War (Grimsted 1998, McKivigan & Harrold 1999). But it did capture municipal reform and the cooperative movement. Gamson's catalog portrays a quickening and broadening of social movement activity in the United States during the later nineteenth century.

Mary Ryan's history of public politics in New York, San Francisco, and New Orleans during the nineteenth century richly illustrates, and generally confirms, the impression of changes offered by Gamson's study. Despite giving greater prominence to ethnic and racial divisions, Ryan's roster of nineteenth-century organizations broadly resembles Gamson's. She reports, for example, activity of New York's Laborers Benevolent Union as a sort of Irish workers' protection society during the 1840s, appearance of a nativist American Party in New Orleans as early as 1856, formation of a Committee of Merchants for the Relief of Colored People in response to the New York draft riots of 1863, New Orleans' hosting of a Convention of Colored Men of Louisiana in 1865, San Francisco workers' parading as the Eight Hour League in 1867, and effective anti-Chinese agitation by the Workingman's Party of California in 1877, as well as racially, ethnically, and occupationally segregated organizations such as the Ancient Order of Hibernians and the Orange Loyal Association (Ryan 1997: 79, 82, 148–50, 173, 229, 262, 282, 290–91). But Ryan also marks the 1863 entry into public politics of New York's National Loyal Women League and of New Orleans' National Equal Rights League (Ryan 1997: 179, 262). Her evidence reveals a wide range of program claims, a spectacular variety of identity claims, and repeated standing claims—including demands for the exclusion of other actors from political rights or even from the country as a whole.

Again paralleling Gamson's observations, Ryan notes the increasing prominence of workers' organizations in her three cities' public politics after the Civil War.

In 1877, when the great railroad strikes consumed smaller cities and towns, a variety of workers took to the streets of big cities for a common cause. Cigar workers announced their militancy on the streets of New Orleans and New York with particular vehemence and solidarity. The New Orleans press reported that they assembled in Congo Square and heard speeches in Spanish, French, and English. Similar work stoppages in New York won favorable notices on the sidewalks and in the press. Of "The Cigar Makers Street Parade" the *Tribune* observed, "The faces of the striking cigar-makers beamed with smiles of triumph as they assembled yesterday in front of Concordia Hall, to take part in the procession of the organization. Men, women, and children came singly and in groups from shops, each bearing a flag and banner with inscriptions." Those flags included the colors of Germany, Bohemia, and Austria and, like the language groups assembled in Congo Square, signaled a new mobilization within the urban public, that of "labor" in multiethnic array. (Ryan 1997: 256)

Ryan sums up the overall trajectories of nineteenth-century American urban politics as running "from differences toward dualism, from representation toward bureaucracy, from a citizenry toward a tax base, from voluntary associations toward social movements" (Ryan 1997: 259). As the festival phase of American urban space declined, disciplined claim-making—and often narrowly self-interested—social movements replaced it. The rise of the social movement, Ryan suggests, tamed the rambunctious street democracy of the early nineteenth century (cf. Vernon 1993 on nineteenth-century England).

Where, When, and Why Social Movements?

What do the nineteenth-century experiences of France, Belgium, the United Kingdom, and the United States add to our knowledge of conditions and causes for social movements? Quite a bit, actually. Most obviously, even these quick snapshots show us how much the fine grain of nineteenth-century social movement activity drew on local and regional culture: songs, slogans, symbols, costumes, and labels that took their meaning from previously existing practices and entities.

Within the convergence on special-purpose associations, public meetings, and demonstrations that occurred in all four countries, we notice continued differentiation that attached claim-making campaigns, social movement performances, and WUNC displays to their immediate contexts and, thus, made them legible to local audiences. Modularity does not mean perfect uniformity: seen from one side a demonstration or a special-purpose association retained recognizable local cultural markers even if from the other its distinctive overall contours transferred easily from one setting to another.

The shift of repertoires we have observed in the four countries had profound implications for popular participation in public politics. House sacking, shaming ceremonies, forced illuminations, and direct attacks on malefactors declined rapidly as ordinary people moved to new forms of claim making and authorities applied more stringent repression to the old forms. The sheer effectiveness of social movement strategies by no means accounts for the change. The older repertoire's direct actions rarely produced political reform at the national level, but they often settled matters locally in a quick, decisive way. Ordinary people in North America, Belgium, France, and the British Isles lost some of their cherished, proven means of retaliation, coercion, supplication, and threat.

Segments of the population lacking connections with political entrepreneurs and special-purpose associations, furthermore, actually lost some of their political leverage. Before the time of Chartism, for example, Great Britain's landless agricultural laborers had at least occasionally been able to exert collective pressure on farmers and local authorities through public shaming, appeals to local patrons, collective destruction of agricultural machinery, and coordinated withholding of labor; by the 1840s their means had dwindled to occasional arson, poaching, and clandestine attacks on animals (Archer 1990). Chartism itself recruited mainly from artisans and skilled workers rather than landless laborers. The repertoire shift produced a dramatic decline in the physical damage to persons and property wrought by collective claim making; most public performances in the social movement mode went off with no violence whatever, and such scuffling as occurred between police and demonstrators generally involved far less damage than had the old repertoire's attacks.

Why did that happen? On the whole, parliamentarization seems to have offered powerful spurs to the creation of social movements in all four of our cases. Remember the two main components of parliamentarization: 1) increase in the absolute power of representative institutions with respect to governmental activities such as taxation, war making, provision of public services, and creation of public infrastructure; and 2) increase in the *relative* power of representative institutions compared to hereditary rulers, great patrons, priests, and local holders of power.

In all four cases, the parliaments in question organized territorially, distributing across the national space. Not all parliaments do so; indeed, the Estates General that constituted France's closest approximation to a national parliament before the Revolution of 1789 specifically represented not French regions but the national memberships of three broad Estates: clergy, nobility, and propertied commoners. Revolutionary struggles of 1789 and 1790 then converted the Estates General into a geographically representative national body (Lepetit 1982, 1988, Margadant 1992, Markoff 1996a, Ozouf-Marignier 1986, Schultz 1982, Tilly 1962, Woloch 1994). In France and elsewhere, such a territorial organization increased social and geographic proximity between national power holders and their constituencies. Rising absolute and relative impacts of parliamentary decisions therefore focused affected citizens on increasingly accessible potential targets of claims, their regions' representatives in the parliament.

Parliamentarization also produced a further set of political effects that, on the average, favored social movement claim making:

- reduction in the political importance of long-established patron-client chains as major conduits for national politics;
- significant new opportunities for political entrepreneurs who could produce temporary links between public officials and multiple groups of aggrieved, connected citizens;
- accentuation of governmental claims to speak on behalf of a unified, connected people; and
- regular semipublic sittings of representative bodies that in turn became geographic and temporal sites for claim making.

In the nineteenth-century United Kingdom, United States, France, and Belgium, parliamentary sessions and deliberations focused many social movement campaigns. Just remember Deneckere's linking of "socialist mass actions" and Belgium's parliamentary move to manhood suffrage in 1893.

Notice, nevertheless, significant differences between the relatively centralized political regimes of France and Belgium, on one side, and the more segmented political structures of the United Kingdom and, especially, the United States, on the other. Although the inventories at hand do not allow precise comparisons, they give a strong impression of social movements' greater focus on the national state in the centralized regimes. Take workers: in France and Belgium, they struck against individual employers but directed demands for rights, policies, and reforms to national authorities; repeated attempts of Belgian workers at general strikes aimed at the state rather than at employers. Parliament did draw a significant share of social movement claim making in the United Kingdom, but so did local and regional authorities. In the United States, leaders of cities and states drew a significant share of social movement claims. National political structures shaped social movement activity.

In a complementary way, the forms of organization already established on the ground also shaped social movements in the four countries. Such organizations as the League of American Wheelmen and the American Party formed precisely in the course of public claim making. Yet even when SMOs came into being in the course of social movement mobilizations, they fed on their organizational environments. Religious congregations, mutual benefit societies, fraternal orders, and ethnic associations, for example, recur as contexts for the coalitions and blanket associations that figured in U.S. social movements. Confrontations between Catholic organizations and their anticlerical opponents loomed much larger in France and Belgium. Even where close collaboration and emulation occur across settings, with the emergence of social movement activity elsewhere we should expect to find a similar grounding of its specific organizational forms in local environments. As a complex form of political interaction, we should not expect to find the social movement diffusing relatively unchanged as do cell phones, slogan-printed tee shirts, and the term "OK."

Political Rights

Behind such differences, state-guaranteed political rights or their absence wielded a large influence. In the histories we have examined, rights to assembly, association, and speech mattered especially (see Anderson & Anderson 1967: chaps. 6 and 7 for a convenient review). Where regimes succeeded in abridging those rights seriously (as during the early years of France's Second Empire), social movements generally declined. Rights to assembly directly affected all the major social movement performances and their concomitant WUNC displays; unlike routines of the older repertoire that flowed out of routine authorized assemblies such as markets and holidays, social movement routines depended intimately on assembly.

Rights to associate proved crucial to the special-purpose organizations and crosscutting coalitions of social movements; clandestine organizations and informal networks could coordinate some forms of claim making, but legal rights to associate greatly facilitated mobilization and coordination of public claims. They also multiplied the number of political actors that a regime's denial of associational rights to any particular interest would threaten even when the actors in question opposed that interest; Belgian promoters of French and Flemish predominance both acquired an investment in the organizational forms their opponents deployed.

Freedom of speech obviously mattered centrally to the public making of claims in all its social movement forms: the meeting, the demonstration, the pamphlet, the media message, and all the rest. Among the cases surveyed earlier, Chartism provides the most dramatic examples; U.K. authorities scanned Chartist activities closely for signs of criminal conspiracy or attempted rebellion that they could prosecute but found themselves hamstrung with regard to restricting public expression. By the 1830s, the United Kingdom's popular activists were fully exercising rights to criticize their rulers and to propose radical political transformations.

This way of describing the situation, however, implies a false scenario: first a regime grants rights, then ordinary people take advantage of those rights. In fact, we have seen popular activists and political entrepreneurs from John Wilkes onward bargaining for rights to assembly, association, and speech. They generally did so by pushing against the limits that attached existing rights to certain populations, activities, organizations, or places. Wilkes's 1768 victory in court, which established powerful precedents in British law for the protection of political speech, provides a dramatic example.

Less visibly but more fundamentally, day-to-day bargaining in the course of contentious claim making pushed the boundaries of existing rights. Citizens who already exercised contained rights to assemble as taxpayers or as members of religious congregations dared to use taxpayers' meetings and church services for the formulation and expression of shared demands. Where members of the ruling classes were already employing similar means of assembly, association, and speech to pursue their own collective ends—as, for example, in prerevolutionary Boston—authorities had a more difficult time restricting the rights of ordinary people to exercise the same rights. That became especially true when dissident members of the elite drew popular followings or deliberately allied themselves with opponents of the regime.

The bargaining process speeded up enormously during nationwide political struggles and revolutions. It could proceed from bottom up or from top down. Bottom up, we see ordinary people increasing their access to assembly, association, and speech as divided elites fight with each other and sometimes reach out for popular followings. Top down, we see reformers or revolutionaries seizing control of central states and instituting rights as matters of principle and/or means of consolidating their power. Viewing the French revolution of 1848 from Lyon, we have seen both the bottom-up and top-down versions of rights extension occurring; workers and other claimants in Lyon took advantage of revolutionary divisions to emerge from the shadows into public politics, but the revolutionaries who captured the French state in February–March 1848 also instituted a legal program supporting assembly, association, and speech. The top-down intervention then promoted a temporary expansion of social-movement activity in Lyon and other French cities. In 1870–1871, Lyon's radicals inverted the process: they seized power over the city against opposition from national authorities and for six months installed a commune whose citizens enjoyed extensive rights of assembly, association, and speech.

One political innovation that always proceeded from the top down greatly promoted the emergence of social movements: the institution of consequential, contested elections. As the histories of Britain and North America amply illustrate, even with narrow, uneven suffrage such elections could promote social movement activity. Consequential, contested elections promoted social movement campaigns, performances, and WUNC displays in several different ways.

1. In a manner similar to official holidays they almost inevitably involved public assemblies from which it was difficult for authorities to exclude nonvoters; those assemblies then became privileged occasions for the public voicing of claims.
2. They provided a model of public support for rival programs, as embodied in competing candidates; once governments authorized public discussion of major issues during electoral campaigns, it became harder to silence that discussion outside of electoral campaigns.

3. Elections magnified the importance of numbers; with contested elections, any group receiving disciplined support from large numbers of followers became a possible ally or enemy at the polls.
4. Candidates often had incentives for displays of popular support, including support from nonvoters; such displays fortified their claims to represent "the people" at large and to command wider support than one's electoral opponents (Morgan 1988).
5. To the extent that voting districts were geographical, both campaigns and polls offered opportunities for injecting local and regional issues into the public discussion.
6. Visible legal divisions between those who did and those who did not have the right to vote promoted claims by the excluded for rights denied as they made exclusion dramatically evident.

In Britain, North America, France, and Belgium, the nineteenth-century institutionalization of national elections promoted social movement activity. Expansion of the franchise then doubly facilitated social movement expansion: increased rights of political participation for the enfranchised, increased incentives to collective complaints by the disfranchised.

Do Social Movements Equal Democratization?

Does all this then amount to a giant tautology: social movements = democratization (Giugni, McAdam, & Tilly 1998, Ibarra 2003, Markoff 1996b)? Certainly our historical cases argue for some general affinity between social movements and democratization. In fact, however, social movements and democratization remain logically, empirically, and causally distinct. Logically, proliferation of social movements does not entail democratization, since the campaigns, performances, and WUNC displays of social movements can in principle operate on behalf of inequality and exclusion rather than equality and inclusion; consider the (very logical) possibility of movements on behalf of expelling recent immigrants. Empirically, antidemocratic movements have formed repeatedly; we need look no further than the nativist mobilizations in William Gamson's catalog for the nineteenth-century United States.

Causally, social movements and democratization also occur in partial independence; in cases of conquest and revolution, for example, new rulers sometimes impose democratic institutions suddenly in the absence of any previous social movement mobilization on behalf of democracy; think about occupied Japan and Germany after World War II. No necessary connection exists between social movements and democracy. The main generalization we can draw from our evidence so far runs rather differently: once democratization does occur, social movements (whether democratic or not) usually follow.

Ruth Berins Collier's comparative study of democratization in Western Europe and South America offers an opportunity to add a little more precision to these claims (for explication and critique of Collier's analysis, see Tilly 2001a). In a systematic effort to detect effects of middle-class and working-class participation in democratic transitions, Collier compares seventeen "historic" cases of democratization, mostly nineteenth-century, with ten "recent" cases occurring from 1974 to 1990. Democratization, for Collier, means establishment of 1) liberal constitutional rule, 2) classical elections, and 3) an independent and popularly elected legislative assembly (Collier 1999: 24). Table 3.3 lists her historic cases, from Switzerland (1848) to Spain (three transitions, all reversed sooner or later, from 1868 to 1931). To sort out the interdependence of social movements and Collier's democratic transitions, we must decide which transitions to emphasize, date the availability of social movements in popular politics, and then match the two dates. As the history of France suggests, that will not always be easy; Collier's dates of 1848 and 1875–1877 for French democratic transitions clearly precede the date of durable social movement establishment indicated by the history of demonstrations, but 1848 certainly did bring France a temporary flowering of associations, meetings, demonstrations, and other social movement performances.

Table 3.3 Ruth Berins Collier's "Historic" Cases of
Democratization, with Transition Dates

Country	Year(s)
Switzerland	1848
France	1848, 1875–1877
Denmark	1849, 1915
Greece	1864
Chile	1874/1891
Great Britain	1884, 1918
Norway	1898
Finland	(1906), 1919
Sweden	1907/1909, 1918/1920
Portugal	1911, 1918
Argentina	1912
Italy	1912 (1919)
Netherlands	1917
Belgium	1918
Germany	1918–1919
Uruguay	1918
Spain	1868, 1890, 1931

Source: Collier 1999: 23.

Key: date/date: elements of democratic rule arrived in segments;
(date): arguable alternative to main date given; repeated dates:
partial establishment followed by reversal(s) or long plateaux

Table 3.4 Order of Social Movements and Democratic Transitions in Collier's
"Historic" Cases

Social Movements First	Transition First
Denmark 1849, 1915	Switzerland 1848
Great Britain 1884, 1918	France 1848, 1875–1877
Norway 1898	Greece 1864
Finland (1906), 1919	Chile 1874/1891
Sweden 1907/1909, 1918/1920	Portugal 1911, 1918
Argentina 1912	Spain 1868
Italy 1912 (1919)	
Netherlands 1917	
Belgium 1918	
Germany 1918–1919	
Uruguay 1918	
Spain 1890, 1931	

Sources: Alapuro 1988, Ballbé 1983, Birmingham 1993, Caramani 2003, Collier 1999, Deneckere 1997, Dolléans & Crozier 1950, Dowe 1970, González Calleja 1998, 1999, Lida 1972, López-Alves 2000, Lundqvist 1977, Öhngren 1974, Paige 1997, Rock 1987, Sabato 2001, Seip 1974, 1981, Skidmore & Smith 1984, Stenius 1987, Tilly 1986, 1995, Wåhlin 1986, Wirtz 1981.

Drawing on Collier's own descriptions plus a variety of historical works, let me nevertheless offer a rough tabulation of Collier's cases. The tabulation distinguishes between instances in which social movement activity clearly proliferated before Collier's transition date and those in which substantial establishment of democratic institutions preceded the extensive growth of social movements. Table 3.4 presents the breakdown. Spain appears twice in the tabulation, with the abortive democratization of 1868 preceding any significant social movement mobilization but with the new transitions of 1890 and 1931 occurring after social movements had begun to proliferate, at least in the country's major cities (Ballbé 1983, González Calleja 1998, 1999). Other countries only appear once, but sometimes with multiple years representing subsequently reversed transitions, partial transitions, or alternative dates. Except for Spain, however, the multiple dates do not blur the decision concerning whether transition or social movements came first.

How do the countries divide? Although social movements preceded Collier's democratic transitions in twelve of the eighteen cases, in the other six narrowly based democratic transitions promoted subsequent social movements where they had previously possessed little political standing or none at all. Regimes that early experienced top-down creation of liberal constitutions, contested elections, and popularly chosen legislative assemblies, on the average, put them into place before social movements developed fully; we have followed just such an experience closely for France. Aside from that obvious point, no strong difference in geographic location or previous type of regime differentiates the two sides.

One geographic exception, however: The Nordic countries—Denmark, Norway, Finland, and Sweden—concentrate early in the "social movements first" column. The Baltic region had long stood out from the rest of Europe for its exceptional combination of powerful (Lutheran) state churches with extensive citizenship rights. Denmark's early creation of a relatively democratic constitution (1849) resulted from the intervention of a young, reforming monarch in the wake of the 1848 revolutions. But even in Denmark peasants, workers, and religious activists had been creating special-purpose associations and deploying them in public politics for a century before then (Wåhlin 1986). Despite the previous chapter's placement of social movement invention in England and North America during the nineteenth century's first decades, then, the Nordic countries might have some claims to coinvention. Their eighteenth-century innovations, however, did not spread early or widely.

Norway, Finland, and Sweden hummed with social movements through most of the nineteenth century. Church-backed organizations provided the initial impetus, but secular liberals, religious opponents of state churches, advocates of cooperatives, supporters of folk nationalism, organized workers, and (especially after 1880) opponents of alcohol mounted vast campaigns, adopted social movement performances, and made regular displays of WUNC integral elements of their claim making (Alapuro 1988, Lundqvist 1977, Öhngren 1974, Seip 1974, 1981, Stenius 1987). In partial independence of democratic transitions, then, regional and national social processes sometimes promoted social movements.

Puzzling Switzerland

Given its reputation for intensive civic participation, Switzerland's appearance at the top of the "transition first" list comes as a surprise. One might have thought that Swiss citizens were busy forming associations, staging demonstrations, and creating social movement campaigns well before 1848. There hangs a tale. Far from easing into democracy as a consequence of age-old habits and culture, Switzerland fashioned democratic institutions as a contested and improvised compromise solution to a revolutionary crisis (for general historical background, see Bonjour 1948, Bonjour, Offler, & Potter 1952, Capitani 1986, Deutsch 1976, Gilliard 1955, Gossman 2000, Kohn 1956, Wimmer 2002: 222–68).

Especially in the highlands, Swiss towns and cantons did have a long history of civic participation, but in the circumscribed old-regime version of European peasant villages and city-states. Some subset of property-holding males and their sons typically formed an assembly that consented to major taxes and expenditures, elected the year's officers, and held veto power in the case of widespread dissent against official actions. But those proud electors generally excluded the propertyless, and often governed dependent territories whose residents had no say in public affairs (Böning 1998, Wyrsch 1983). Oligarchy would be a better name for the system than democracy.

The French Revolution shook Switzerland's economic and political ties to France. It also exposed Swiss people, especially its commercial bourgeoisie and its growing industrial proletariat, to new French models and doctrines. From 1789 onward, revolutionary movements formed in several parts of Switzerland. In 1793 Geneva (not a federation member, but closely tied to Switzerland) underwent a revolution on the French model. As the threat of French invasion mounted in early 1798, Basel, Vaud, Lucerne, Zurich, and other Swiss regions followed the revolutionary path. Basel, for example, turned from a constitution in which only citizens of the town chose their canton's senators to another giving urban and rural populations equal representation.

Conquered by France in collaboration with Swiss revolutionaries in 1798, then receiving a new constitution that year, the Swiss regime as a whole adopted a much more centralized form of government with significantly expanded citizenship. The new regime incorporated the territories of the cantons St. Gall, Grisons, Thurgau, Ticino, Aargau, and Vaud on equal terms with the older cantons but followed French revolutionary practice by reducing the cantons to administrative and electoral units. The central government remained fragile, however; four coups occurred between 1800 and 1802 alone. At the withdrawal of French troops in 1802, multiple rebellions broke out. Switzerland then rushed to the brink of civil war. Only Napoleon's intervention and imposition of a new constitution in 1803 kept the country together.

The 1803 regime, known in Swiss history as the Mediation, restored considerable powers to cantons but by no means reestablished the Old Regime. Switzerland's recast federation operated with a national assembly, official multilingualism, relative equality among cantons, and freedom for citizens to move from canton to canton. Despite some territorial adjustments, a weak central legislature, judiciary, and executive survived Napoleon's defeat. Survival only occurred, however, after another close brush with civil war, this time averted by Great Power intervention, in 1813–1815. In the war settlement of 1815, Austria, France, Great Britain, Portugal, Prussia, Russia, Spain, and Sweden accepted a treaty among twenty-two cantons called the Federal Pact (now adding Valais, Neuchâtel, and Geneva) as they guaranteed Switzerland's perpetual neutrality and the inviolability of its frontiers.

The victors of 1815 did not give Swiss central authorities adequate means for managing their country's complexity. Switzerland of the Federal Pact operated without a permanent bureaucracy, a standing army, common coinage, standard measures, or a national flag but with multiple internal customs barriers, a rotating capital, and incessant bickering among cantonal representatives who had no right to deviate from their home constituents' instructions. At the national scale, the Swiss lived with a system better disposed to vetoes than to concerted change. At that point, social movements played no significant part in Swiss public life.

At France's July 1830 revolution, anticlericalism became more salient in Swiss radicalism. After 1830, Switzerland became a temporary home for many exiled revolutionaries (for example Giuseppe Mazzini, Wilhelm Weitling and, more surprisingly, future emperor Louis Napoleon), who collaborated with Swiss radicals in calling for reform. Historians of Switzerland in the 1830s speak of a Regeneration Movement pursued by means of "publicity, clubs, and mass marches" (Nabholz, von Muralt, Feller, & Bonjour 1938: II, 406). But that "movement" resembled the narrow, top-down mobilizations we have already observed in France and Belgium before 1848. A great spurt of new periodicals and pamphlets accompanied the political turmoil of 1830–31 (Andrey 1986: 551–52). Within individual cantons, empowered liberals began enacting standard nineteenth-century reforms such as limitation of child labor and expansion of public schools. Nevertheless, the new cantonal constitutions installed during that mobilization stressed liberty and fraternity much more than they did equality.

Between 1830 and 1848, Switzerland underwent a contradictory set of political processes. Although the era's struggles unquestionably activated many convinced democrats, they pitted competing conceptions of democracy against each other. They played out, furthermore, over a substratum of competition for control of the Swiss federation as a whole. The country's richer, more Protestant cantons struggled their way toward their own versions of democracy. Those cantons installed representative institutions instead of the direct democracy of male citizens that had long prevailed in highland communities and cantons. Activists based in reformed cantons then used armed force to drive their unreformed neighbors toward representative democracy. They did so first in military raids across cantonal boundaries, then in an open, if short-lived, civil war, the Sonderbund War of 1847 (Bucher 1966, Remak 1993). Only after the liberal side won the civil war decisively did negotiations resulting in a democratic constitution begin.

During the crisis, furthermore, confessional qualifications for citizenship became even more salient. As astute observer Alexis de Tocqueville put it shortly after the civil war,

> Nowhere else has the democratic revolution that is now stirring the world occurred in such complicated, bizarre circumstances. One people composed of multiple races, speaking multiple languages, adhering to multiple faiths and various dissident sects, two equally established and privileged churches, every political question soon pivoting on religious questions and every religious question leading to political questions, really two societies, one very old and the other very young, married to each other despite the difference in their ages. That is Switzerland. (Tocqueville 1983: 635–36)

Switzerland as a whole actually dedemocratized between 1830 and 1847. Yet the settlement of 1848 clearly advanced democracy at a national scale beyond the level it had reached in 1798, 1803, 1815, or even 1830. Swiss democratization rapidly generated opportunities for social movements. Soon after 1848, Swiss citizens began creating a wide range of social movements closely tuned to the consultative institutions—for example, referenda at cantonal and national levels—established by the constitutional peace settlement. They created the intensely participatory Swiss public politics we know today (Frey & Stutzer 2002: chaps. 8–9, Kriesi, Levy, Ganguillet, & Zwicky 1981, Steinberg 1996, Stutzer & Frey 2002, Trechsel 2000).

Social Movements in Argentina

Let us look at one more puzzling national placement. Argentina stands in the column of countries where social movements preceded democratic transitions. With the country's political history of caudillos, colonels, and repressive regimes, we might have expected Argentina to resemble Greece, Chile, or Portugal. In fact, the country's very uneven relationship between center and periphery left space for islands of social movement activity. At least in Buenos Aires, social movement politics became visible quite early. As Argentine historian Hilda Sabato summarizes,

> In the 1860s and 1870s, the people of Buenos Aires often mobilized in order to encourage, protest, or otherwise influence government action. Important demonstrations were staged, for example, in 1864, to support Peru in its conflict with Spain; to support the War of the Triple Alliance against Paraguay in the following year; to sympathize with Cuba in 1869 and 1873; to oppose the death penalty when Pascual Castro Chavarría was sentenced to death in 1870; to object to the official organization mounted on occasion of the yellow fever epidemics of 1871; to protest the restitution of the church of San Ignacio to the original owners, the Jesuits, in 1875; to resist the law of 1878 that imposed an additional tax on liquor, tobacco, and playing cards; to demonstrate for peace in the face of the revolutionary events of 1880. (Sabato 2001: 118)

Social movement activity continued into the 1880s. In 1889, Buenos Aires students formed an organization called the Youth Civic Union (*Unión Cívica de la Juventud*) to oppose government policies. The organization soon attracted nonstudent followers and evolved into a general Civic Union. In 1890 the union staged a Buenos Aires demonstration with thirty thousand participants. Later that year a popular militia aligned with the union attacked government forces in a failed rebellion, only to discover that major politicians who had encouraged the attack had made a deal behind its back to change the government. The 1890s brought organization-based popular politics onto the national scene, but against a distinctive Argentine background of military and strongman politics.

Between 1890 and 1914, associational life flowered in Argentina. A broad, semiconspiratorial movement of people who called themselves radicals connected numerous local middle-class political clubs with a hierarchy of party committees. They adopted standard social movement means, including mass meetings and demonstrations. Several anarchist federations organized workers in the Buenos Aires region. In addition to their own demonstrations on such occasions as May

Day and New Year's Day, anarchists originated half a dozen general strikes in and around Buenos Aires between 1899 and 1910. When they threatened to sabotage festivities for the centennial of Argentine independence in 1910, however, the government began arresting anarchists as vigilantes and smashed their meeting places.

Meanwhile, Argentine socialists (who distinguished themselves sharply from the anarchists) initiated standard social movement campaigns for working-class credit, housing, education, divorce, women's suffrage, and an eight-hour day. Their Socialist Party, founded in 1894, brought together workers with professionals and some small manufacturers. By the time the party elected its first member of Argentina's Chamber of Deputies in 1904, social movement politics had taken firm root in the country. Thus Argentine social movements unquestionably long preceded the democratic transition that Ruth Berins Collier marks at 1912, when the Sáenz Peña Law enacted suffrage and the secret ballot for men eighteen and over.

To be sure, Collier's and my assignment of dates to Argentina brushes past a vexing problem that all of the cases actually hide: variability in access to both democracy and social movements within each regime. As of 1912, Buenos Aires had become a cosmopolitan capital of a large, prosperous country. But most of the country remained agricultural, significant regions still hosted indigenous populations that were little involved in national politics, and large parts fell under the control of great landlords, ranchers, and regional strongmen (Rock 1987: 179–83). In all our countries, the dates in question neglect great unevenness in access to democratic institutions and social movements. They mark essentially the time when some substantial segment of the national population first gained that access.

Internationalization of Social Movements

One more important observation emerges from the nineteenth-century national experiences this chapter has surveyed. Although the timing and character of social movements depended chiefly on the changing structure of national politics, international connections made a significant difference. We have already observed the close interaction between British and North American activists during the eighteenth century, in the social movement's very formative days. From early on, antislavery took a very international turn. Throughout the nineteenth century, international connections mattered in three different ways.

1. Social movements responded to changes produced by international contacts such as flows of migrants; American nativist movements provide a case in point.
2. Seeking to outflank national authorities, social movement entrepreneurs deliberately organized across international boundaries. We have glimpsed the

International Workingmen's Association at work during the 1860s and 1870s, but we might also have traced the great influence of Irish exiles and sympathizers in nineteenth-century Irish nationalist movements.

3. International connections among rulers and claimants to rule also affected social movement activity, as rulers and claimants sought external validation of their politics. Claiming that your regime or your opposition movement represented a unified, committed people opened either side to demands for proof as a condition for international support. As the century wore on, furthermore, rulers' claims that their regime was a democracy and opposition claims that the regime was *not* a democracy increasingly drew scrutiny and even intervention by outsiders.

Claims to legitimate rule, in turn, invited oppressed peoples to adopt social movement strategies—campaigns, repertoires, and WUNC displays—on the way to gathering external support against their oppressors. The Indian National Congress (founded in 1885) originated in just such an effort. During its early years, the Congress made its claims in the manner of an orderly British pressure group, by lobbying, petitioning, and drafting addresses; it acted as a social movement organization (Bose & Jalal 1998: 116–17, Johnson 1996: 156–62). Nevertheless, the spread and internationalization of social movements both greatly accelerated during the twentieth century. Our nineteenth-century story has concentrated very heavily on Western Europe and North America. The twentieth-century story will be different.

4

TWENTIETH-CENTURY EXPANSION AND TRANSFORMATION

Teleology and wishful thinking often coincide. We tell stories about the past in which all history conspired to produce our tolerable present and our glorious future. In 1962, on behalf of the Soviet Communist Party's Central Committee, the High Party School's Department of the History of the International Working and National Liberation Movement applied the principle faithfully. It published two fat volumes surveying, yes, the international working and national liberation movement from the eighteenth century to the recent past. The two volumes broke, significantly, at 1917, year of the Bolshevik Revolution. Up to 1917 merited 644 pages, from 1917 to 1939, 634 pages. Before 1917, they seemed to say, preparation; from 1917 onward, fulfillment. The past, for them, offered a vindicating vision of the future (Bogolyubov, R'izhkova, Popov, & Dubinskii 1962).

Each volume contained commissioned essays on major events, economic changes, workers' movements in industrial areas, and liberation movements in nonindustrial areas. It set down summaries for country after country, region after region, across the world. Here are titles of the two volumes' introductory and concluding chapters:

Volume I, chapter 1: Formation of a Producing Proletariat and the First Independent Appearances of Workers in England, France, and Germany.
Volume I, chapter 33: Workers' and National-Liberation Movements During the First World War.
Volume II, chapter 1: The World-Historical Significance of the Great October Socialist Revolution.
Volume II, chapter 27: International Workers' Movements 1917–1939. The Communist International.

We see unfolding an updated Communist Manifesto story of class formation and crystallization of popular action in militant movements, with the Bolshevik

Revolution now figuring as the harbinger of worldwide collective action against tyranny. The second volume's final chapter concluded with this summary of conditions in 1939:

> Despite the impossibility of holding a Comintern congress in the conditions of the war's outbreak and the difficulty of maintaining contacts between individual parties and the Comintern's leading organs, the communist parties of most countries managed to offer correct analyses of conditions and interconnections of class forces and to work out correct tactical lines, to rally around themselves the broad popular masses in the battle for the interests of workers, for freedom and independence of their countries, for democracy, against reaction and Fascism. Here we have described the huge role played by the Communist International in the development of the world communist movement. (Bogolyubov, R'izhkova, Popov, & Dubinskii 1962: II, 625)

While to a twenty-first-century reader the forty-year-old party-line prose, with its "correct analyses" and "correct tactical lines," reeks of musty antiquity, it expresses a common inside view of social movement activity during the twentieth century: we are fulfilling history, and we will prevail.

Although they certainly stressed communist parties and the Comintern, these Soviet historians of 1962 took a broad view of relevant movements across the world. Their second volume's chronologies for 1935 and 1936 appear in table 4.1. During those eventful years, the chronologies of major events included the emphatically noncommunist American New Deal legislation that finally authorized industrial (as opposed to craft) unions, antifascist action whether communist-organized or not, and electoral victories of Left coalitions in Spain and France. (Unsurprisingly, the chroniclers omitted the lethal purges of the Soviet Communist Party, wholesale transfers of rural populations, and massive expulsions of suspected counterrevolutionaries from Moscow and Leningrad that Stalin was orchestrating during the same years.) For the part of the twentieth century up to 1939, the chronologies portray an international workers' movement sometimes facing setbacks such as fascist countermobilizations and defeated rebellions but generally gaining strength, increasing in international scope, and—after the fateful year of 1917—taking inspiration from the Soviet Communist Party.

The compilation's nineteenth-century chronologies enumerate a number of events already familiar to us from our own survey of the century. They include the partial legalization of workers' organizations in England (1824), Lyon's workers' insurrections of 1831 and 1834, Britain's Chartist movement, the French revolution of 1848, and the formation of militant workers' parties, combined with major strike waves in the United States from the 1860s onward and the foundation of the Argentine Socialist Party (1896). France gets a great deal of attention, partly because of its revolutionary tradition and partly because Marx, Engels, and Lenin wrote quotable analyses of the country's nineteenth-century political history.

Table 4.1 Soviet Historians' Movement Chronologies for 1935 and 1936

1935	
July	Wagner Act, or law on industrial relations in the USA
July	Antifascist demonstrations in Paris and other French cities
July–August	Seventh Congress of the Comintern
1 August	Address of the Chinese Communist Party to the Chinese people calling for creation of a united anti-Japanese front
October	Conference of the German Communist Party in Brussels
October	Italian anti-Fascist conference in Brussels
all year	Mass anti-Fascist movement in Poland, with general strikes in Lodz, Cracow, and Lvov
1936	
January	Publication of the Popular Front program in France
February	Victory of the Popular Front in Spanish elections
May	Victory of the Popular Front in French elections
July	Fascist uprising in Spain. Beginning of the Spanish people's national-revolutionary war against Fascist rebels and German-Italian interventionists
July	Beginning of international mass anti-Fascist movement for the defense of the Spanish Republic

Source: Bogolyubov, R'izhkova, Popov, & Dubinskii 1962: II, 633.

Outside of Europe and the United States, the chronologies also signal Latin American independence struggles (1810–1826), the Opium War of England and China (1839–1842), China's Taiping Rebellion (1851–1864), Indian rebellions against English rule (1857–1859), founding of the Indian National Congress (1885), creation of Sun Yat-sen's (Sun Yixian's) Society for the Regeneration of China (1894), Cuba's rebellion against Spain (1895–1898), formation of the Chilean Socialist Party (1897), and the Boxer Rebellion in China (1899–1900).

Yet some of the Soviet book's silences sound loudly, at least to ears tuned for social movements. Despite substantial chapters on English industrialization and the American Civil War, antislavery mobilizations make no appearance in the nineteenth-century history. Catholic emancipation, parliamentary reform, and female suffrage disappear from the British roster. In the United States, we hear nothing of nativism, temperance, and municipal reform. Argentina's Unión Cívica makes not a sound. The years 1847–1848 abound with revolutionary movements, but not the Swiss civil war. Researchers of the Department of the History of the International Working and National Liberation Movement took their mandate seriously. They were not surveying all the world's social movements and political struggles but only those that bore somehow on the mission of bringing the world's workers into a communist-led collective fight for freedom.

Within that more restricted scope, what picture of nineteenth-century social movements does the Soviet survey project? From its retrospect of 1962, it portrays a century of great promise: European and North American workers begin early to show signs of class consciousness as Latin American masses throw over their Spanish masters. Soon Chinese, Indian, and Latin American peoples are beginning to resist other varieties of colonialism and to make connections with the worldwide worker's movement.

As the Soviet movement history enters the twentieth century, the Russian Revolution of 1905 joins Russia to the nineteenth-century revolutionary tradition, but it reveals a proletariat still unready to seize power. The Bolshevik Revolution then consolidates the nineteenth century's hopeful projects by offering a concrete model of proletarian revolution and a communist regime strong enough to lend muscle for workers' efforts everywhere. Between 1917 and the chronology's terminus in 1939, we encounter a round of revolutionary struggles immediately after World War I, founding of the Comintern, and extension of progressive mobilization from its pre-1917 sites to Japan, Korea, Mexico, Indonesia, Iran, Turkey, Uruguay, Mongolia, Egypt, Hong Kong, Syria, the Philippines, and elsewhere, followed in the 1930s by formation of a far-reaching antifascist coalition. Soviet historians writing in 1962 knew, of course, that the German and Italian fascist regimes had collapsed in World War II and that a battered Soviet Union had emerged from the war on the winning side. Their vantage point helps explain the combination of teleology and wishful thinking that informed their history of movements up to 1939.

If the same group of experts had extrapolated their account forward through the remainder of the twentieth century, what features of the period from 1939 to 2000 would they have gotten right? They might have taken credit for having anticipated anticolonial mobilization, stressing how often leaders of independence movements styled themselves socialists and drew encouragement from China or the Soviet Union. They might also have drawn some satisfaction from the formation of vigorous workers' movements in Japan, Korea, Brazil, and other rapidly industrializing countries. At least after the fact, they could probably have accommodated the American civil rights movement of the 1960s. They would, however, have encountered three very large surprises: proliferation of what Western observers eventually came to call new social movements, disintegration of almost all state socialist regimes, and the connections that later historians would start to make between new social movements, on one side, and opposition to state socialism, on the other.

The Social Movement Surge of 1968

Of all the twentieth-century years after the Soviet historians wrote, 1968 and 1989 probably would have surprised them most. As of 1968, for example, West Berlin, walled off from communist-run East Berlin, formed a western island in the midst of the solidly communist German Democratic Republic (for a sophisticated world survey of 1968, see Suri 2003: chap. 5). During 1968, nevertheless, West Berlin's Free University became the base for massive demonstrations against American involvement in Vietnam and against the West German government itself. Italy then hosted the most powerful communist party outside of state socialism. In Italy of 1968, not just communists but a wide variety of workers, students, Catholic parishioners, and middle-class citizens—sometimes independently, sometimes in concert—started a round of claim making that continued into the early 1970s (Tarrow 1989).

Most famously, French students and workers joined in partially coordinated attacks on the regime of Charles de Gaulle and Georges Pompidou; they looked as though they might bring the regime down. In May 1968, the left-leaning magazine *Nouvel Observateur* published an interview of twenty-three-year-old French-German student leader Daniel Cohn-Bendit by none other than Jean-Paul Sartre. The interview opened with this exchange:

> JEAN-PAUL SARTRE: In a few days, with no call for a general strike, France was essentially paralyzed by strikes and factory occupations. All that because students took over the streets in the Latin Quarter. How do you analyze the movement you've started? How far can it go?

> DANIEL COHN-BENDIT: It grew beyond what we could have predicted at the start. Our objective is now to overthrow the regime. But it's not up to us whether that happens or not. If the Communist Party, the General Confederation of Labor, and the other national unions really shared our aims, there would be no problem: the regime would fall in a fortnight because it has no means of fending off a show of strength by the whole workforce. (Bourges 1968: 86)

History ruled otherwise: Pompidou's well-timed concessions to organized labor split the temporary worker-student alliance, and a June referendum brought a landslide for de Gaulle. But the movement certainly shook France's regime.

The mobilization of 1968 extended far beyond Western Europe. In Canada, almost every university hosted its own uprising, and forty thousand Québecois students staged a general strike on behalf of an independent socialist state (Westhues 1975: 392–94). In Mexico, student demands for civil liberties led to campus general strikes and swelling demonstrations reaching one hundred thousand participants or more. They led to the 2 October gathering at the Plaza de las Tres Culturas in Tlatelolco at which the army and police killed hundreds of demonstrators as they arrested more than two thousand. In state socialist Poland, students and intellectuals united in a campaign of meetings, demonstrations, and petitions on behalf of political rights and economic reform despite severe repression. In Prague, dissident intellectuals spoke out against communist censorship and helped bring reformist Alexander Dubček to leadership of the Czechoslovak Communist Party. The 1968 Czech mobilization opened a season of liberalization that ended after dramatic resistance when Soviet-backed troops and tanks invaded the country in August.

The United States also participated energetically in 1968's movements:

- the American Indian Movement made its appearance on the national scene;
- protests against the Vietnam War accelerated;

- the assassination of Martin Luther King Jr. incited collective attacks on property and struggles with police in mainly black neighborhoods of about 125 cities;
- radical students at Columbia University and elsewhere shut down their schools;
- the Oakland-based Black Panthers distributed copies of Chairman Mao's writings on the University of California's Berkeley campus;
- the guerrilla image of Che Guevara (recently executed by Bolivian troops) became stylish across a wide variety of dissident groups;
- a Poor People's March brought thousands of protesters to Washington;
- President Lyndon Johnson declined to run for a second term in the face of widespread opposition;
- the Chicago nominating convention of the Democratic Party generated a wave of demonstrations and street fighting; but
- Republican nominee Richard Nixon went on to beat Democrat Hubert Humphrey in a fiercely contested election.

Although the year's social movement organizers clearly fell far short of their announced objectives, 1968 marked a significant transition in American public politics and a substantial expansion in the range of social movement activity.

From reactions to 1968's conflicts in the United States and elsewhere developed the idea that "old" social movements on behalf of power for workers and other exploited categories had passed their prime. "New" social movements oriented to autonomy, self-expression, and the critique of postindustrial society, many observers thought, were supplanting the old. French sociologist Alain Touraine, a veteran analyst of workers' movements in Western Europe and Latin America, articulated some of the most influential ideas along this line and taught some of its most widely read proponents. Before 1968 ended, Touraine published a major statement under the title *The May Movement, or Utopian Communism.* National liberation struggles were succumbing to the power of the world's dominant states, he declared, while the Cold War had deadlocked the earlier open struggle between capitalism and socialism. The sheer power of governments, corporations, and mass media to produce stifling conformity, continued Touraine, had become the enemy of creativity and change.

Social movements of a new type, according to Touraine, held out the hope of breaking the bureaucratic stranglehold. The crucial task, he concluded, was

> to reveal what forces and social conflicts are operating in this new type of society, still too new to be aware of its nature and its problems. It is this new class struggle, between domination by the control apparatus and those who are experiencing change, that lends the May movement its importance, that makes it not the pivotal moment of a crisis but the beginning of new struggles that will be just as fundamental and lasting in our society as was the workers' movement in the course of capitalist industrialization. (Touraine 1968: 279)

Touraine's language promoted a comparison between resistance to state socialism and attacks on the rulers of capitalist democracies; both could forward liberation from oppressive systems of top-down control. Social movements of a new type could play vital roles in either setting.

Soon the term "new social movement" expanded to include mobilizations on behalf of expressive feminism, homosexual rights, psychedelic drugs, indigenous peoples, the environment, and a variety of other causes that did not map easily into Touraine's own critique of postindustrial oppression. Activists and commentators began speaking of "identity" as the key, in contrast to the ostensibly instrumental aims of earlier social movements (Cohen 1985). They also began connecting new social movements hopefully with the creation of vibrant, autonomous civil societies in both capitalist and postsocialist countries (Cohen & Arato 1992). Reporting a massive French-Polish collaborative research effort on the Polish worker-based movement Solidarity, Alain Touraine and his colleagues asked:

> What is the aim of this social movement? Seize power, establish a proletarian dictatorship or the rule of workers' councils? Not at all. First because the agreements of Gdansk, which have from the start constituted Solidarity's fundamental law, explicitly recognize the party's leading role in the state. Second because militants themselves are trying to free themselves from the grip of power and not to win power. The repeatedly stated aim of Solidarity is to free society from the party's totalitarian domination. (Touraine, Dubet, Wieviorka, & Strzelecki 1982: 93)

Unlike their sedulously interest-oriented predecessors with their aims of wringing power and benefits from the existing system, ran the argument, identity-centered new social movements could recast the very framework of social life.

Craig Calhoun deftly punctured that balloon. In an article wittily titled "New Social Movements of the Early Nineteenth Century," Calhoun pointed out how regularly nineteenth-century mobilizations on behalf of ethnic minorities, women, religious revival, and workers' rights also stressed demands for autonomy and identity. We need to consider, concluded Calhoun, "the possibility that proliferation of NSMs is normal to modernity and not in need of special explanation because it violates the oppositions of left and right, cultural and social, public and private, aesthetic and instrumental that organize so much of our thought" (Calhoun 1995: 205; for similar doubts based on close study of Italian social movements, see Tarrow 1989: 194–95). In this book's terms, Calhoun was emphasizing how often identity claims accompany program and standing claims, sometimes becoming the focus of social movement activity. Social movements are always making new claims in at least one of these regards. When new political actors appear on the social movement scene, assertions of identity become crucial to the actors' impacts on constituencies, competitors, potential allies, and the objects of their program or standing claims. The distinction between "identity" and "interest" movement dissolves.

Crises and Transitions in 1989

What of 1989? Selected headlines from the 1989 *New York Times* (table 4.2) tell stories that surely would have amazed the Soviet chroniclers of 1962. In terse summaries, we witness the flourishing of Poland's Solidarity movement, the installation of competitive electoral politics in most of Europe's state socialist regimes, lip-service to democratization in even such hidebound authoritarian regimes as Albania's version of state socialism, mobilization leading to the destruction of the Berlin Wall, vast demonstrations in Budapest, Berlin, and Prague, a combination of social movement with civil war in Romania, and—perhaps most astonishing—a month during which students, workers, and city residents seized control of central Beijing's public spaces and even held back the army before a bloody military sweep (4 June) broke the movement. Yugoslavia began to tremble with demands for autonomies and distinctive regimes for its federated republics.

Table 4.2 *New York Times* Social Movement Headlines from the State Socialist World, 1989

6 February	(Warsaw) Warsaw Opens Parley with Solidarity
26 March	(Moscow) Soviets Savor Vote in Freest Election since '17
2 April	(Havana) Gorbachev Begins His Visit to Cuba with Castro's Hug
4 May	(Beijing) Urging Chinese Democracy, 100,000 Surge Past Police
13 May	(Tirana) Albanian Leader Says the Country Will Be Democratized but Will Retain Socialism
13 May	(Beijing) China's Hero of Democracy: Gorbachev
17 May	(Beijing) A Million Chinese March, Adding Pressure for Change
4 June	(Beijing) Troops Attack and Crush Beijing Protest; Thousands Fight Back, Scores Are Killed
8 June	(Warsaw) Warsaw Accepts Solidarity Sweep and Humiliating Losses by Party
11 June	(Beijing) Democracy Movement: Over, for the Time Being
16 June	(Budapest) Hungarian Who Led '56 Revolt Is Buried as a Hero
15 October	(West Berlin) East German Movement Overtaken by Followers
4 November	(East Berlin) 500,000 in East Berlin Rally for Change; Émigrés Are Given Passage to West
20 November	(Prague) 200,000 March in Prague as Calls for Change Mount
25 November	(Prague) Prague Party Leaders Resign; New Chief, 48, Surprise Choice; 350,000 at Rally Cheer Dubcek
26 November	(Budapest) Hungarians Hold First Free Vote in 42 Years, Shunning a Boycott
27 November	(Prague) Millions of Czechoslovaks Increase Pressure on Party with Two-Hour General Strike
4 December	(Prague) Protest Rallies Resume in Prague in Effort to Oust New Government
24 December	(Bucarest) Rumanian Army Gains in Capital but Battle Goes On

Source: Gwertzman & Kaufman 1991.

Social movements, long banned from the public politics of state socialism, seemed to be exploding the old socialist system. Among visible state socialist regimes, only Albania and Cuba managed to maintain close control. Even in Cuba a state visit of Soviet leader Mikhail Gorbachev (2–5 April) embarrassed Fidel Castro's regime as Gorbachev chose the occasion to deliver a speech that renounced the policy of exporting revolution.

Warsaw and Moscow started the year, but Beijing soon grabbed the headlines. Confrontations in Beijing eventually brought a resounding defeat for democracy, but along the way they focused world attention on Chinese popular mobilization. Table 4.3 offers an abbreviated summary of events in Beijing alone;

Table 4.3 Chronology of the Beijing Student Movement, 1989

16 April	At death of Hu Yaobang, former secretary general of Chinese Communist Party, students post wreaths and elegiac couplets in Tiananmen Square and many Beijing colleges.
17 April	Students march to Tiananmen to memorialize Hu Yaobang.
20 April	Skirmishes between police and students at Xinhua Gate; some students begin class boycott.
22 April	Hu's funeral in Great Hall of the People; about fifty thousand students march to Tiananmen to participate; numerous student actions include kneeling on the Great Hall's steps to deliver a petition and request a meeting with premier Li Peng.
23 April	Students form Beijing Student Autonomous Union Provisional Committee.
26 April	*People's Daily* calls student mobilization "planned conspiracy," "turmoil."
27 April	About one hundred thousand students march to Tiananmen and protest the editorial. State Council announces willingness to meet with students.
29 April	Senior government officials meet with forty-five selected students from sixteen Beijing universities, but other students challenge both the dialogue and the student representatives.
4 May	Students march in commemoration of the May 4th Movement (of 1919).
5 May	Students form Beijing Student Dialogue Delegation. Most students end class boycott.
13 May	Three hundred students start hunger strike at Tiananmen, numbers eventually rising to three thousand strikers, thousands of supporters.
14 May	High-level state delegation meets student activists, chaotic discussion ensues because of student divisions, students withdraw from the talks.
15 May	Mikhail Gorbachev arrives for a state visit; because of Tiananmen's occupation, government holds its official reception at the Beijing airport.
17 May	More than a million Beijing residents march in support of students and hunger strikers.
19 May	Government declares martial law, but residents and students block the troops. Students from outside Beijing continue to arrive in the city.
3 June	Military repression begins, with hundreds of people killed by government troops.
4 June	Troops encircle remaining four thousand students at Tiananmen; students leave the square.

Source: Adapted from Zhao 2001: xxv–xxvi.

in fact, by June, students and workers all over the country were participating in one version or another of the Beijing events. When connected dissidents face authoritarian regimes, they commonly have three choices: bide their time in silence, engage in forbidden and clandestine acts of destruction, or overload the narrow range of tolerated occasions for assembly and expression. In the third case, criticism of regimes often occurs in the course of public holidays and ceremonies—Mardi Gras, inaugurations, funerals, royal weddings, and the like—when authorities tolerate larger and more public assemblies than usual. The Beijing events started exactly that way, with student memorials to the dead Hu Yaobang, a former secretary general of the Chinese Communist Party who had been quite unpopular with students while in office but who retroactively acquired the reputation of having been sacked in 1987 for his excessive sympathy with student demands.

Students soon converted a ceremonial occasion into a mobilization having distinctive Chinese properties, yet in other regards greatly resembling social movement mobilizations elsewhere. When the government held a state funeral for Hu in Tiananmen's Great Hall of the People on 22 April, some fifty thousand students gathered at the square for the ceremonies. In an old, recognizable routine, groups of students regularly arrived at Tiananmen carrying banners representing the school units to which they belonged (Perry 2002: 313). Some of them reenacted old regime rituals by kneeling on the Great Hall's steps to present a petition and ask humbly for a meeting with premier Li Peng. Over the period from mid-April to the beginning of June, groups of students played hide-and-seek with the government's armed forces; they marched despite prohibitions against assemblies, chanted slogans, staged hunger strikes, resisted orders to evacuate public spaces, and tossed bottles or shoes at the police. Meanwhile, a state visit of Mikhail Gorbachev on 14 and 15 May embarrassed the regime's leaders (blocked from giving Gorbachev the customary state reception at Tiananmen) and encouraged students to call for Gorbachev-style reforms.

By that time, thousands of nonstudents had joined student activists in open challenges to the regime. As our two chronologies show, a million or more people marched through Beijing on 17 May in support of student demonstrators and hunger strikers. Demonstrators and their supporters blocked the one hundred thousand troops sent to clear Tiananmen during the night of 19–20 May. Private entrepreneurs contributed money, services, and equipment such as battery-powered megaphones for student speakers. Despite considerable discouragement from student organizers (until mounting threats of repression changed the organizers' minds), substantial numbers of workers also provided aid and encouragement for the Tiananmen mobilization (Perry 2002: 318–23). Recent student arrivals from outside of Beijing, furthermore, increasingly swelled the crowds at the square. The mobilization was starting to overflow the organizations of Beijing students.

As martial law forces assembled in and around Beijing, residents often insulted and attacked the soldiers. But when troops began their assault on Tiananmen the night of 3 June, they brought in overwhelming force. On their way to retaking the city, they killed about 250 people and suffered half a dozen deaths of their own men. Between 4:30 and 6:30 A.M. on the 4th, the remaining students marched out of Tiananmen through columns opened by the military (Zhao 2001: 203–7). By the end of 1989, public mobilization of students and workers on behalf of civil liberties had entirely subsided across China.

Social movement mobilization in Eastern Europe had more durable success. The *Annual Register* began its commentary on Eastern Europe's whirlwind year with a comparison to the French Revolution that had started exactly two centuries earlier.

> As we look back on 1989, the bicentenary celebrations of the start of the French Revolution in July seem like an historical overture to the actual drama of events in Eastern Europe, from October onwards, which by their range and speed gained a revolutionary label. Between the storming of the Bastille and the breach of the Berlin Wall, each an inaugural and symbolic incident of a far wider transformation of Europe, there was indeed a certain ancestral affinity. For the Declaration of the Rights of Man, which became the ideological manifesto of the French Revolution, was great-great-grandfather to the demand for personal freedom and political democracy which suddenly overwhelmed the fortress of authoritarian rule in East Germany, and then in Czechoslovakia, following more gradual but still radical reforms in Poland and Hungary, and followed in turn by reluctant changes in Bulgaria and by a triumphant uprising in Romania. (*Annual Register* 1989: 1)

Although the word "movement" recurred in the *Annual Register* accounts of particular countries' politics, the editorialist did not describe the events of 1989 as a social movement or a series of social movements. Indeed, the anonymous author invoked the authority of *Annual Register* founder Edmund Burke to warn: "He correctly foresaw that if you launch off from the claims of individuals, distinct from the societies to which they belong, you end with the despotism of a central authority as the incarnation of the sovereignty of the people" (*Annual Register* 1989: 3). One could hardly signal more emphatically the worrisome connection between social movement claim making and calls for popular sovereignty. Eastern European activists were making just such claims. As distinguished from the previous few decades' participation of East German, Russian, Chinese, Polish, Hungarian, Czech, and Romanian ordinary people in public politics, 1989 featured the combination of campaigns, WUNC displays, and performances from the social movement repertoire to a startling degree.

Take the case of Czechoslovakia, where a repressive regime remained unshaken well into 1989. Regime forces, for example, ruthlessly dispersed a 21 August Prague gathering to commemorate the anniversary of the Warsaw Pact's 1968 invasion of Czechoslovakia. When police and militia again broke up a 17 November student commemoration of a student murdered by the Nazi government in

1939, however, students and theater groups used their national connections to call for a general strike. A new group called Civic Forum backed a declaration drafted by playwright Václav Havel that called for punishment of the repressive forces at the 17 November demonstration and demanded establishment of civil liberties. An estimated three-quarters of the Czechoslovak population observed a two-hour strike on 27 November. Then,

> when Prime Minister Adamec proposed a reform government on December 3, 1989, in which members of the Communist Party maintained a majority, Civic Forum rejected it and again threatened to strike. On December 7, the government capitulated and Adamec resigned. After two days of hurried negotiations between the civic movements and representatives of the Leninist regime, President Gustav Husák announced the formation of a Government of National Understanding in which members of Civic Forum had a majority, and then he himself resigned. With the nomination of Civic Forum spokesperson Václav Havel as president on December 30, 1989, the rapid demise of the Communist Party in Czechoslovakia was completed. (Glenn 2001: 8)

A stunning spread of social movement strategies accompanied and hastened the rapid collapse of a previously resistant state socialist regime.

At varying tempos, similar scenarios played out in much of Eastern Europe. Concentrating on the Soviet Union and its successor states, Mark Beissinger has taken the most comprehensive look at deployment of the social movement repertoire in Eastern Europe before, during, and after 1989. From a wide variety of sources he catalogued two sorts of events: public demonstrations of one hundred persons or more, and "mass violent events" in which fifteen or more people gathered to attack persons or property (Beissinger 2002: 462–65). Beissinger points out that demonstrations and attacks did occur occasionally in the Soviet Union before Mikhail Gorbachev began his reform programs. In April 1965, for example, one hundred thousand people gathered in Yerevan, Armenia, to commemorate victims of the Ottoman expulsion and massacre of Armenians fifty years earlier (Beissinger 2002: 71). But under that repressive regime, both demonstrations and collective attacks by anyone other than state authorities remained very rare.

The arrival of reformer Gorbachev at the head of the Communist Party (1985), however, touched off an enormous expansion of claim making in the social movement style: not just mass demonstrations, but also special-purpose associations, strikes, press campaigns, and appeals for international support. (Those appeals often included demonstration signs not in the local language but in English.) Although the earlier claims of Soviet social movements focused on political and economic reform, nationalist demands soon predominated. Russians themselves sometimes demanded special recognition within the Soviet Union; Boris Yeltsin first came to power as a Russian nationalist. But the bulk of the demands—as well as the mass violent events—centered on recognition, autonomy, or independence for ethnically labeled subdivisions of the Soviet Union such as Estonia, Armenia, and Chechnya.

The relative timing of violent and nonviolent, nationalist and nonnationalist events tells a story of its own. Nonviolent demonstrations centering on nonnationalist claims reached their peak in 1989–90, as a variety of claimants made bids to influence the form of government, the distribution of benefits, the provision of security, and related issues of civic participation. Nonviolent demonstrations concerning ethnic and national rights did rise significantly in 1989, but they became even more frequent in 1991 before starting to dwindle. Violent attacks centered on nonnationalist questions never became very frequent, but they did occur more often after 1989. The most dramatic shift occurred in nationalist violence: despite secondary spurts in 1989 and 1990, it reached unprecedented heights in 1992 before tailing off rapidly (Beissinger 2002: 105, 284). Beissinger explains the sequence as a consequence of a political cycle: early risers, on the average, either gained some advantages or demobilized peacefully, but those who persisted despite previous failures or arrived on the social movement scene late— especially if their program centered on political autonomy or independence— encountered rising resistance and engaged increasingly in claim making that incited or entailed violence.

Grzegorz Ekiert and Jan Kubik prepared a similar catalog of "protest events" in Poland for 1989 through 1993. (An event qualified as a protest if participants made specific demands in nonroutine ways and if three or more people—from one person upward in the case of self-immolation and other "extreme" acts—took part.) In Poland, mass demonstrations accompanied the 1989 overthrow of the communist regime, but a new surge of demonstrations arrived in 1991, as a wide variety of claimants publicized their programs, identities, and political standings. On the 1993 calendar:

> In January, approximately 7,000 people demonstrated against the president and burned his effigy in front of his residence. In March, over 10,000 public sector employees marched through the streets of Warsaw demanding higher wages and increased state spending on education and health. In May, 4,000 farmers dumped stacks of hay in front of the government building, protesting the government's agricultural policies and demanding price controls, protective tariffs, and credit guarantees. In June, several thousand demonstrators clashed with police on the streets of Warsaw and ended the protest by burning the image of a red pig in front of the government building. (Ekiert & Kubik 1999: 108)

These were merely the most visible of the 250 Polish protest events Ekiert and Kubik uncovered for 1993. Considering Poland's recent exit from state socialism, the events stand out, ironically, for their utter familiarity: despite specific idioms, such as a red pig to represent the former communist rulers, they greatly resemble demonstrations elsewhere across the democratic and democratizing world.

Were These Social Movements?

To what extent do the popular mobilizations of 1989 under authoritarian regimes therefore qualify as social movements? We tread on delicate, shifting ground. Across most of Eastern Europe, if not in China, social movements of a sort easily recognizable from our nineteenth-century survey eventually became widely available as means of political claim making. Looking at Poland or the Czech Republic today, we repeatedly see the combination of campaigns, WUNC displays, and performances in the social movement repertoire such as mounting of demonstrations, releases to the press, and formation of special-interest associations devoted to specific public programs. We notice that many other groups, not just political dissidents, employ these means for making claims. But at what point in time and political process can we reasonably declare that the social movement synthesis of campaign, repertoire, and WUNC display became widely available across groups, issues, and objects of claims? The question matters here for two reasons: first, because it bears on the general causal connections between social movements and democratization; second, because if in fact each regime invented its own social movements more or less independently, that fact would challenge the story of one-time invention and subsequent diffusion with adaptation that I have drawn from the eighteenth- and nineteenth-century histories in previous chapters.

Let us return attentively to the three test questions we have already applied to similar decisions: 1) *Resemblance:* Does this particular campaign, performance, or WUNC display resemble those that commonly occur in full-fledged social movements? 2) *Combination:* Does this particular campaign combine performances and WUNC displays in a recognizably similar manner to social movements elsewhere? 3) *Availability:* In this setting, is the characteristic combination of campaign, performances, and WUNC displays now widely available for different issues, claimants, and objects of claims? Once we pose the problem this way, it becomes fairly easy to recognize that, at their start, the state socialist mobilizations of 1989 all qualified under the first heading: with due allowance for such local idioms as kneeling on the Great Hall's steps and burning images of red pigs, they all involved some clear analogs to familiar social movement activities elsewhere. At that point, however, none had reached the third stage, that of making campaigns, performances, and WUNC displays widely available in popular public politics. All were located somewhere in the middle ground, early or late in the process of synthesizing campaign, performances, and WUNC displays into durable social movements pressing claims for regime change.

All the countries involved had two sources of models for social movement action: their own earlier histories and their knowledge of social movements in the nonsocialist world. Before their moves into socialism, China, Russia, Poland, Hungary, East Germany, Romania, and Czechoslovakia had all passed through substantial twentieth-century periods in which at least some sectors of their population had engaged feverishly in the association building, meeting, demonstrating, communicating, and campaign planning of social movements. Those earlier efforts still remained as available models. Through radio, television, electronic messaging, and occasional travel in both directions, furthermore, many citizens of state socialist regimes received information about public politics in North America, Western Europe, and East Asia's capitalist countries. From at least the 1968 West Berlin student movement onward, East Germans in particular had wide access to social movement models from West Germany. From syntheses of local history and available models, dissidents in the state socialist regimes of 1989 were starting to construct their own social movement sectors.

By that time, social movements had become regular features of public politics in a number of countries outside of Western Europe and North America. The upsurge of 1968 has already shown us Mexican students participating in social movement claim making. Elsewhere in Latin America, social movements likewise proliferated during 1989. In Argentina, for example, struggles over the transfer of power from Radical Raúl Alfonsín to Peronist Carlos Saúl Menem—Argentina's first peaceful change of presidential party since 1916—produced large mobilizations by trade unions, human rights groups, military veterans, and the Madres de la Plaza de Mayo. No social movements surfaced, however, in authoritarian Chile (still ruled by General Pinochet), Paraguay (where a coup toppled long-term dictator Alfredo Stroessner but replaced him with another general), or Cuba (where Fidel Castro's special version of state socialism included tight controls over popular expression).

All of these authoritarian countries had passed through earlier periods of social movement activity, but despots and dictators had shut that activity down. In Cuba, for example, social movements had flourished prior to Fulgencio Batista's coup of 1952 and continued intermittently in moments of regime weakness up to the Castro-led revolution of 1959. In 1955

> a series of developments marked the anti-Batista movement. *Auténticos, ortodoxos,* and other *politicos* regrouped and seemed to be better coordinated. University students elected new leadership and expressed renewed discontent. Toward the end of the year, independence war veteran Cosme de la Torriente formed the Friends of the Republic Society and called for a civic dialogue and a new round of elections. Except for the July 26th movement, every other opposition sector participated. Although Batista accepted the invitation, he would not concede to elections before their scheduled date of 1958. His intransigence bolstered those who argued that armed struggle was the only way to challenge his rule. (Pérez-Stable 1993: 56)

Despite calling itself the July 26th Movement, once it seized power in 1959 Castro's force rapidly suppressed opposition campaigns, performances, and WUNC displays (Pérez-Stable 1993: 52–81). In short, as of 1989, the Latin American map of social movements corresponded approximately to the map of relatively democratic regimes. Latin America's many authoritarian rulers still discouraged the combination of bottom-up campaigns, social movement performances, and WUNC displays.

By century's end, the basic generalization applied to the entire world: wherever relatively extensive democratic institutions operated, so too did social movements. What is more, wherever rapid steps toward democracy occurred—South Korea, Taiwan, South Africa, and elsewhere—those steps typically brought the flowering of campaigns, performances, and WUNC displays in the social movement vein. Sometimes, to be sure, it seemed that social movements had swept the whole world, democratic or authoritarian; television, for example, occasionally showed the paraphernalia of demonstrations—gathering in public places, marching in ranks, shouting slogans, bearing signs, and so on—from remote corners of the earth. But it helps to recall our three-part test: 1) resemblance, 2) combination, and 3) availability.

By the year 2000, almost every country anywhere sometimes met test 1, with supporters or opponents of the regime adopting one element or another resembling those in the social movement array. Since the vast majority of countries declared themselves democracies of some sort, the sheer presence of international mass media called forth at least some staged performances of popular public claim making by means of campaigns, social movement activities, or (especially) WUNC displays. Only a minority of regimes, however, unambiguously met test 3. In another substantial minority, some privileged sectors of the population could engage in limited social movement claim making, so long as they stayed within their prescribed limits and avoided offending the regime's most powerful actors. Students (who were often, of course, children of the ruling class) enjoyed that precarious privilege in a number of semiauthoritarian regimes.

Indonesia provides a clear case in point. Although contested elections began producing genuine changes of government in Indonesia during the late 1990s, the Indonesian military retained great power in and behind the government, administered a number of rebellious areas, and used force widely with little fear of punishment. As of 2000, the New York–based democracy monitoring organization Freedom House rated Indonesia at the midpoint of its scales for political rights and civil liberties, labeling the regime as "partly free" (Karatnycky 2000: 235). After delayed announcement of results from a national election held in June 1999,

> on September 23, students in Jakarta put the government on notice that they would take to the streets if it took decisions that went counter to reform. That day, the parliament passed an army-backed bill on national security that would have given the army sweeping powers to declare states of emergency at the regional or national level. Pro-democracy groups and student organizations mobilized thousands in protest, and in the ensuing clash with security forces, four people were killed, including one policeman. On September 24, the government announced that it was suspending implementation of the law. (Human Rights Watch 2000: 193–94)

As this small opening for performances in the social movement style appeared in Jakarta, however, much of Indonesia engaged in a very different sort of politics, what Human Rights Watch calls "communal riots" involving religious factions, separatists, strongmen's militias, or all three.

Where peaceful protests did occur, furthermore, they did not much resemble the interactions of social movements. In February 1999, for example,

> in what was billed as a "national dialogue" on Irian Jaya's future political status, one hundred prominent public figures from Irian Jaya presented President Habibie with a statement expressing the aspirations of the people of Irian Jaya for independence. The government rejected any discussion of independence, and in April, after participants in the meeting tried to disseminate the results of the meeting to a larger public at home, the Irian Jaya chief of police banned any further discussion. In August, news leaked out that five prominent Irianese had been banned from leaving Indonesia as of June 28. The ban, initiated by the military and imposed by immigration officials, was justified on unspecified national security grounds. (Human Rights Watch 2000: 195)

Although the Soviet Union and its successor states of 1989–1992 hardly qualified as entrenched democracies, Beissinger's analysis of claim making there and then makes it clear that the Soviet Union had come much closer to institutionalizing social movements by 1989 than had Indonesia by 1999.

In both cases, nevertheless, the international arena made a large difference to social movement performances and their suppression. Just as the Soviet Union's demonstrators for political autonomy were addressing potential external supporters at the same time as they confronted Soviet authorities, Jakarta's students could take to the streets in part because of their membership in a national elite, but also in part because international television would broadcast their demands—and perhaps their struggles with the police—the very next day. On our three-step test, we might be able to place some Indonesian student mobilizations in test 2, but we could certainly not assign Indonesia as a whole to the list of countries that, as of the twentieth century's end, had fully institutionalized social movements.

Twentieth-Century Transmutations

In the minority of national regimes that had regularized social movement claim making by 2000, a century of substantial change in the character and distribution of social movements lay behind them. The more important twentieth-century trends included:

- routinization of (some) relations between social movement organizers and local authorities, especially police specializing in public order and crowd control;
- evolution of campaigns, social movement performances, and WUNC displays in response to changing means of communication;

- adoption of social movement campaigns by opponents of radical and reformist movements; and
- substantial adaptation of social movement campaigns, repertoires, and WUNC displays to local and national political cultures in countries outside the zone of early social movement development.

Over the century, impressive changes occurred in relations between social movement activists and authorities. At the twentieth century's end, many social movement participants still considered police and local authorities their enemies; they told repeated stories of brutality and repression. Yet as compared with a century earlier, the legal environment had altered significantly. Where social movements occurred regularly, authorities might still require permits for meetings and demonstrations, demand that suspect organizations register, hound those organizations by means of surveillance, infiltration, conspiracy prosecutions, or tax assessments, limit access of dissidents to the media, shield public figures from attack, or avert their eyes from dirty tricks by a movement's opponents. As compared with shooting down demonstrators, incarcerating movement activists as subversives, and wholesale banning of dissident organizations, prevalent late-twentieth-century practices in the major centers of social movement activity revealed a sea change in relations between activists and regimes.

To recognize the change more clearly, we can crank the century's film back to Berlin at the start of the twentieth century. German historian Thomas Lindenberger has done a splendid, detailed study of Berlin's "street politics" from 1900 to 1914. He speaks of the "little everyday war between police and public." As reference points for his wide-ranging study of street contention, Lindenberger assembled three substantial catalogs: of "little street wars," of industrial strikes, and of street demonstrations. In the case of street wars, Lindenberger prepared a catalog resembling those of Deneckere, Beissinger, Ekiert, and Kubik. His 405 "street disorders" collected from the neighborhood reporting in the daily *Vossische Zeitung* included occasions in which an estimated twenty or more people gathered in a public place and police intervened—whether or not the event began with a civilian-police encounter (Lindenberger 1995: 107–8). Official statistics, police reports, and periodicals supplied him with ample documentation on strikes. Extensive police reporting plus the *Vossische Zeitung* and the socialist newspaper *Vorwärts* also allowed him to prepare an exhaustive inventory of major street demonstrations through the period. Let us focus on the demonstrations.

In parallel with our news from nineteenth-century France, Lindenberger points out that, before the early twentieth century, most quasi demonstrations occurred in the context of funeral marches and public holidays (Lindenberger 1995: 308–16). Likewise in parallel with France, May 1st became an unofficial workers' holiday, and the occasion for assertive gatherings, around 1890. But police generally broke up the frequent efforts of participants in indoor meetings to take to the streets at meetings' end. When the campaign for working-class voting rights began in 1906, however, the situation changed. From then until World War

I, Berlin resounded with street demonstrations despite strenuous efforts of the city authorities and police to suppress them. "At least in the initial phase up to 1910," remarks Lindenberger, "street demonstrations occurred against the background of a struggle against the police for control of the streets" (Lindenberger 1995: 386).

Table 4.4 describes the major demonstrations occurring in Berlin during ten weeks of 1910. They give a picture of a regime grudgingly making concessions to social movement activists but using public order as grounds for containing or banning public performances such as meetings and demonstrations by regime opponents. Despite the presence of Social Democratic and Democratic Alliance deputies in the national legislature, the Berlin police kept a tight rein on street activities by both parties. As a consequence, the most frequent approach to demonstrating was to hold an authorized public meeting (with a police officer present to take notes and to call in reinforcements if necessary) and for people leaving the

Table 4.4 Demonstrations in Berlin, February–May 1910

13 February	Two hundred thousand participants in forty-two Social Democratic meetings across the city with subsequent street demonstrations involving tens of thousands.
15 February	Meetings of the city's women's movement followed by small demonstrations.
20 February	Meeting of freethinkers with a short demonstration afterward.
27 February	Eight thousand participants in a meeting of left-liberal intellectuals followed by a demonstration involving a few thousand in front of the royal palace.
6 March	Demonstration announced in *Vorwärts* but forbidden by the authorities: a "right to vote stroll" shifted overnight from Treptow Park to the Zoo, where about 150 thousand people demonstrated. Police went to both Treptow Park and the Zoo on foot and horseback, using bared swords against people in the gathering.
13 March	Five thousand participants in a meeting of the left-liberal Democratic Alliance, followed by a demonstration.
15 March	Forty-eight Social Democratic meetings across metropolitan Berlin without demonstrations, but with police decrees against any displays in public.
17 March	Social Democratic meeting in Spandau, followed by a demonstration.
18 March	Altercations between police and Social Democrats after a meeting at the cemetery of Friedrich Woods.
10 April	Three authorized open-air gatherings of Social Democrats and the Democratic Alliance in Treptow Park, Friedrich Woods, and Humboldt Woods with about twenty-five thousand participants.
1 May	May Day celebrations after the authorized late morning period had ended, but without police-demonstrator violence.

Source: Lindenberger 1995: 326–27.

meeting to make their presence known briefly on the street under the watchful eyes of the police. At that point, we might think of Germany as making a stumbling entry into our test 3: widespread availability of social movement campaigns, performances, and WUNC displays. Until it collapsed with the Nazi seizure of power (1933), the Weimar Republic that followed World War I offered wider scope to social movement claim making.

Leap forward to the later twentieth century. German authorities never stopped watching social movements closely, but after the repressive hiatus of the Nazi regime and World War II they conceded an open legal space in German politics to conjoined campaigns, social movement performances, and WUNC displays. Summing up her comparison of "protest policing" in Germany and Italy between 1950 and 1990, Donatella della Porta concludes that

> in Italy as well as in Germany, from 1950 to 1990, protest control evolved toward more flexible forms based on a more liberal understanding of demonstration rights. In both countries, public order policies became more tolerant, more selective, more oriented toward prevention, more respectful of democratic procedures, and "softer," even though this evolution was hardly linear (both countries experienced "relapses," as it were, when political conflicts escalated into violent forms). We can add that, over time, cross-national differences seemed to diminish, probably because of international cooperation and cross-national flows of information involving both movement organizations and law enforcers. (della Porta 1995: 71; see also della Porta & Reiter 1998)

Social movements waxed and waned to the rhythms of a particular country's political history. The rise of regime-threatening social movements almost always stimulated attempts to repress them. But on the average and over the long run, authorities, police, and social movement organizers negotiated routines that provided broad opportunities for nonviolent campaigns, WUNC displays, and employment of the social movement repertoire.

Movements and Media

From the eighteenth-century days of incipient social movements onward, newspapers, magazines, pamphlets, and other print media conveyed campaign messages, announced forthcoming movement activities, evaluated those activities, and provided news reports on their successes or failures. Nevertheless, twentieth-century alteration and expansion of communications media offered unprecedented opportunities and exposure to social movements. Radio, television, electronic messaging, opinion polls, and worldwide proliferation of the press all triggered shifts in campaigns, social movement performances, and WUNC displays.

As compared to direct attacks and person-to-person negotiation, broadcast of movement claims by means of public media reaches far more third parties. Those third parties include powerful figures other than the ones to whom activists are directing their claims. But they also include publics that will be making relevant judgments in elections, purchases, opinion polls, and other expressions of support; potential recruits to the cause; and, for that matter, allies of the target(s) who might reconsider their positions (Koopmans 2004). Thus, the broadcast of movement claims with regard to program, identity, and standing through such mass media as newspapers and magazines amplified the audience for social movements and WUNC displays.

Movement involvement with mass media also produces a sort of echo chamber in which activists hear how others are interpreting their claims to program, identity, and standing. Both the extent and the character of reporting, therefore, become objects of movement strategy. By no means, however, did twentieth-century social movements establish dominant or even equal relations with mass media. Movements attracted attention to the extent that their campaigns, performances, and WUNC displays became newsworthy: big, colorful, locally relevant, and/or oriented to issues already under widespread public discussion (Hocke 2002, McCarthy, McPhail, & Smith 1996, Oliver & Maney 2000, Oliver & Myers 1999, Scalmer 2002a, Tilly 2002b). This built-in asymmetry meant that activists could rarely count on media coverage, had little control over their portrayal in the media, and usually came away dissatisfied with the media treatment they received.

Over the long run, the most telling effect of new media was not to reshape movements in the images of those media. It was instead to connect activists with the circumscribed audiences reached by those media and therefore to *disconnect* them from people excluded by the same media. Newspapers had a narrowing effect on social movement audiences so long as literacy was low and readership sparse. The Internet, with its very unequal access—about 6 percent of world population in 2000 (*Le Monde* 2001: 33)—surely has a similar effect. It reaches far beyond any activist's immediate circle, but it reaches very selectively.

Media differ significantly in asymmetry. Print media, radio, and television permit little feedback from recipients, despite letters to editors, op-ed columns, talk shows, and other gestures toward symmetry. Telephones and the Internet, in contrast, permit greater symmetry between sender and receiver; twentieth-century social movement organizers, for example, often used preestablished telephone trees to bring out participants in movement performances. As commercial calling, Internet advertising, and Web sites indicate, however, even that symmetry butts up against serious limits; it may equalize relations among parties that already define themselves as equal, but it also offers opportunities for well-organized purveyors to dominate the circulation of information.

Let us therefore avoid technological determinism: the mere invention of new communications media did not single-handedly change the character of social movements. What happened typically was that some social movement organizers adapted newly available media to an activity they were already pursuing; most such adaptations fizzled, but a few did so well that they produced changes in the organization that made them and offered models to other organizations that were pursuing similar campaigns.

Take the example of Charles Edward Coughlin. The Canadian-born Catholic priest became one of the United States' most influential social movement leaders of the 1930s until the church silenced him, returning him to parish work in 1942. Born in 1891 and educated in Toronto, Father Coughlin first taught at Assumption College near Windsor, Ontario, across the river from Detroit. In 1923, he became assistant pastor of a parish in Kalamazoo, Michigan, before moving to a parish in downtown Detroit. Recognizing Coughlin's eloquence and organizing talent, Detroit's bishop soon made him pastor of a small village, then offered him appointment as head pastor of a church in Royal Oak, a northern suburb where the Ku Klux Klan had been burning crosses to intimidate Catholics.

At that point, commercial radio was a new medium, only in operation for a half dozen years. In 1926, as a fund-raising effort, Coughlin went on the radio in a broadcast that began as a children's program. His radio talks soon shifted to politics and economics in a populist vein. As Samuel Eliot Morison's general history of the United States described Coughlin: "a consummate radio orator, his Irish humor attracted attention to his theories; and as a free-silver and paper-money man he appealed to the old populist faith that gold was the root of all evil and New York bankers the devils" (Morison 1965: 972). Coughlin became so popular that the Columbia Broadcasting Service (CBS) took him national.

According to wildly varying estimates, Coughlin's Sunday afternoon broadcasts soon attracted ten million to forty million listeners; Coughlin himself claimed forty-five million (Brinkley 1983: 304). His Radio League of the Little Flower was soon financing not only Coughlin's Shrine of the Little Flower Church but also a national movement promoting his version of social justice. From the start, he attacked the Soviet Union as a bastion of irreligion and a threat to sound family values. When he started attacking government policies and such eminent capitalists as Henry Ford, CBS dropped his show (1931), whereupon Coughlin created his own radio network. In 1932, Coughlin stridently opposed President Herbert Hoover's reelection campaign and by implication supported Franklin D. Roosevelt's presidential candidacy against the incumbent. (As a Catholic priest, Coughlin did not then dare to offer an explicit public endorsement of a presidential candidate. Later in his career, he overcame that scruple.) After Roosevelt's victory, Coughlin's organizations campaigned for creation of a national central bank, formed unions to compete with those he saw as tainted by communism, and joined with Huey Long to support the Bonus Bill for veterans of World War I. They engaged extensively in social movement activity.

Roosevelt soon disappointed Coughlin. By 1934, Coughlin was forming a National Union for Social Justice in explicit opposition to Roosevelt's New Deal. In 1935, Coughlin almost single-handedly blocked Senate endorsement of Roosevelt's proposal to enter the League of Nations' World Court (Brinkley 1983: 135–36). As the Union Party, his organization even backed its own populist third-party presidential candidate in 1936. After that party's resounding defeat in a Roosevelt landslide, Coughlin replaced the National Union with the isolationist, increasingly anticommunist Christian Front, named in explicit contrast to Europe's leftist Popular Fronts. His magazine *Social Justice* carried the message to millions of Americans. It even began publishing the forged anti-Semitic *Protocols of the Elders of Zion.*

From that point on, Coughlin's weekly broadcasts became increasingly rabid on the subject of FDR's "communist conspiracy" and more openly anti-Semitic to boot. In 1940, Coughlin called for Roosevelt's impeachment on the grounds that transferring military equipment to Britain and continuing to support the Soviet Union constituted abuse of office. Once the United States entered World War II, the government had him indicted under the Espionage Act, canceled the second-class mailing privileges that played so important a part in his solicitation of funds, and thus gave Detroit's bishop a long-awaited opportunity; the bishop confined his diocese's increasingly intemperate gadfly to parish work at Little Flower, where Coughlin served until 1966. Coughlin did not remain entirely silent, however; he continued to write anticommunist pamphlets up to his death in 1979.

Father Coughlin pioneered the use of radio as a vehicle of social movement organizing, and radio certainly did not disappear from the social movement scene with the departure of Father Coughlin. On the contrary, it continued to grow in importance during and after World War II. Radio news disseminated information about movement activities such as marches in the making and, more rarely, actually transmitted movement messages containing program, identity, and standing claims. As recently as 2003, American leftists were deploring their exclusion from the widely followed talk-show circuit, and at least one group of left-leaning venture capitalists was planning to finance "liberal" broadcasts to counter the influence of right-wing bigots (Gans 2003: 29, Hertzberg 2003). From the 1960s, nevertheless, television became an even more influential medium in the representation of American social movements.

My Columbia University colleague Todd Gitlin served as national president of a quintessential American 1960s social movement organization—Students for a Democratic Society (SDS)—in 1963 and 1964, remaining active in the organization until 1966. He then began withdrawing from SDS activities and, by the late 1960s, "grew steadily more estranged from the direction of the national organization" (Gitlin 1980: 294; for historical context, see Fendrich 2003). He concluded, among other things, that its interaction with the news media was driving the SDS to strike ineffectual radical poses that invited repression instead of promoting progressive change.

Instead of simply stomping off and fulminating, however, Gitlin eventually constructed a close study of interaction between this New Left organization and the media. His study concentrated on news coverage by CBS television and the *New York Times* from 1965 to 1970. Adopting an idea that entered sociology through Erving Goffman, Gitlin examined how interpretive "frames" in the news affected the telling of stories and the reflections of themselves received by activists. Gitlin concluded that media coverage encouraged the activists to remain newsworthy by means of innovations that did not necessarily advance their cause, to substitute what news media told them for direct observation of their actions' effects, to give disproportionate attention to eye-catching symbols, slogans, dress, and performances, and, in the absence of solid information about their own accomplishments and failures, to alternate between despair and hubris. (Recall Daniel Cohn-Bendit, about the same time, telling Jean-Paul Sartre that his movement can bring down the French regime if only workers' organizations will cooperate.)

For all his pessimism, Gitlin demonstrates two major points for our analysis: 1) that the sheer availability of a medium did not in itself alter movement campaigns, performances, and WUNC displays, and 2) that movement organizers themselves played an active part in integrating media access into their own campaign planning. That media commitments often produce unintended or untoward consequences is, of course, an important part of the story. More recent analyses of media-movement interaction point in the same direction (see, e.g., Granjon 2002, Hocke 2002, Oliver & Maney 2000). However, even in our high-tech time, media do not in themselves cause social movements.

Annelise Riles uncovered use of an impressive array of media by activists as she coupled a survey of organizations participating in the United Nations Fourth World Conference on Women (Beijing 1985) with an ethnographic study of movement activity in Fiji after the conference. She found the organizations actively employing the Internet, fax networks, telephones, satellite communications, and newsletters. She did discover some enthusiasts extending their information, contacts, and influence through these media (Riles 2000: 54–55), but for the most part activists did their work by ignoring the media or subordinating them to the maintenance of existing interpersonal relations.

Just as the prodigious expansion of cellular telephones and portable text-messaging devices seems to be serving primarily to facilitate communication among people who are already closely tied, Fijian feminists preferred those means that reinforced established connections. "Those working in bureaucratic institutions in Suva had numerous ways of sharing information at their disposal," Riles comments.

> They might walk across the street from one office to the next to meet face to face; at lunchtime, they were bound to encounter one another at one of Suva's handful of professional lunch spots. They could send letters, exchange faxes or memoranda, or send their drivers to deliver messages. They also could convene meetings and conferences. Yet the most popular means of day to day communication was the telephone. The telephone was useful precisely because it was regarded as personal (as opposed to institutional), private (in contrast to the collective office spaces in which face to face meetings take place), and informal. As described to me by networkers, as well as observed and practiced on my part, these were lengthy telephone conversations; it was not unusual for people to spend an hour or more on the telephone. (Riles 2000: 67)

In this bureaucratized setting, we might conclude that the activists had abandoned the mounting of campaigns, the deployment of social movement perfor-

mances, and the creation of WUNC displays. That would be wrong: they continued to press women's issues in their relatively unresponsive environment. But they
did so in the style of late-twentieth-century nongovernmental organizations.

Right-Wing Appropriation of Social Movement Forms

As twentieth-century social movements worked out partial accommodations with
authorities and integrated new media into their repertoires, they also expanded to
include a wider range of right-wing claim making. Although American nativism
and proslavery mobilization remind us that nineteenth-century social movements
did not always move in progressive directions, right-wing appropriation of social
movement forms grew much more extensive during the twentieth century. It often occurred through countermobilization against reformist and radical movements as they began to threaten conservative interests. Europe's authoritarian
mobilizations against labor, the left, and/or Jews in Germany, Italy, Spain, France,
Romania, and elsewhere provide the most spectacular examples (Birnbaum 1993,
Brustein 1998, Paxton 1995).

Let one well-documented case suffice. Rudy Koshar's masterful study of
organizational life in the university town of Marburg from 1880 to 1935 shows
how Nazis entered a flourishing organizational landscape and turned it to their
own advantage. The number of voluntary associations in Marburg rose steadily
from 10 per thousand people in 1913 to 15.9 per thousand—1 organization for
every sixty-three people—in 1930 (Koshar 1986: 136). During that period, socialist trade unions were mostly losing strength, while veterans, housewives, and
property owners associations expanded enormously and student organizations held
their own. As the Nazi party took root in Marburg from 1923 onward, it first
drew its few members mainly from existing right-wing, nationalist, and anti-Semitic
organizations. Its activists paraded, burned red flags, and shouted against left-
wingers but had little influence on local politics until 1929. (Anheier, Neidhardt,
& Vortkamp 1998 documents a parallel 1929 surge of Nazi organizational activity in Munich; see also Anheier & Ohlemacher 1996 for national trends in Nazi
membership.)

At the end of the 1920s, Nazis began speaking widely, proselytizing in the
countryside, and engaging actively in electoral campaigns. They also infiltrated
existing organizations at the university and in the community at large. Their anti-
Semitic and anti-Bolshevik appeals reinforced well-entrenched political positions
in Marburg. In contrast to prewar Berlin, many of Marburg's police belonged to
the Social Democratic Party and thus split with conservative city officials whose
own response to Nazi organizing ranged from worried toleration to encouragement. "Deepening social roots," concludes Koshar,

> established the NSDAP [National Socialist Party, or Nazis] at the center of an
> evolving *völkisch* [racist-nationalist] polity. The success of Hitler's visit to Marburg

in April 1932, which attracted 20,000 people from the city and countryside, was only partly due to the charisma of the *Führer*. It was also a direct outgrowth of the party's stance as a vehicle of popular involvement in local public life. Hitler was an attraction because the party was; the party was attractive in part because of its positive image in conversations in the marketplace, local stores, university classrooms, fraternity houses, meeting halls, soccer fields, and homes. Hitler's seemingly mysterious mass appeal could hardly have been so extensive without the unplanned propaganda of daily social life. (Koshar 1986: 204)

The party did not simply impose its will on the Marburg public, at least not before the Nazi seizure of power in 1933. It adapted to the local organizational environment, combining membership in existing non-Nazi associations with creation of parallel organizations under party sponsorship. By 1932 it was receiving half or more of the votes in Marburg's elections. It far outshadowed the city's communists and Social Democrats, with whom Nazi squads sometimes engaged in street fighting. On its way to power, it adopted the performances, campaigns, and WUNC displays of social movements at large.

International Adaptation of Social Movement Forms

The case of Marburg reveals the importance of local implantation for national social movements. The lesson is more general. As our glances at China, Indonesia, and Fiji have already shown, social movement campaigns, performances, and WUNC displays do not simply migrate intact from one political culture to another (Chabot 2000, Chabot & Duyvendak 2002, Scalmer 2002b). Precisely because social movement organizers are most often addressing regional or national audiences on regional or national issues, they have no choice but to employ at least some familiar idioms, display some known symbols, and draw on existing organizational forms, however much they also innovate and borrow from elsewhere. The twentieth century's unprecedented spread of social movement activity across the world ironically produced both commonality and diversity. It produced commonality because social movement performances such as the demonstration or the creation of fronts, coalitions, and special-purpose associations provided models for emulators everywhere. It produced diversity because each region's organizers found ways of integrating social movement strategies into local conditions.

Again let a single case suffice, this time a very large one. India, the world's second-most populous country and most populous democracy, has hosted forms of social movement activity at least since the formation of the Indian National Congress in 1885. Mohandas Gandhi was a genius at organizing associations, marches, declarations, campaigns, and—preeminently—WUNC displays in his own version of the social movement style. He had become a veteran organizer of nonviolent opposition in South Africa. After a stop in England to organize an

Indian corps for war service, Gandhi returned to India from his twenty-year South African sojourn in 1914.

Back in India, Gandhi supported the British war effort, which sent Indian troops to Europe, Mesopotamia, Palestine, Egypt, and East Africa. But he also played a crucial part in expanding the political role of the Indian National Congress and in forging its alliance with the All-India Moslem League. The Hindu-Muslim coalition often worked uneasily, since Muslim activists generally opposed dismantling the Ottoman Empire (still the world's leading Muslim power), which was, after all, a major aim of the British war effort. Indeed, in 1915 a conspiratorial Muslim Indian group sought German support for an uprising against the British in India and Afghanistan.

As WWI ground on, the Congress and the All-India Moslem League began demanding an elected Indian legislative assembly as a first step toward self-government. In 1916, they even agreed on a program Indian nationalists had previously resisted: separate earmarked electorates for Muslim voters. In parallel with European events, the war's end brought an increase in popular mobilization. Gandhi led a campaign of strikes, demonstrations, and passive resistance as the colonial government struck back with repression. Authorities arrested Gandhi in April for violating an order to keep his organizing efforts out of the Punjab region. A low point arrived in April 1919, when a British general ordered his troops to fire on a large protest meeting in Amritsar, Punjab. As troops blocked the only exit from the meeting place, their volleys killed 379 demonstrators and wounded 1,200 more. The government then compounded its problems by declaring martial law and imposing severe punishments on participants. Those displays of colonial vengeance included public whipping and forced crawling through the streets. Widespread campaigns of condemnation in both India and Great Britain accelerated the introduction of moves toward self-government—or at least greater inclusion of Indians in the government of India.

The reform split Congress, with Gandhi's group bitterly opposing Britain's partial measures. In 1920, Congress launched a major campaign of noncooperation with British authorities and boycott of British goods. Indians rallied around the watchwords *satyagraha* (soul force), *hartal* (boycott), and *swaraj* (home rule), each of which had multiple religious, moral, and political overtones. The program included resignation from public office, nonparticipation in elections, withdrawal from school, and avoidance of law courts. It also involved spectacular actions such as a monster bonfire of foreign cloth, which Gandhi lighted in Bombay (August 1921). By that time, Indian nationalists were energetically creating their own distinctive forms of social movement claim making, but directing them against the forms of British rule.

Meanwhile, militant Muslims organized their own campaigns to maintain the Ottoman sultan (emperor) as leader of the world's Muslims, restore the Ottoman Empire as it was in 1914, and reestablish Muslim control of all the faith's holy places in the Near East. The predominantly Hindu Congress hesitantly backed their Muslim allies' program. Although Gandhi and his followers insisted on nonviolence, in many parts of India people attacked landlords, moneylenders, and officials. Muslim attacks on Hindu landlords, in fact, led to wider Hindu-Muslim battles and repeated splits in the movement for self-government. As conflicts escalated in 1922, the colonial government imprisoned Gandhi, thus cutting short a great, turbulent civil disobedience campaign. Through repeated imprisonments, nevertheless, Gandhi continued to act as India's most visible social movement organizer until his assassination by a dissatisfied Hindu nationalist in 1948. He was, of course, an inspiring religious model, but he was also a consummate political entrepreneur.

Gandhi's disappearance by no means terminated Indian social movements. After Indian independence (1947), Hindu leaders continued to employ and invent distinctive versions of the social movement repertoire. Consider an extraordinary, turbulent campaign to build a Hindu temple on the site of a Muslim shrine and thus to assert Hindu historical, religious, and political priority. Ayodhya, Uttar Pradesh, India, long sheltered a sixteenth-century mosque, Babri Masjid. The first Mughal (and Muslim) emperor Babur is supposed to have built the mosque in 1528. Ayodhya attracted worldwide attention on 6 December 1992, when Hindu militants destroyed Babri Masjid, began construction of a Hindu temple on the same site, and launched a nationwide series of struggles that eventually produced some twelve hundred deaths (Bose and Jalal 1998: 228; Madan 1997: 56–58; Tambiah 1996: 251; van der Veer 1996).

The campaigns behind that newsworthy event had, however, begun much earlier. During the nineteenth century, a platform marking the supposed birthplace of Ram, epic hero of the Hindu classic Ramayana, stood adjacent to the mosque. It represented the historical assertion that during his sixteenth-century conquest the Mughal emperor had demolished an ancient Hindu temple and built a mosque in its place.

The platform supplied the occasions for repeated Hindu-Muslim confrontations and for the program of building a Hindu temple on the site (Brass 1994: 241). Colonial authorities scotched the program. Shortly after independence, fifty to sixty local Hindus occupied the site one night and installed Hindu idols there. In response to Muslim demands, however, the newly independent (and avowedly secular) Indian government seized and locked up the mosque. During the 1980s, militant Hindu groups started demanding destruction of the mosque and erection of a temple to Ram. Just before the 1989 elections, Bharatiya Janata Party (BJP) activists transported what they called holy bricks to Ayodhya and ceremoniously laid a foundation for their temple.

The following year, President Lal Advani of the BJP took his chariot caravan on a pilgrimage (*rath yatra*) across northern India, promising along the way to start building the Ram temple in Ayodhya. Advani started his pilgrimage in Somnath, fabled site of yet another great Hindu temple destroyed by Muslim marauders. "For the sake of the temple," he declared en route, "we will sacrifice not one but many governments" (Chaturvedi & Chaturvedi 1996: 181–82). Advani's followers had fashioned his Toyota van into a version of legendary hero

Arjuna's chariot, an image familiar from Peter Brook's film *Mahabharata*. As the BJP caravan passed through towns and villages, Advani's chariot attracted gifts of flower petals, coconut, burning incense, sandalwood paste, and prayer from local women. Authorities arrested Advani before he could begin the last lap of his journey to Ayodhya, but not before many of his followers had preceded him to the city. When some of them broke through police barricades near the offending mosque, police fired on them, killing "scores" of BJP activists (Kakar 1996: 51).

Both sides represented their actions as virtuous violence—one side as defense of public order, the other side as sacrifice for a holy cause. Hindu activists made a great pageant of cremating the victims' bodies on a nearby river bank, then returning martyrs' ashes to their homes in various parts of India. Soon the fatalities at Ayodhya became the cause of widespread Hindu-Muslim-police clashes. Those conflicts intersected with higher-caste students' public resistance to the national government's revival of an affirmative action program on behalf of Other Backward Classes (Tambiah 1996: 249).

The dispute continued into the twenty-first century, with militant Hindu leaders frequently vowing to build (or, as they insisted, rebuild) their temple on the Babri Masjid site. In 2003, the Uttar Pradesh state court ordered the Archaeological Survey of India (ASI) to bring its scientific expertise to bear on the site. ASI excavations identified fifty pillar bases plus other artifacts in patterns characteristic of North Indian temples. Instead of settling the matter with the cool calm of science, however, the new discoveries incited sharp disagreements among archaeologists as they brought cries of triumph from Hindu activists. Lal Advani himself declared that the ASI report "gladdens crores [tens of millions] of devotees of Lord Rama" (Bagla 2003: 1305). A few weeks later, an Uttar Pradesh court dismissed criminal charges against Advani (now a plausible candidate for prime minister if the BJP wins the 2004 general election) that stemmed from his incitement of the 1992 attack on the Ayodhya mosque.

These dramatic events could not have unfolded anywhere else than in India. Yet they combined a campaign (not only to build a Hindu temple but also to attract political support for the BJP), a series of social movement performances (associations, meetings, processions, and more) along with sensational displays of worthiness, unity, numbers, and commitment. In those regards, the political work of India's Hindu organizers resembled that of nationalist social movement leaders across the earth, complete with the strident nationalist claim that "we were here first." Just as Gandhi and his collaborators pioneered a distinctive Indian variety of social movement claim making oriented to the British colonial system and taking the British government itself as one of its targets, the BJP integrated visibly Hindu references into its campaigns, performances, and WUNC displays as it sought power within a nominally secular Indian state. Indian campaigns could hardly have made the distinctive duality of social movements—simultaneously local and international in their forms, practices, and meanings—clearer.

By the twentieth century's end, social movements had become available as vehicles of popular politics throughout the democratic and democratizing world.

They had become available to programs that would have horrified many of the early-nineteenth-century social movement's pioneers. They had adopted cultural forms and technical means that no nineteenth-century social movement activist could have imagined. In Western democracies, at least, social movement organizers, authorities, and police had negotiated routines that greatly minimized the violence of social movement claim making. Organizers had also begun creating international alliances even more actively than their nineteenth-century predecessors had managed. But that process brings us into the twenty-first century.

5

SOCIAL MOVEMENTS ENTER
THE TWENTY-FIRST CENTURY

Toward midnight on Tuesday 16 January 2001, text-messaging mobile phones in and around Manila, Philippines, began transmitting the message *Go 2EDSA, Wear blck*. Within an hour, tens of thousands arrived at Epifanio de los Santos Avenue, which Manileños call Edsa. The avenue already featured a People Power shrine, Our Lady of Peace. The shrine stood at the spot where in 1986 praying nuns had faced down the tanks of President Ferdinand Marcos and helped drive Marcos from power. Over the next four days in 2001, more than a million people, many of them wearing black clothing, gathered in downtown Manila, calling for President Joseph Estrada to step down. A defeated Erap (as Filipinos commonly called Estrada) actually abandoned his office on 20 January.

On the 16th, Estrada's impeachment trial had reached an impasse when the Senate's impeachment court voted 11–10 not to examine one crucial piece of evidence, whereupon the Senate's president had resigned. Late that night, demonstrators started gathering at Edsa, spreading word of their action by mobile phone. At that point, prosecutor Oscar Moreno declared, "The forum is now on the streets, no longer in the Senate halls. It is now in the bar of public opinion and I'm sure the Filipinos will rise up to the occasion." On the 17th, prosecutors in the case followed the Senate president's lead by resigning as well. Over the next two days, numerous groups across the Philippines began joining the movement with calls for the president's resignation.

Arriving from Hong Kong, for example, former president Fidel Ramos led a protest march of about three hundred supporters from the airport to Edsa, where former president Corazon Aquino and People Power patron Cardinal Jaime Sin addressed the crowd, likewise demanding a presidential resignation. Throughout the Manila region, two hundred thousand workers walked off the job to attend anti-Estrada rallies (*Philippine Star* 18 January 2001). On the evening of 18 January, a 10-kilometer hand-in-hand human chain stretched from the monument in memory of Ninoy Aquino (whose assassination by Marcos forces in 1983 had indirectly precipitated the People Power movement of 1986) to the Edsa shrine.

On Friday the 19th, anti-Estrada forces took even more serious steps against the beleaguered president. That day, 150 thousand demonstrators gathered at the People Power monument, the army's head appeared before them to announce his defection from the president's camp, and Vice President Gloria Macapagal-Arroyo (daughter of an earlier Philippine president) started describing herself as "commander in chief." In the course of the day, a number of top police and military officers deserted the president and authorized a march on the presidential palace.

Meanwhile, streets filled with rock groups, high school marching bands, chanting Estrada opponents, and banners calling for the president's ouster. As street demonstrations continued, army chiefs sent a high-ranking officer and former presidential aide to inform Estrada—by now half drunk—unambiguously that the military were no longer backing him. Although the president never quite filed a formal resignation, by late on the 19th Gloria Macapagal-Arroyo had assumed power, receiving quick recognition as president by the country's major authorities. Estrada finally left the presidential palace on the 20th (Ananova 2001, *Philippine Star* 2001).

A nonviolent but visibly momentous assembly of Philippine citizens had again helped produce a major transfer of power in that troubled country. A week later, *Time Asia* reflected:

> What transpired last week in Manila had all the makings of democracy on the hoof: protesters, rousing speeches, People Power—just like the glorious revolution that ousted dictator Ferdinand Marcos so dramatically and virtually bloodlessly, nearly 15 years ago. The emotion of the moment carried the day, and one felt cynical questioning the motives of the people or the alleged corruption of departed President Joseph Estrada. But what actually happened behind the scenes to bring about People Power II? And could those very powers—and people— that have brought about the downfall of yet another Philippine President be the same forces that will make it difficult for anyone, including freshly sworn in President Gloria Macapagal Arroyo, to govern the Philippines effectively? (*Time Asia* 2001)

In other words, did all that commotion in Manila's streets provide nothing but camouflage for the decisive political steps taken by an establishment that had already decided to rid itself of an inconvenient figurehead and that would manipulate his successor as well?

The magazine's worries raised questions that spill far beyond a tumultuous week in January in Manila. Would the twenty-first century finally bring social movements to the long-dreamed culmination of People Power across the world? Would technologies of communication such as the text-messaging mobile telephones that carried the word so swiftly through Manila provide the means for activists and ordinary people to shift the tactical balance away from capitalists, military leaders, and corrupt politicians? Or, on the contrary, did the assembly of thousands in the streets there and elsewhere merely mark the last churning of popular politics in the wake of globalization's dreadnaught?

Technology analyst Howard Rheingold takes the Philippine adventure as a harbinger of what he calls "smart mobs": "people who are able to act in concert even if they don't know each other" (Rheingold 2003: xii). He stresses the enormous enthusiasm of Filipinos for Short Message Service (SMS) since its introduction in 1995. As of 2000, the Philippines' 84 cellular mobile subscribers per thousand people topped richer countries such as Costa Rica (52) and Belize (70), despite falling far short of Iceland's spectacular 783 and Norway's almost equally remarkable 751.

The Philippines, furthermore, fell into a special communications class in one relevant regard. The only countries in the world to have more than twice as many cellular mobile phone subscribers as mainline telephone connections were then Paraguay, Gabon, Congo, and the Philippines (UNDP 2002: 186–89). Satellite-backed cellular phones and text messaging begin to look like serious alternatives to fixed-line telecommunication, especially where poverty, political turmoil, and/or forbidding geography impede the creation of government-backed telecommunications infrastructure. At least superficially, the mobile systems have the populist attraction of not falling easily under governmental control.

Rheingold goes further, however. He argues that smart mobs connected by text messaging are already taking over from conventional twentieth-century social movements. He cites these examples:

- On 30 November 1999, autonomous but internetworked squads of demonstrators protesting the meeting of the World Trade Organization used "swarming" tactics, mobile phones, Web sites, laptops, and handheld computers to win the "Battle of Seattle."
- In September 2000, thousands of citizens in Britain, outraged by a sudden rise in gasoline prices, used mobile phones, SMS, e-mail from laptop PCs, and CB radios in taxicabs to coordinate dispersed groups that blocked fuel delivery at selected service stations in a wildcat political protest.
- A violent political demonstration in Toronto in the spring of 2000 was chronicled by a group of roving journalist-researchers who webcast digital video of everything they saw.
- Since 1992, thousands of bicycle activists have assembled monthly for "Critical Mass" moving demonstrations in San Francisco, weaving through the streets en masse. Critical Mass operates through loosely linked networks, alerted by mobile phone and e-mail trees, and breaks up into smaller, telecoordinated groups when appropriate. (Rheingold 2003: 158)

Undoubtedly early-twentieth-first-century social movement activists have integrated fresh new technologies into their organizing and into their very claim-making performances. Serious questions, however, start there: Are new technologies transforming social movements? In what ways? If so, how do they produce their effects? How do new tactics and new forms of organization interact in twenty-first-century social movements? More generally, to what extent and how do recent alterations in social movements result from the changes in international connectedness that people loosely call globalization?

This chapter shows that significant changes in social movements are, indeed, occurring during the early twenty-first century. As compared with the twentieth century, internationally organized networks of activists, international nongovernmental organizations, and internationally visible targets such as multinational corporations and international financial institutions all figure more prominently in recent social movements, especially in the richer and better-connected parts of the world. Even domestically oriented movements such as the anti-Estrada campaign in the Philippines receive, on the average, more international attention and intervention than their twentieth-century counterparts.

Yet this chapter also issues four stern warnings.

1. Avoid technological determinism; recognize that most new features of social movements result from alterations in their social and political contexts rather than from technical innovations as such.
2. Notice that, as they did during the nineteenth and twentieth centuries, twenty-first-century communications innovations always operate in a two-sided way: on one side, lowering the costs of coordination among activists who are already connected with each other; on the other, excluding even more definitively those who lack access to the new communications means and, thus, increasing communications inequality.
3. Remember that most twenty-first-century social movement activity continues to rely on the local, regional, and national forms of organization that already prevailed during the later twentieth century.
4. While noting that globalization is shaping the world distribution of social movements, avoid the supposition that the confrontation of globalization and antiglobalization now dominates the social movement scene.

To ignore these warnings would blind you to the actual social changes that are affecting collective claim making worldwide as well as to the persistence of local, regional, and national issues in social movements.

Globalization

Let us first get globalization right. Any time a distinctive set of social connections and practices expands from a regional to a transcontinental scale, some globalization is occurring. Each time an existing transcontinental set of social connections and practices fragments, disintegrates, or vanishes, some deglobalization occurs. Only when the first sort of process is far outrunning the second does it clarify matters to say that humanity as a whole is globalizing.

During the half millennium since 1500, three main waves of globalization have occurred. The first arrived right around 1500. It resulted from the rapidly spreading influence of Europe, growth of the Ottoman Empire, and parallel expansions of Chinese and Arab merchants into the Indian Ocean and the Pacific. The Ottomans extended their control into southern Europe, northern Africa, and the Near East while Western Europeans were building commercial and territorial empires in Africa, the Pacific, and the Americas. Meanwhile, seafaring Muslim merchants continued to connect Africa, the Near East, and Indian Ocean ports. In Asia, European and Muslim commercial activity interacted with China's energetic expansion into Pacific trade under the Ming Empire (1368–1644).

Ottoman expansion ended in the nineteenth century, and Europeans partly displaced Muslim merchants across the Indian Ocean and the Pacific. But Europeans and the Chinese continued their shares of the first post-1500 globalizing process into the twentieth century. Europeans began colonizing the more temperate zones of their empires in Africa, the Americas, and the Pacific. Chinese migrants by the millions likewise moved into Southeast Asia and the Pacific. Here is one sign of the world's increasing connectedness: by the seventeenth century, large amounts of silver mined in South America were ending up in Chinese treasuries, drawn by the export of precious Chinese commodities to the West.

We can place the second major post-1500 wave of globalization approximately at 1850–1914. Consider the fury of long-distance migration between 1850 and World War I: three million Indians, nine million Japanese, ten million Russians, twenty million Chinese, and thirty-three million Europeans. During this period, international trade and capital flows reached previously unmatched heights, especially across the Atlantic. Improvements in transportation and communication such as railroads, steamships, telephone, and telegraph lowered the costs of those flows and speeded them up. Massive movements of labor, goods, and capital made prices of traded goods more uniform across the world and reduced wage gaps among countries that were heavily involved in those flows. The chief beneficiaries included Japan, Western Europe, and the richer countries of North and South America. For the world as a whole, globalization's second wave increased disparities in wealth and well-being between those beneficiaries and everyone else. Except for European settler areas such as Australia, European colonies did not generally share in the prosperity.

Migration, trade, and capital flows slowed between the two world wars. But as Europe and Asia recovered from World War II, a third post-1500 surge of globalization began. This time intercontinental migration accelerated less than between 1850 and 1914. In comparison with 1850–1914, fewer economies felt acute labor shortages and labor organized more effectively to bar immigrant competition. As a consequence, long-distance migration bifurcated into relatively small streams of professional and technical workers, on one side, and vast numbers of servants and general laborers, on the other. Because differences in wealth and security between rich and poor countries were widening visibly, potential workers from poor countries made desperate attempts to migrate into richer countries, either permanently or long enough to earn substantial money for their return home. Whole industries grew up around the facilitation of illegal, semilegal, and legal but brutal forms of migration into richer countries.

Flows of goods and capital accelerated even beyond nineteenth-century levels. Many of those flows occurred within firms, as multinational companies spanned markets, manufacturing sites, headquarters, and sources of raw materials in different countries. But international trade among countries and firms also accelerated. High-tech and high-end goods produced in East Asia, Western Europe, and North America became available almost everywhere in the world. Capitalists based in the richest countries invested increasingly in manufacturing where labor costs ran lower than at home, often bringing clothing, electronic devices, and other goods produced in low-wage countries back to compete in their own home markets. At the same time, political institutions, communications systems, technology, science, disease, pollution, and criminal activity all took on increasingly international scales. During the early twenty-first century, the third wave of post-1500 globalization was moving ahead with full force.

The globalization waves of 1850–1914 and of 1950 onward differed conspicuously. Despite imperial outreach and the rising importance of Japan, nineteenth-century expansion centered on the Atlantic, first benefiting the major European states, then increasingly favoring North America. Its twentieth- and twenty-first-century counterpart involved Asia much more heavily. As sites of production, as objects of investment, and increasingly as markets, China, Japan, Korea, Taiwan, India, Pakistan, Bangladesh, Indonesia, Malaysia, Singapore, Thailand, the Philippines, and other Asian countries participated extensively in global growth.

Another difference: during the wave of 1850–1914, economic expansion depended heavily on coal and iron. As a consequence, capital and workers flowed especially to a limited number of smokestack regions, producing the characteristic grimy concentrations of industrial cities along waterways and rail lines. By the late twentieth century, oil, natural gas, hydroelectric generators, and nuclear reactors had largely displaced coal as sources of power in the world's richer regions. Post-1945 globalization featured such high-tech industries as electronics and pharmaceuticals. Those industries depended on important clusters of scientific and technical expertise such as Paris-Sud and Silicon Valley, California. But with goods of high value and relatively low transport cost, they could easily subdivide production according to the availability of labor and markets. Service and information industries pushed even farther in the same direction: low-wage data-processing clerks in southern India, for example, processed information for firms based in New York and London, with fiber-optic cable and satellite connections transmitting data instantly in both directions.

Globalization in its nineteenth-century version consolidated states. It augmented their control over resources, activities, and people within their boundaries as it increased their regulation of flows across those boundaries. Between 1850 and World War I, for example, the world's states regularized national passports and their firm attachment of citizens to particular states (Torpey 2000). In the process, uneasy but effective working agreements emerged among governments, capital, and labor at the national scale. Organized labor, organized capital, organized political parties, and organized bureaucrats fought hard but made deals. Those bargains eventually turned states from free trade toward protection of industries that combined large labor forces with extensive fixed capital. Chemicals, steel, and metal-processing industries led the way.

The variety of globalization found in the twentieth and twenty-first centuries, in dramatic contrast, undermined the central power of most states, freeing capital to move rapidly from country to country as opportunities for profit arose. Post-1945 states also lost effectiveness when it came to containing accelerated flows of communication, scientific knowledge, drugs, arms, gems, or migrants across their borders. Even the predominant United States failed to block substantial flows of contraband, tainted capital, and illegal migrants. Most other states lost control more dramatically than the United States.

At the same time, nongovernmental and supergovernmental organizations escaped partially from control by any particular state. The newly powerful nonstate organizations included multinational corporations, world financial institutions, the United Nations, political compacts such as the European Union, military alliances such as the North Atlantic Treaty Organization (NATO), and international activist groups such as Doctors Without Borders. An irony appears: the United States sponsored or at least supported the initial formation of many such transnational organizations. In their early phases, the United States often bent them to its national interests. Yet as the twenty-first century began, even the United States, the world's greatest financial and military power, could not simply order these organizations around.

Globalization and Social Movements

As a context for changes in social movements, we can see the operation of globalization more clearly by distinguishing among top-down connectedness, bottom-up adaptation, and a middle ground of negotiation. From the top down, globalization produces connections among centers of power: commercial connections among financial nodes, coercive connections among military forces, cultural connections among religious or ethnic clusters, and combinations of the three. From the bottom up, globalization looks different; it includes such connections as long-distance migration streams, telephone calls across borders and oceans, remittances and gifts sent by migrants to their home villages, and sharing of lore by social movement organizers. As critics often complain, it certainly involves the spread of standardized consumer goods and services across the world. Yet it also involves a surprising range of adaptations that integrate those goods and services into local cultures rather than simply homogenizing and flattening those cultures (Zelizer 1999).

In the intermediate zone of negotiation, people respond to opportunities and threats generated by top-down processes, employing bottom-up networks to create new relations with centers of power. That intermediate zone contains not only coordinated confrontations such as the worldwide mobilization against American invasion of Iraq on 15 February 2003 but also globe-spanning trade in contraband, such as illegally acquired minerals, drugs, timber, and sexual services. The intermediate zone depends largely on connections produced by the top-down and bottom-up versions of globalization. For example, flows of contraband often pass from their points of origin to and through well-connected emigrants, the more profitable forms of illicit trade use international financial circuits to launder their money, and international contacts among far-flung social movement activists often originate at conferences staged by international organizations.

Since Howard Rheingold and many other technology enthusiasts claim that new communications technologies are entirely remapping social movement organization and strategy, it helps to recognize that from the start social movement activists have responded to mass media. We have already noticed how the vast increase of print media during the nineteenth and twentieth centuries gave new resonance to social movements long before the electronic age. Radio and television played important parts during the twentieth century. Table 5.1 lists some crucial dates for relevant technological innovations.

We should take great care before adopting communications determinism in either its general or its particular form: generally by supposing that each of these innovations in itself transformed social life and political action, particularly by imagining that the Internet or the cellular telephone affords so much greater communications power that it detaches people from previously existing social relations and practices. In a thoughtful, comprehensive recent survey of Internet use, Caroline Haythornthwaite and Barry Wellman offer a summary concerning social impact in general.

Table 5.1 New Communications Technologies

Year	Technology
1833	introduction of the telegraph
1876	introduction of the telephone
1895	Marconi's demonstration of radio
1920s	experimental television
1966	initiation of satellite communication
1977	first mobile telecommunications system (Saudi Arabia)
1978	first computer modem
1989	initial plan for World Wide Web
1995	public Internet established in United States
1996	Wireless Application Protocol

Source: Adapted from UNDP 2001: 33.

Even before the advent of the Internet, there has been a move from all-encom-passing, socially controlling communities to individualized fragmented personal communities. Most friends and relatives with whom we maintain socially close ties are not physically close. These ties are spread through metropolitan areas, and often on the other side of countries or seas. Mail, the telephone, cars, air-planes, and now email and the Internet sustain these ties. Most people do not live lives bound in one community. Instead, they maneuver through multiple specialized partial communities, giving limited commitment to each. Their life is "glocalized": combining long-distance ties with continuing involvements in households, neighborhoods, and worksites. (Haythornthwaite & Wellman 2002: 32)

Of course, these observations apply with greater force to rich Western countries than to the world as a whole. But they clarify the sense in which integration of communications innovations into existing social relations and practices extends projects that people already have underway and, especially, accentuates connec-tions that were already in play but costly to maintain. The observations reinforce two crucial points that came up as we examined the adoption of new media such as radio in twentieth-century social movements. First, each new form of com-munications connection facilitates a specific set of social relations as it excludes oth-ers—the others who do not have access to the relevant communications medium. Second, communications media differ dramatically in their degree of symmetry and asymmetry; newspapers, radio, and television exhibit massive asymmetry among par-ticipants, while digital communications redress the balance to some extent.

Looking chiefly at economic relations in a similar light, Viviana Zelizer astutely recognizes the existence of social relations she calls "commercial circuits." Each of those circuits includes four elements: 1) a well-defined boundary with some control over transactions crossing the boundary; 2) a distinctive set of eco-nomic transactions; 3) distinctive media (reckoning systems and tokens of value) employed in the pursuit of those transactions; and 4) meaningful ties among par-ticipants (Zelizer 2004). Cases in point include credit networks, mutual-aid con-nections among professionals in different organizations, and specialized currency systems. Such circuits create an institutional structure that reinforces credit, trust, and reciprocity within its perimeter but organizes exclusion and inequality in re-lation to outsiders. Circuits cut across the limits of communities, households, and organizations but link their participants in significant forms of coordination, com-munication, and interdependence.

The idea extends easily to what we might call *political circuits:* not simply networks of connection among political activists but the full combination of bound-aries, controls, political transactions, media, and meaningful ties. Social move-ments build on, create, and transform political circuits. In this regard, the com-munications media their members employ make a difference for precisely the reasons just mentioned: because each medium in its own ways reinforces some connections, facilitates other connections that would otherwise be costly to establish or sustain, and excludes a great many other possible connections. Once involved in a political circuit, participants negotiate matches among media, transactions, and meaningful social ties as they establish and control boundaries between insiders and outsiders. Instead of communications determinism, we find political participants actively engaged in organizational innovation.

All of the technological innovations listed earlier or their applications eventually became available to social movement organizers and activists. In general, they reduced communication costs as they increased the geographic range covered by social movement communications. They also tied social movement participants more firmly to other users of the same technologies as they separated participants from nonusers of those technologies; they had significant selection effects in that regard.

In their times, similarly, transportation breakthroughs such as intercity steam trains, electrical street cars, and jet aircraft facilitated social movement contact at a distance but actually impeded contact with like-minded people who lived away from major transport lines. Neither in communications nor in transportation, however, did the technological timetable dominate alterations in social movement organization, strategy, and practice. Shifts in the political and organizational context impinged far more directly and immediately on how social movements worked than did technical transformations as such.

A little reflection on the world distribution of communications connections, in any case, dispels the illusion that electronic messages will soon coordinate social movements across the entire globe. Table 5.2 presents relevant data for an array of countries from relatively poor (e.g., Congo) to very rich (e.g., Norway). Note the wide disparities in the numbers of telephone lines, mobile telephones, and Internet connections. Telephone lines run from 7 connections for every 10 people (Iceland and the United States) to 1 connection for every 143 people (Congo). Mobile telephone ownership varies to about the same extent across countries, and Internet connections vary even more widely. As the ratios comparing 2000 to 1990 indicate, some small equalization among countries is occurring with respect to fixed-line telephone access. But when it comes to cellular telephones and Internet connections, rapid expansion of those services in richer countries is actually increasing worldwide inequalities. Within the Internet, furthermore, inequality runs even deeper than these figures indicate; U.S. producers, for example, dominate the world's Web sites, making English the World Wide Web's lingua franca (DiMaggio, Hargittai, Neuman, & Robinson 2001: 312).

Two conclusions follow. First, to the extent that internationally coordinated social movements rely on electronic communication, they will have a much easier time of it in rich countries than poor ones. Second, electronic communications connect social movement activists selectively both across countries and within countries. Anyone whom a Norwegian organizer can reach electronically in, say, India or Kazakhstan already belongs to a very small communications elite. In a more distant future, diffusion of high-tech communications facilities may eventually equalize social movement opportunities internationally. For the medium term, this important aspect of globalization is making the world more unequal.

Table 5.2 Communications Connections for Selected Countries, 1990–2000

Country	Telephone lines per thousand people, 2000	Ratio, 2000/1990	Cellular mobile subscribers per thousand, 2000	Ratio, 2000/1990	Internet hosts per thousand, 2000	Ratio, 2000/1990
Australia	525	1.2	447	40.6	85.7	5.0
Canada	677	1.2	285	131.3	77.4	6.1
China	112	18.7	66	—	0.1	—
Congo	7	1.0	24	—	—	—
Czech Republic	378	2.4	424	—	15.4	7.3
Gabon	32	1.5	98	—	—	—
Iceland	701	1.4	783	20.1	143.0	4.6
India	32	5.3	4	—	—	—
Indonesia	31	5.2	17	—	0.1	—
Israel	482	1.4	702	234.0	29.5	6.0
Kazakhstan	113	1.4	12	—	0.5	—
Norway	532	1.1	751	16.3	101.1	5.2
Paraguay	50	1.9	149	—	0.2	—
Philippines	40	4.0	84	—	0.3	—
Saudi Arabia	137	1.8	64	64.0	0.2	—
United Kingdom	589	1.3	727	38.3	28.2	3.8
United States	700	1.3	398	19.0	295.2	12.8
World	163	1.6	121	60.5	17.8	10.5

— = either no data or 0 in 1990

Source: UNDP 2002: 186–89.

Within the high-tech world, to be sure, organizers of international social movements have widely incorporated digital communications technologies into their performances. Web sites, online petitions, electronic discussion lists, person-to-person e-mail messages, and coordination of local actions by means of cellular telephones or portable radios all speed up communications and increase the range of persons with whom any particular individual can maintain contact. Tough questions start there: Is the introduction of digital technologies into social movement practices transforming those practices more rapidly and extensively than did earlier communications and transport technologies such as the telephone, television, and long-distance buses? Are new sorts of relationships among activists emerging as a consequence? Are social movement campaigns, repertoires, and WUNC displays therefore changing character more dramatically than ever before?

In a field full of hyperbole, Lance Bennett's exceptionally thoughtful and balanced review of the subject (Bennett 2003) argues that digital media are changing international activism in several important ways, including

- making loosely structured networks, rather than the relatively dense networks of earlier social movements (Diani 2003), crucial to communication and co-ordination among activists;
- weakening the identification of local activists with the movement as a whole by allowing greater scope for introduction of local issues into movement discourse;
- reducing the influence of ideology on personal involvement in social movements;
- diminishing the relative importance of bounded, durable, resource-rich local and national organizations as bases for social movement activism;
- increasing the strategic advantages of resource-poor organizations within social movements;
- promoting the creation of permanent campaigns (e.g., antiglobalization or for environmental protection) with rapidly shifting immediate targets; and
- combining older face-to-face performances with virtual performances.

Bennett concludes that these changes, in turn, make social movements increasingly vulnerable to problems of coordination, control, and commitment.

Even Bennett does not claim, however, that the trends he describes amount to established fact; he is sniffing the wind with a sensitive nose. Let us move cautiously, in case a storm is indeed coming. Reflecting on the place of communications technologies in social relations at large as well as in earlier social movements, we should remain skeptical of straightforward technological determinism. Most likely some of the changes Bennett detects result less from the adoption of digital technologies as such than from alterations in the political and economic circumstances of social movement activists (DiMaggio, Hargittai, Neuman, & Robinson 2001, Sassen 2002, Tarrow 2003, Wellman 2000, 2001a, 2001b). Proliferation of international organizations (both governmental and nongovernmental); increasing prominence of transnational corporations and financial networks; diminishing capacity of most states to control flows of goods, persons, capital, or contraband; and expansion of communications among likely targets of social movement claims all contribute to the changes on Bennett's list. They all pose new challenges for social movement activists, and they all encourage formation of new political circuits as bases of social movement mobilization.

That brings us back to globalization. In principle, how might we expect the three currents of globalizing change—top down, bottom up, and in between—to affect social movements across the world? Let us think separately about campaigns, repertoires, and WUNC displays:

- Since top-down, bottom-up, and intermediate changes all increase connectedness among sites that share interests and, on the average, reduce the cost of communication among those sites, we might expect an increase in the frequency of *campaigns* involving similar or identical targets simultaneously at many different sites.
- As for *repertoires,* we might expect decreasing reliance on expressions of program, identity, and standing claims that require the physical copresence of all participants in favor of locally clustered performances connected by long, thin strands of communication. At the extreme, that trend would yield virtual performances requiring no physical copresence whatsoever.
- When it comes to *WUNC displays,* despite the example of wearing black in Manila during January 2001 we might expect an interesting bifurcation: on one side, ways of signaling worthiness, unity, numbers, and commitment that gain instant recognition anywhere in the world; on the other side, increasingly localized WUNC codes that announce the relations of participating clusters to their local environments. Indonesian demonstrators wearing locally intelligible headbands but holding English-language signs up to television cameras illustrate the bifurcation.

The expected changes in campaigns and repertoires have almost certainly been occurring since the late twentieth century. In the absence of detailed event catalogs, the bifurcation of WUNC displays remains uncertain but plausible. If my speculation is correct, detailed comparisons of episodes will show that (as compared with more localized social movements) internationally oriented performances combine codes linking participants closely to their own localities and groups with other WUNC codes of worldwide currency such as peace signs and chanting in unison.

Just as we should avoid simple technological determinism, we should guard against attributing every twenty-first-century change in social movements to globalization; coincidence does not prove causation. In particular, we should not allow the spectacular occasions on which activists coordinate their claim making across seas and continents to persuade us that the days of local, regional, and national social movements have faded away. International connections still bind together people who continue to act mainly within bounded countries and who continue to take the governments of those countries seriously. Many observers and participants describe all international connections as if they were global and, therefore, transcend the old politics of bounded, centralized states. In fact, states remain salient actors, targets, and sites of early-twenty-first-century social movements. Manila's mobilization around the Philippine presidency provides one example. The enormous presence of the United States as actor, target, and site in the new century's social movement politics makes the point even more emphatically.

Back to the Philippines

Return to the Philippines of 2000 and 2001 will help clarify the place of social movements in twenty-first-century public politics—and provide some grounds for skepticism that new communications technologies are sweeping all before them. After long periods of colonization by Spain and then by the United States, the Philippines had by 2000 spent more than half a century as an independent country. It retained strong ties to the United States through the substantial presence of American military forces, a population more than nine-tenths Christian, extensive trade flows, substantial migration to the United States, and alternation between English and Filipino (the latter based closely on Tagalog) as the major languages of public life.

Between 1946 and 2001, the Philippines swung between relatively democratic competition for high offices within the archipelago's landed and commercial elites, on one side, and strongman rule just barely conforming to democratic procedures, on the other (Anderson 1998: 192–226). The presidency of Ferdinand Marcos (1965–1986), with its "crony capitalism," brought the high point of strongman rule at a national scale. In 1986, however, a vast popular mobilization called People Power sent Marcos packing to Hawaii and brought (equally elite) Corazon Aquino to the presidency. Over the next fifteen years, fairly free competitive elections produced more or less orderly successions of legislatures and presidents. Film star Joseph Estrada won the presidency in 1998 on a populist program, backed by a loosely structured party called Party for the Filipino Masses. But, like some of his predecessors, Estrada soon started dipping into the public till. Two years later, on a scale from 1 (high) to 7 (low), Freedom House rated the Philippines a relatively high 2 on political rights and 3 on civil rights, putting the country in the company of Argentina, Benin, and Bulgaria but below the 2+2 of Botswana, Chile, and Guyana. Major regional, religious, and ethnic conflicts plus doubts about the president's actual democratic commitments kept the Philippines from higher ratings (Karatnycky 2000: 389–90, 596–97).

By no means did all of Filipino popular public politics of the time, in fact, involve social movements. In many rural areas of the Philippines, militias and strongmen still predominated. In Mindanao, Islamic guerrillas had been fighting for an independent state since 1971. Although the mainline Moro National Liberation Front (MNLF) had settled with the central government in 1996, the twelve thousand to fifteen thousand armed members of its splinter Moro Islamic Liberation Front (MILF, which broke off from the MNLF in 1984) continued to conduct guerrilla warfare. Elsewhere, the communist New People's Army (NPA, perhaps eleven thousand strong), in loose alliance with the MILF, conducted its own campaign for a Marxist state (SIPRI 2001: 39–40).

Joseph Estrada's predecessor, Fidel Ramos, had managed the 1996 pacification of the MNLF while working out partial accommodations with the MILF and the NPA. Under Estrada, those agreements had started unraveling. Worse yet for the new president, unknown assailants (widely rumored to be members of the Abu Sayyaf group of militant Islamic separatists) kidnapped tourists, foreign journalists, and Philippine citizens in both the Philippines and Malaysia. They only released some of their hostages on payment of large ransoms. Meanwhile a lethal series of bombs exploded in Manila, once again being attributed without firm evidence to Abu Sayyaf (*Annual Register* 2000: 326–27). All of these unresolved conflicts shook popular support for Estrada.

The constitutional crisis that produced Estrada's departure from office in January 2001 actually began two months earlier. After credible allegations that the president had received huge kickbacks from illegal activities, the Philippine Congress voted to impeach him on 13 November. The twenty-two-member Senate, constituted as a trial court, needed a two-thirds vote to convict Estrada, hence the widespread upset at the court's 11–10 vote to suppress evidence on 16 January. As corruption accusations surfaced and before impeachment proceedings began, Vice President Macapagal-Arroyo (a U.S.-trained economist who had been elected independently of Estrada with a significantly larger share of the popular vote) resigned her post as social security minister, joining with former president Corazon Aquino and Cardinal Jaime Sin in the leadership of an anti-Estrada coalition. If People Power brought down Joseph Estrada, it did so with powerful elite backing.

Table 5.3 describes some of the context, as conveyed in headlines from the Manila daily *Philippine Star.* (In almost every case, the events reported at a given dateline occurred on the previous day.) By early December, the headlines reveal, Filipino political entrepreneurs were preparing an extensive campaign, complete with planned marches to the Senate, to Edsa, and to the presidential palace, Malacañang. Among a number of other less-radical organizations, the Philippine communist party (CPP) supported the anti-Estrada campaign. Estrada courted popular and church support with a ceasefire on the guerrilla front, commutations of death sentences, and release of prisoners. But his credibility suffered more blows as bombings continued in the provinces and then (at the end of December) in Manila's public transport system. Early in January, Estrada switched tactics by reopening military action against the MILF.

Despite Estrada's attempts to ban demonstrations against his regime, they continued in Manila and elsewhere. Pickets from the Akbayan Action Party, for

Table 5.3 Selected Headlines from the *Philippine Star,* December 2000 and January 2001

1 December	Anti-Estrada Forces Launch Civil Disobedience Plan
2 December	Government Declares Holiday Ceasefire with NPA, MILF
8 December	Anti-Estrada Protesters Prevented from Marching to Senate
8 December	United States Expresses Concern Over Coup Rumors Amid Estrada Trial
9 December	Cotabato Cathedral, Jollibee Outlet Bombed; 4 Wounded
11 December	Estrada Woos Church, Left: Commutes All Death Sentences to Life, Frees Political Prisoners
18 December	Edsa Rally Set Today
24 December	Acquittal to be Met with Massive Civil Disobedience
27 December	CPP Warns vs Suppressing Anti-Estrada Protests
28 December	Miriam to Supreme Court: Stop Rallies in My Home
31 December	Bombs Kill 11 in Metro
7 January	Estrada Renews War with MILF
9 January	Rallyists Maul Senate Driver
10 January	Protesters to Defy Senate Rally Ban
15 January	Police Use Water Cannons to Break Up Antipolo Protest
16 January	Malacañang Ready to Crush Anarchy
16 January	Antipolo Residents Attack Dump Trucks
17 January	Cyberwarriors Vow to Block Miriam's Bid for International Court Post
18 January	Edsa II to Erap: Resign
19 January	Edsa Protesters Form Human Chain
19 January	Nationwide Work Stoppage Set Today
19 January	Estrada Loyalists Chase Students with Clubs
20 January	Estrada Government Collapses
20 January	Rallyists Clash in Makati
21 January	3 Hurt, 6 Nabbed in Mendiola Clash
21 January	Supreme Court: People's Welfare is the Supreme Law
21 January	United States Recognizes GMA [Gloria Macapagal-Arroyo] Government

example, marched outside the Quezon City home of Senator Miriam Defensor-Santiago, an Estrada ally who belonged to the impeachment court. On 27 December she made an unsuccessful appeal to the Philippine Supreme Court for a legal ban of those marchers. A few weeks later, organizers of a Web site originally created to collect signatures for an electronic petition advocating Estrada's resignation—150 thousand people "signed" the petition—extended their campaign to oppose nomination of Senator Defensor-Santiago ("Miriam") to the International Court of Justice.

Not all the social movement activity of the time, however, directly concerned the campaign to remove Joseph Estrada from office. The "Antipolo protest" of 14 January, for example, had little direct connection with Manila's mobilization and much connection with Manila's garbage. Manila suffers from vast accumulations of refuse in its congested streets. Estrada had ordered reopening of the garbage dump that overlapped the towns of San Mateo and Antipolo, 30 kilometers east of Manila. One thousand protesters from Antipolo (which has six hundred thousand residents), led by Antipolo's mayor, blocked the highway and kept Manila's garbage trucks from getting through until police dispersed them with water cannons. On the 15th, unidentified men fired at garbage trucks passing through Antipolo and threw rocks that shattered the trucks' windows. Commentators said that local officials supported the protests because they feared defeat in approaching local elections if they publicly accepted the landfill.

As the impeachment crisis deepened, nevertheless, Philippine social movement action centered increasingly on encounters between pro-Estrada and anti-Estrada forces organized around the issue of impeachment. Up to 19 January, government spokesmen at the presidential palace (Malacañang) continued to threaten antigovernment demonstrators, and Estrada's popular supporters (drawn especially from Manila's poorest neighborhoods and from migrant networks of servants, drivers, and other service workers) kept on battling those demonstrators. By the 20th, however, metropolitan police were beginning to contain and arrest Estrada counterdemonstrators in such Manila neighborhoods as Makati (the city's financial district) and Mendiola (adjacent to Malacañang and site of a bridge where major confrontations had occurred during the ouster of Ferdinand Marcos). The tide had turned. U.S. recognition of the Macapagal-Arroyo regime that same day capped the transition.

Estrada's support did not entirely melt away. On 25 April, the Macapagal-Arroyo government fulfilled an early promise by arresting Estrada, treating him as an ordinary criminal. At that, organizers of Estrada's party (now called Force of the Masses) and allied religious groups brought their own demonstrators to Edsa for vocal demands on behalf of their leader. On 1 May, a similar group of Estrada supporters marched to the presidential palace (now occupied by Macapagal-Arroyo), destroying more than 20 million pesos worth of property along the way. Two demonstrators and two police officers died in struggles between Estrada activists and governmental forces in Mendiola. Like their enemies, the Estrada side continued to draw on its own version of the social movement repertoire (Rafael 2003: 422–25).

What do the Philippine struggles of 2000 and 2001 tell us about twenty-first-century social movements? First, they establish that, despite guerrilla warfare in some parts of the country, at least the Philippine capital region had institutionalized social movements in recognizable forms. With plenty of local color, the marches, picketing, and press releases of December and January clearly belonged to the international social movement repertoire, formed part of a sustained campaign to bring down the president, expressed program, identity, and standing claims, and involved repeated displays of WUNC. The confrontation over garbage dumping in Antipolo, furthermore, indicates that social movement tactics extended beyond the anti-Estrada campaign. The Philippines' incomplete democracy offered a favorable environment for social movements. As we have already observed for the later twentieth century, across the world democracy and social movements kept each other company during the early twenty-first century.

Second, by the same token the Philippines fell into the substantial category of socially and geographically segmented countries with regard to social movements. Despite the performances of Estrada's Manila supporters and their leaders, participants in recent Philippine social movements came overwhelmingly from the middle classes (Rafael 2003). Geographic differences divided the Philippines even more sharply than class differences. In such embattled regions as Mindanao, public politics did not involve social movements but warlords, religious leaders, bandits, hostage takers, patron-client networks, militias, and guerrilla forces. Nearby Malaysia and Indonesia similarly segmented into capital regions where social movement campaigns maintained political footholds and large areas where no one could hope to make political gains by combining nonviolent social movement performances and WUNC displays in sustained campaigns. Not only authoritarian countries but also authoritarian segments of partly democratic countries remained outside the world of social movements.

Third, international connections clearly mattered in this momentous national conflict. Most obviously, U.S. officials monitored the anti-Estrada campaign closely and managed almost instant diplomatic recognition of the Macapagal-Arroyo regime. Intense international media coverage (stimulated in part by deliberately staged parallels with the 1986 ouster of Ferdinand Marcos) meant that Manila's activists had no choice but to act on the local and world stages simultaneously. Does that make the events of 2000–2001 an instance or consequence of globalization? Not in the sense that intensification of international connections constituted or precipitated the mobilization against Estrada. At most we can say that by the start of the twenty-first century the Philippines had integrated sufficiently into worldwide circuits of power and communication that Philippine rulers lacked the options of obfuscation, seclusion, and repression that remained available to their counterparts in Myanmar, Belarus, and Liberia.

Fourth, the widespread use of mobile telephones and text messaging does not in itself make the case for the anti-Estrada campaign as a new sort of media-driven social movement. Manila's crowds may have formed more rapidly or in larger numbers than before because of cheap, quick communications. But the overall contours of popular mobilization in December and January—at least as seen from this distance—greatly resemble those of earlier, pre–cellular phone Philippine social movements as well as earlier social movements elsewhere in the democratic and semidemocratic worlds: plans for civil disobedience, published challenges to authorities, calling up of previously established organizations, assemblies in symbolically charged locations, demonstrations, marches, human chains, and prominent involvement of national leaders.

The fourth point, however, marks the limits of knowledge based on such sources as the *Philippine Star* alone. Media reports help us greatly in specifying what sorts of actions we must explain, what major actors (individual and collective) appear in public, and which publicly avowed alliances form among actors. But by themselves they do not answer the worrisome questions raised by the correspondents of *Time Asia:* To what extent did the popular mobilization exert an independent influence on the outcome? Could a cabal of Macapagal-Arroyo, Sin, and Aquino plus invisible backers in the military and finance have incited street politics as camouflage for a power grab? Without much closer observation of interactions among the campaign's participants, we cannot say for sure.

The most plausible reading of the evidence at hand, as I see it, runs like this: Organizations and political entrepreneurs long opposed to Estrada played a significant part in mobilizing widespread popular dissatisfaction with Estrada into a sustained campaign. The Senate's impeachment trial provided a visible focus for that campaign. Vast marches and demonstrations ratified the campaign to national and international audiences as they reduced Estrada's capacity to use force against his opponents. The fact that Estrada's supporters (who continued their agitation long after January 2001) also employed social movement tactics suggests both that genuine social movement politics came into play during January 2001 and that—at least in the Manila region—the social movement had become widely available as a way of pressing popular claims.

Going International

Across much of the world, meanwhile, social movements were internationalizing. We have of course encountered international connections within social movements since the very start: remember the prominence of British symbols, such as John Wilkes's number forty-five, in the Charleston, South Carolina, of June 1768? Abolitionism soon became a transatlantic movement with branches extending into a number of countries on both sides of the ocean. Through the nineteenth century, movements on behalf of temperance, women's rights, and Irish independence continued to generate cooperation around the Atlantic (Hanagan 2002, Keck & Sikkink 2000).

We are searching, then, not merely for examples of international social movement interactions but for indications of a significant change in the orientations of social movements. Figure 5.1 schematizes internationalization. It distinguishes between a) *claimants* (for example, campaigners against the World Trade Organization) that make program, identity, and standing claims by means of WUNC displays integrated into social movement performances, and b) *objects of claims* (for example, the World Trade Organization), whose response, recognition, or removal claimants seek. Over the two-century history of social movements this book surveys, both claimants and objects have ranged from local to regional to national to international. Most often the two have operated at the same level: local claimants with local objects, regional claimants with regional objects, and so on. But an increasingly common pattern matched coordinated claims by multiple claimants at one level with objects at a higher level, as when abolitionists in Boston

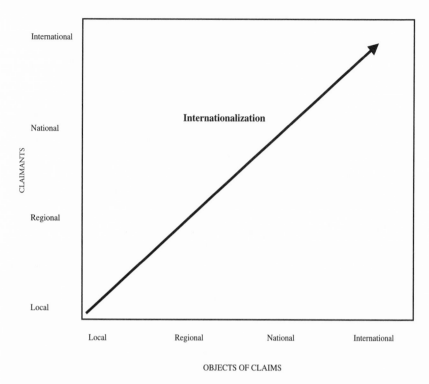

Figure 5.1 Internationalization of Social Movements

and Philadelphia joined to petition Congress for an end to slavery or when local Nazi activists in Marburg and other cities began concerting their claims for Hitler's placement as German ruler.

Similarly, national-level claimants such as supporters of independence from the Soviet Union within USSR republics or Soviet satellite states in 1989 simultaneously targeted Soviet rulers and international authorities including the European Union and the United Nations. The second case constituted a major step in the direction of internationalization. It fell short of the maximum—the upper-right-hand corner of figure 5.1—because it activated regional and national claimants rather than actors who spoke decisively on behalf of an international "we." Nevertheless, the international construction of "we" became an increasingly familiar feature of twenty-first-century social movements.

Objects of claims also internationalized. As transnational corporations and national corporations operating in many countries—think of Nike, McDonald's, Coca-Cola, and Royal Dutch Shell—expanded and multiplied, they provided targets for multinational social movement coordination. Creation of international authorities such as the United Nations, the North Atlantic Treaty Organization, the European Union, and the World Trade Organization (WTO) likewise produced consequential actors whose influence, policies, and interventions attracted social movement claims from multiple countries (see, e.g., Deibert 2000, Wood 2003). When those actors held visible high-level meetings, the meetings themselves invited internationally coordinated protests of their policies. Jackie Smith describes mobilization around the WTO's Seattle meeting of November 1999:

> On the evening of November 29, 1999, Seattle business and political leaders hosted an elaborate welcoming party in the city's football stadium for delegates to the World Trade Organization's Third Ministerial Conference. At the same time, thousands of activists rallied at a downtown church in preparation for the first large public confrontation in what became the "Battle of Seattle." Protesters emerged from the overflowing church and joined thousands more who were dancing, chanting, and conversing in a cold Seattle downpour. They filled several city blocks and celebrated the "protest of the century." Many wore union jackets or rain ponchos that proclaimed their opposition to the World Trade Organization. Several thousand marchers . . . progressed to the stadium, and around it formed a human chain—three or four people deep—to dramatize the crippling effects of the debt crisis. The protest deterred more than two-thirds of the expected 5,000 guests from attending the lavish welcoming event. The human chain's symbolism of the "chains of debt" was part of an international campaign (Jubilee 2000) to end Third World debt. It highlighted for protesters and onlookers the enormous inequities of the global trading system, and it kicked off a week of street protests and rallies against the global trade regime. (Smith 2002: 207)

Jubilee 2000 had originally formed as a coalition of United Kingdom nongovernmental organizations oriented to questions of economic and social development. The coalition soon focused on the cancellation of Third World debt. It pioneered the human chain maneuver at a 1998 meeting of international financial leaders in Birmingham, England. Bringing together activists from Jubilee 2000 and a great many other political networks, the Battle of Seattle became a model for international organizers who targeted international institutions.

To understand internationalization of claimants and objects of claims, we must recognize two other aspects of internationalization: a) proliferation of intermediaries specialized less in making claims on their own than in helping others coordinate claims at the international level, and b) multiplication of lateral connections among groups of activists involved in making similar claims within their own territories. Human rights organizations such as Amnesty International and Human Rights Watch led the way, monitoring human rights abuses across the world, publishing regular ratings and reports on those abuses, intervening to call down sanctions from major states and international authorities on human rights abusers, but often providing templates, certification, connections, and advice to claimants. Movements of self-styled indigenous peoples across the world benefited substantially from that identification of themselves as participants in a worldwide cause.

In partial independence of professional intermediaries, however, movement activists in similar causes—e.g., environmentalism, women's rights, and opposition to low-wage sweatshops producing in poor countries for rich markets—have also created enduring connections across oceans and continents. As we have seen with Fijian feminist activists, some of those connections form initially at international meetings convened by international organizations including the United Nations. Others form through Internet contacts mediated by discussion lists and Web sites.

Despite ample precedents, internationally coordinated social movement performances and international backing for regional and national social movement performances occurred with increasing frequency from the final decades of the twentieth century. Activists and analysts became ever more likely, furthermore, to claim regional and national events for worldwide movements variously labeled antiglobalization, global justice, or global civil society (Bennett 2003, Koopmans 2004, Rucht 2003, Tarrow 2002).

Under the heading of global civil society, a group of analysts at the London School of Economics began in 2001 to issue yearbooks on organization-based connections among activities most of which qualify as parts of social movements in one part of the world or another. Table 5.4 summarizes the yearbook's chronology for January and February 2001. It includes the Philippines' now-familiar People Power II. But it also enumerates a number of other activities well known to advocates of antiglobalization and global justice: the trial of McDonald's attackers in France; the World Social Forum of Porto Alegre, Brazil; militant counterconferences at the World Economic Forums of Davos, Switzerland, and Cancún, Mexico; a much-publicized march of Zapatistas in Mexico, and more. Two months' events cannot, of course, establish a trend. But the calendar helps explain why so many early-twenty-first-century observers took to speaking of social movements as globalizing apace. Most of these episodes emphatically involved internationally organized claimants, internationally prominent objects of claims, or both.

What do we see when we place the early twenty-first century in a longer time perspective? In the absence of comprehensive catalogs for social movements across the world (and with the tedious but essential warning that social movements by no means reduce to social movement organizations), we can get some sense of expansion into the twentieth century from counts of foundings for international nongovernmental organizations (INGOs). Those foundings ran at two or three per year during the 1870s and 1880s, and five or six per year during the 1890s, increasing to thirty or so per year before World War I. Founding of INGOs then declined during and after the war before rising close to forty during the 1920s, declining again through World War II, then soaring to eighty, ninety, and finally above one hundred new foundings per year during the 1980s (Boli & Thomas 1997: 176; for counts of existing INGOs 1900–2000, see Anheier & Themudo 2002: 194).

The evidence displays striking correspondence between formation of INGOs and creation of governmental or quasi-governmental organizations such as the

Table 5.4 "Global Civil Society Events," January–February 2001

15–16 January	Montpellier, France: members of Confédération paysanne face appeals court for destruction of a McDonald's restaurant in Millau, 1999.
17–20 January	Manila, Philippines: People Power II.
22 January	Zamfara State, Nigeria: teenage girl sentenced to one hundred lashes for nonmarital sex, which generates widespread condemnation of the sentence, notably by the Canadian government and NGOs.
25–30 January	Porto Alegre, Brazil: World Social Forum brings together eleven thousand activists to discuss programs opposing neoliberalism and capitalist globalization.
26 January	Gujarat, India: earthquake killing twenty thousand people elicits worldwide contributions of aid and intervention.
29 January–3 February	Davos, Switzerland: World Economic Forum attracts anticapitalist protesters who try to demonstrate until driven back by water cannon.
3 February	Argentina: in response to pressure from NGOs in Argentina, Spain, and Mexico, Mexican authorities turn over Argentine ex-captain Ricardo Miguel Cavallo to Spanish courts to stand trial for abuses under the 1976–1983 military dictatorship.
10 February	Addis Ababa, Ethiopia: one thousand-plus women march against domestic violence, backed by Ethiopian Women's Lawyers Association.
12 February	Philippines: more than twenty thousand workers and friends of slain labor leader Felimon Lagman march, wearing red shirts and calling for justice.
17 February	Osogbo, Nigeria: police disperse march of pro-democracy protesters mobilized by the National Conscience Party.
20 February	Syria: government takes steps to restrict civil forums that began operating after President Bashar al Assad came to power in 2000.
22–27 February	Cancún, Mexico: anticapitalists and allies such as Greenpeace run extensive protest activities to parallel meeting of (capitalist) World Economic Forum.
25 February–6 March	Mexico: Zapatistas conduct march from Chiapas to Mexico City under the label Zapatour, with participants from across the world.
26 February	Edo State, Nigeria: youths invade oil and gas stations belonging to Shell Oil.

Source: Summarized from Glasius, Kaldor & Anheier 2002: 380–81.

Table 5.5 Number of Transnational Social Movement
Organizations (TSMOs), 1973–2003

Year	Number of TSMOs
1973	183
1983	348
1993	711
2000	959
2003	1011

Source: Smith 2003:32; see also Smith 1997.

League of Nations, the International Labor Office, the United Nations, and the World Bank; indeed, Boli and Thomas find that, year by year, the correlation between foundings of INGOs and foundings of intergovernmental organizations runs at .83 (Boli & Thomas 1997: 178). The Boli-Thomas data also reveal broad parallels between INGO founding and the rough timetable of globalization I proposed earlier.

Concentrating more narrowly—and, for our purposes, more cogently—on "free-standing nongovernmental associations that were specifically organized to promote some type of social or political change goal" and had members in at least three countries, Jackie Smith has pinpointed changes in the number of existing organizations (not the number of new foundings) from 1973 to 2003. Table 5.5 shows her counts of all such transnational social movement organizations (TSMOs), including an estimate for 2003.

The number roughly doubled during each decade from 1973 to 1993, then increased by another half between 1993 and 2003. More TSMOs in Smith's catalog dealt with human rights and environmental issues than with peace, women's rights, development, global justice, ethnic self-determination, or right-wing causes. During the 1990s, however, organizations committed to ethnic issues declined as economic issues became more prominent. What people loosely call antiglobalization movements drew especially on organizations specializing in economic issues, but they often formed alliances with organizations focusing on human rights, the environment, and other prominent objects of international social movement claims.

As the available data suggest, organizational bases of international social movement activity expanded approximately in time with proliferation of international connections in other regards (see also Keck & Sikkink 1998). Internationally active nongovernmental organizations based themselves disproportionately in cities that also lodged major decision-making institutions. Brussels, seat of many European Union institutions, led the world with 1,392 INGOs. As of 2001, the leading sites for all the world's INGOs were Brussels (1,392), London (807), Paris (729), Washington, D.C. (487), New York (390), Geneva (272), Rome (228), Vienna (190), Tokyo (174), and Amsterdam (162) (Glasius, Kaldor, & Anheier 2002: 6). Internationally coordinated social movement actions, furthermore, likewise concentrated in or near major centers of political and economic power, including the temporary centers created by such events as meetings of the World Trade Organization.

In the long run, alas, we cannot rely on counts or descriptions of organizations—international or otherwise—as proxies for the campaigns, repertoires, and WUNC displays of social movements. Someone must do the hard work of cataloguing social movement actions as such. Lesley Wood has made an important preliminary effort. Wood cleverly traced an important aspect of internationalization by using movement-originated electronic sources as well as standard news media to examine participation in five "days of action" against neo-liberalism organized to coincide with meetings of international trade bodies from 1998 to 2001 (Wood 2003):

16–20 May 1998: Group of 8 meeting (Birmingham, UK) and World Trade Organization (WTO) ministerial meeting (Geneva)

18 June 1999: Group of 8 meeting (Cologne, Germany)

30 November 1999: WTO ministers (Seattle, US)

26 September 2000: International Monetary Fund and World Bank meetings (Prague, Czech Republic)

9 November 2001: WTO ministers (Doha, Qatar)

A day of action combined deliberately organized presence at or near the site of the official trade meeting with coordinated, simultaneous meetings, demonstrations, and press releases in a number of other visible places far removed from that site.

Wood's days of action include not only the "Battle of Seattle," but also four of the other most prominent international mobilizations of the four-year period. They actually influenced their targets as well as popular views of those targets. The *Annual Register* commented:

> Following what one reporter called its "fall from grace" at the ministerial meeting at Seattle in late 1999, the WTO spent 2000 in a period of "convalescence" or, in a less charitable characterisation, "paralysis." Little was achieved in resolving the complicated issues that had surfaced so dramatically at the 1999 session. Friction continued between developed and developing nations over the latter's demand for greater WTO influence. The economic powerhouses, most notably the EU, Japan, and the USA, still could not agree on a timetable and agenda for a proposed new round of global trade negotiations. And protests by antiglobalisation activists persisted, attacking, amongst other things, the perceived negative effect of WTO activity on labor standards and environmental protection and arguing that the poverty in many countries was being exacerbated, not ameliorated, by WTO decisions. (*Annual Register* 2000: 385–86)

Similarly, in September 2003, when trade representatives gathered in Cancún, Mexico, to negotiate policy for international exchanges of foodstuffs, observers noted that street demonstrators and the newly formed Group of 21 developing country food exporters had formed a formidable alliance that the European Union and the United States, with their extensive subsidies to farmers, could hardly ignore (Becker 2003). Still, the draft WTO agreement that emerged from the Cancún meeting made only minor concessions, mostly rhetorical, to the Group of 21 and their backers on the street (Thompson 2003). In fact, the talks collapsed when the Group of 21 withdrew in protest against the meagerness of rich countries' proposals. It would therefore take a much closer analysis to detect the precise impact of such action days on WTO behavior. But at a minimum the international activist networks succeeded in shaping public discussion of that behavior.

Wood singled out explicitly associated events during which at least ten people assembled in public to make their claims (Wood 2003). In each case, international activist networks or INGOs such as People's Global Action, Jubilee 2000, and the International Conference of Federated Trade Unions not only tried to establish a presence at or near the trade bodies' meetings but also called for parallel protest events in strategic locations elsewhere. Over the five days, Wood catalogued 462 associated events, or about 90 per mobilization. The largest number of events took place in Western Europe, followed by the United States and Canada, but a substantial minority occurred in Eastern or Central Europe, Oceania, Asia, Africa, and Latin America. Overall, the number of events per mobilization rose from 43 in 1998 to 158 in 2001. Wood's evidence does not tell us whether such internationally coordinated actions were increasing as a share of all social movement performances anywhere. But it certainly demonstrates the rise of geographically dispersed simultaneous performances as a tactic of international activists.

Let us not confuse a wave's leading edge, however, with the whole wave. Doug Imig and Sidney Tarrow have conducted one of the most precise analyses of internationalization, in this case within the European Union (EU) from 1984 to 1997. Imig and Tarrow scanned Reuters online news services to identify "contentious events" roughly equivalent to the contentious gatherings described in chapter 2. They then asked which of the events a) involved cross-national coordination among claimants and/or b) directed claims to the EU or one of its agencies. Of the 9,872 events in the Imig-Tarrow catalog, only 490—5 percent—involved claims on the EU (Imig & Tarrow 2001: 32–34). Of those 490, furthermore, only 84 involved international coordination; the other 406 gestured toward the EU but remained within national boundaries and directed their primary claims at authorities within their own countries. Between 1994 and 1997, it is true, the proportion of all events directly targeting EU agencies swelled from about 5 to 30 percent of the total. For 2002, follow-up research by Trif and Imig showed some 20 percent of European events as transnational in coordination but still only 5 percent directed at EU agencies as such (Trif & Imig 2003). At the turn of the new century, a modest internationalization of Europe's social movement activity was finally starting to occur.

We can cast the Imig-Tarrow evidence in two very different ways. Since the trend displays a recent increase in the proportion of international claimants and claims, we might project that trend forward into the twenty-first century, forecasting a vast internationalization of social movements (see, e.g., Bennett 2003, Smith 2002). Plenty of anecdotal illustrations support such a reading, especially international mobilizations against the North American Free Trade Agreement, the World Trade Organization, and transnational corporations.

From another angle, however, the Imig-Tarrow results show us a late-twentieth-century European world in which most social movement claim making continued to occur within state boundaries, with claims directed mostly at objects within the same state. What is more, such international networks as Jubilee 2000, for all their spectacular efficacy at initiating one-time actions including electronic petitions and simultaneous human chains, have generally fragmented or withered over time; on the whole, nongovernmental organizations based near major world centers of power have proven more durable (Anheier & Themudo 2002). Since Western Europe and North America still contain the bulk of such centers and since their activists were almost certainly more heavily engaged in international social movement claim making than any other large regions of the world, serious worldwide internationalization still had a long way to go.

If Howard Rheingold and Lance Bennett have described the character of digitally mediated social movements correctly, indeed, supporters of democracy may actually want to cheer the current incompleteness of internationalization. Neither smart mobs nor weakly linked networks enjoy the capacity for sustained political work on behalf of their programs that earlier centuries' histories have shown us as the accompaniment of social movement repertoires. Quick mobilization of millions in opposition to WTO policies or McDonald's hamburgers sensitizes their targets to public relations and encourages them to defend their perimeters. It does not obviously give ordinary people voice in decision making. Indian activist-analyst Neera Chandhoke worries about a triple threat: that INGOs will evade democratic accountability to the same degree that the WTO or the IMF evades it, that organizations and activists based in the global north will dominate international claim making to the detriment of organizations and people in poorer, less well-connected countries, and that the division between skilled political entrepreneurs and ordinary people will sharpen.

> We have cause for unease. For much of the leadership of global civil society organisations appears to be self-appointed and nonaccountable to their members, many of whom are passive and confine their activism to signatures to petitions circulated via e-mail. Also note that, whereas we see huge crowds during demonstrations against the WTO or in alternative forums such as the World Social Forum, between such episodes activity is carried on by a core group of NGOs. It is possible that participants in demonstrations are handed a political platform and an agenda that has been finalized elsewhere. This is hardly either democratic or even political, it may even reek of bureaucratic management of participatory events. It may even render people . . . consumers of choices made elsewhere. (Chandhoke 2002: 48)

Perhaps social movements are splitting: on one side, older styles of action and organization that sustain continuous political involvement at points of decision-making power; on the other, spectacular but temporary displays of connection across the continents, largely mediated by specialized organizations and entrepreneurs. If so, we must think hard about the effects of such a split on democracy, that faithful companion of social movements throughout their history.

6

DEMOCRATIZATION AND SOCIAL MOVEMENTS

No social movements occurred in Kazakhstan this year. None occurred last year, and none will occur next year. Plenty of conflict, however, has occurred in Kazakhstan recently. Cossacks have been demanding more autonomy; Russians, guarantees of their language and privileged positions; members of Kazakh hordes, rights to priority in their homeland; Muslims, the Islamization of public life; and many contenders, larger shares of graft or contraband. Since the inauguration of formally competitive elections in 1989, multiple parties have appeared on Kazakh ballots. Responding in 1999 to reporters' questions about forthcoming parliamentary elections, President (and Soviet holdover) Nursultan Nazarbayev portrayed himself as a democratic teacher:

> Of course, when we have such economic hardships, political forces in the country become more active. For the first time in the history of Kazakhstan, there will be parliamentary elections by party lists. That is normal, but if the political struggle becomes more acute in the period to elections, I think I myself, as leader of the country, must educate my nation on how to introduce democracy to the country. We never had any sort of democracy before. (Radio Free Europe 1999: 2)

As he administered that education, schoolmaster Nazarbayev rapped knuckles energetically. In preparation for the series of hastily scheduled national elections then at issue, which were to begin on 10 October, Nazarbayev arranged prosecution for tax evasion of former prime minister and likely rival Akezhan Kazhegeldin. Kazakh courts obligingly disqualified Kazhegeldin's candidacy on the ground of his participating in an unsanctioned political meeting. Kazhegeldin left the country. Early in September, Russian authorities acted on a Kazakh extradition request by arresting Kazhegeldin when he arrived in Moscow on a flight from London (Miller & Levine 1999).

Kazhegeldin was not the only victim of Kazakh repression. Human Rights Watch's 1999 Kazakhstan report recounted:

- 273 state violations of the country's own Law on the Press during 1997;
- detention, prosecution, and disqualification of numerous opposition politicians in 1997 and 1998;
- police beatings;
- suppression of unsanctioned demonstrations; and
- numerous other state infringements of civil liberties.

All occurred in the name of national security (Human Rights Watch 1999; see also CSCE 1998, Olcott 1997, United Nations 1995). Nazarbayev's own security forces deploy violence in virtual immunity from judicial control. As of 2002, the U.S. Department of State reported that

> the Government's poor human rights record worsened, and it continued to commit abuses. The Government severely limited citizens' right to change their government and democratic institutions remained weak. Members of the security forces mistreated detainees on some occasions. Police tortured, beat, and otherwise mistreated detainees. Government officials acknowledged that abuses by police constituted a serious problem. Prison conditions remained harsh; however, the Government took an active role in efforts to improve prison conditions and the treatment of prisoners. The Government continued to use arbitrary arrest and detention, and prolonged detention was a problem. Corruption in the judiciary remained deeply rooted. Amendments to several laws governing the authority of prosecutors further eroded judicial independence by, among other provisions, allowing prosecutors to suspend court verdicts. The Government infringed on citizens' privacy rights, and new legislation granted prosecutors broad authorities to monitor individuals. (U.S. Department of State 2002: 1)

When a new Kazakh political party called All Together formed in 2003, its leader turned out to be media magnate Dariga Nazarbayeva, the president's daughter and possible successor (*Economist* 2003c: 41). As a result, nothing much resembling a social movement goes on in Kazakhstan these days (Tilly 1999). Nor, for that matter, have the remaining fragments of the Soviet Union seen much social movement activity since 1989 (Barrington 1995, Beissinger 1993, 1998a, 1998b, Drobizheva, Gottemoeller, Kelleher, & Walker 1996, Kaiser 1994, Khazanov 1995, Laitin 1998, 1999, McFaul 1997, Nahaylo & Swoboda 1990, Smith, Law, Wilson, Bohr, & Allworth 1998, Suny 1993, 1995).

Breakaway Soviet republic Belarus, for instance, looked as though it would produce an entire social movement sector during the early 1990s. Alexander Lukashenka won the Belarus presidency in a 1994 popular election as a crusader against "corruption." But as soon as he had consolidated his hold on office, Lukashenka instituted censorship, smashed independent trade unions, fixed elections, and subjugated the legislature. He thus reversed the country's modest previous democratic gains (Mihalisko 1997, Titarenko, McCarthy, McPhail, & Augustyn 2001). Opposition leaders and journalists soon found themselves liable to arbitrary imprisonment, torture, kidnapping, and murder (Human Rights Watch 2000: 249–53, Karatnycky 2000: 76–78).

The *Annual Register* described the Belarusan social movement situation for 2000 in this way:

> In Belarus, Russia's closest ally, supporters of the opposition came under continued pressure. A large-scale demonstration took place peacefully in March, although some journalists and foreign observers as well as opposition activists were arrested. President Alyaksandr Lukashenka, who had been out of the country at the time, subsequently dismissed the Interior Minister and described the arrests as "a misunderstanding and a mistake." Former Prime Minister Mikhas Chygir received a three-month prison sentence in May for what he insisted were politically motivated charges. In June two opposition leaders received suspended prison sentences for their part in organising a demonstration the previous October. (*Annual Register* 2000: 133–34)

With public confirmation from his ally, Russian president Vladimir Putin, to be sure, Lukashenka told the rest of the world that his regime was functioning democratically. But by the early twenty-first century the small space that had opened up for Belarusan social movements in 1991 was closing rapidly. As a politically battered world staggered into 2004, neither in the Soviet Union's old central territories (Russia and Belarus) nor in its Central Asian borderlands (Kazakhstan and neighboring countries) were social movements thriving.

I report this unsurprising news because during the early 1990s many observers of communist regimes' last days thought that the destruction of centralized superstructures in those states would rapidly open the way to social movements, which would then facilitate construction of a democratic civil society. Many analysts followed an analogy with the market's expected transformation of economic activity. Through most of the former Soviet Union, neither the explosion of social movements nor the sweeping market transformation has happened (Nelson, Tilly, & Walker 1998). In fact, as of 2004 most of the world's people still lacked access to social movements as a way to voice popular claims. Despite Tiananmen and a variety of subsequent popular struggles, to take the most obvious point, the quarter of the world's population living in China during the early twenty-first century had no regular recourse to social movements (Bernstein & Lü 2002). Where democracy fell short, social movements remained sparse.

Previous chapters repeatedly identified a broad correspondence between democratization and social movements. Social movements originated in the partial democratization that set British subjects and North American colonists against their rulers during the eighteenth century. Across the nineteenth century, social movements generally flourished and spread where further democratization was occurring and receded when authoritarian regimes curtailed democratic rights. The pattern continued during the twentieth and twenty-first centuries: the maps of full-fledged social movements and of democratic institutions overlapped greatly.

Yet we have also learned that social movements do not necessarily espouse or promote democracy. Movements form far more frequently around particular interests and grievances than around demands for democratization as such. From early on, relatively democratic movements regularly provoked undemocratic countermovements such as the United Kingdom's early-nineteenth-century opponents of Catholic rights. In more or less functioning democracies, furthermore, social movements recurrently pursue antidemocratic programs such as exclusion of racial, ethnic, and religious minorities. Sometimes they even pursue the abolition of democracy itself in the name of a totalitarian creed such as Mussolini's Fascism and Hitler's Nazism.

Circumstances in which democracy and social movements do *not* coincide set an especially perplexing challenge to the tracing of their causal connections. Chapter 4 demonstrated, for example, that across the historical cases analyzed by Ruth Collier, democratization and social movements sometimes preceded and sometimes followed each other; neither depended entirely on the other's existence. Social movements occasionally form in democratic crevices of segmented or otherwise authoritarian regimes, as we have seen in Indonesia and the Philippines. In moments of partial democratization—witness many of the Soviet satellite states in 1989—social movements can form without necessarily becoming permanent features of the political landscape. Clearly, more than a mechanical relationship between democracy and social movements is operating. How does it work?

The incomplete overlap of social movements and democratization poses three questions that are crucial both for explaining social movements and for gauging their futures.

1. What causes the broad but still incomplete correspondence between social movements and democratic institutions?
2. To what extent and how does democratization itself cause social movements to form and prosper?
3. Under what conditions, and how, do social movements actually advance democracy?

(Question number 3 forces us to think about a further unpleasant question we have so far mostly avoided: Under what conditions, and how, do social movements damage democracy?) It is time to reflect on the social movement's history in search of answers to these pressing questions. In order to do so, we have to think about the character and causes of democratization before moving on to relations between democratization and social movements.

How Will We Recognize Democracy and Democratization?

Like almost all other regimes elsewhere in the world, former members of the Soviet Union generally claim to be democracies. Article 1 of the Kazakh constitution, for instance, reads as follows:

The Republic of Kazakhstan proclaims itself a democratic, secular, legal and social state whose highest values are an individual, his life, rights and freedoms.

The fundamental principles of the activity of the Republic are public concord and political stability; economic development for the benefit of all the nation; Kazakhstan patriotism and resolution of the most important issues of the affairs of state by democratic methods including voting at an all-nation referendum or in the Parliament. (Kazakhstan 2003)

Clearly, constitutions alone will not tell us whether regimes qualify as working democracies. Even today, visibly viable democracies remain a minority among the world's forms of rule.

How will we recognize democracy and democratization when we see them? Many widely used definitions of democracy concentrate on the character of relations among citizens: whether they are just, kind, considerate, egalitarian, and so on. Others stress legal criteria: contested elections, representative institutions, formal guarantees of liberty, and related political arrangements (for reviews of definitions and measures, see Collier & Levitsky 1997, Geddes 1999, Inkeles 1991, Lijphart 1999, Przeworski, Alvarez, Cheibub, & Limongi 2000: 55–59, Vanhanen 2000). Here, however, let me insist that, like tyranny and oligarchy, democracy is a kind of regime: a set of relations between a government and persons subject to that government's jurisdiction. The relations in question consist of mutual rights and obligations, government to subject and subject to government.

Democracies differ from other regimes because instead of the massive asymmetry, coercion, exploitation, patronage, and communal segmentation that have characterized most political regimes across the centuries they establish fairly general and reliable rules of law (Tilly 2004). A regime is democratic to the extent that:

1. regular and categorical, rather than intermittent and individualized, relations exist between the government and its subjects (for example, legal residence within the government's territories in itself establishes routine connections with governmental agents, regardless of relations to particular patrons or membership in specific ethnic groups);
2. those relations include most or all subjects (for example, no substantial sovereign enclaves exist within governmental perimeters);
3. those relations are equal across subjects and categories of subjects (for example, no legal exclusions from voting or officeholding based on gender, religion, or property ownership prevail);
4. governmental personnel, resources, and performances change in response to binding collective consultation of subjects (for example, popular referenda make law); and
5. subjects, especially members of minorities, receive protection from arbitrary action by governmental agents (for example, uniformly administered due process precedes incarceration of any individual regardless of social category).

Thus democratization means formation of a regime featuring relatively broad, equal, categorical, binding consultation and protection. Note the word *relatively:* if we applied these standards absolutely, no regime past or present anywhere in the world would qualify as a democracy; all regimes have always fallen short in some regards when it has come to categorical regularity, breadth, equality, consultation, and protection. Democratization consists of a regime's moves *toward* greater categorical regularity, breadth, equality, binding consultation, and protection, and dedemocratization consists of moves *away* from them.

If democracy entails relatively high levels of breadth, equality, consultation, and protection by definition, as a practical matter it also requires the institution of citizenship (Tilly 1999). Citizenship consists, in this context, of mutual rights and obligations binding governmental agents to whole categories of people who are subject to the government's authority, those categories being defined chiefly or exclusively by relations to the government rather than by reference to particular connections with rulers or to membership in categories based on imputed durable traits such as race, ethnicity, gender, or religion. It institutionalizes regular, categorical relations between subjects and their governments.

Citizenship sometimes appears in the absence of democracy. Authoritarian regimes such as Fascist Italy institutionalized broad, regular, categorical and relatively equal relations between subjects and their governments but greatly restricted both consultation and protection. Powerful ruling parties and large police apparatuses inhibited democratic liberties. Citizenship looks like a necessary condition for democratization but not a sufficient one.

Our survey of the nineteenth century showed the United Kingdom, Scandinavia, the United States, Switzerland, and Argentina all instituting limited degrees of citizenship—still exclusive in many regards, but diminishing the political influence of patron-client ties, outright coercion, and membership in culturally defined communities, at least within the charmed circle of those who enjoyed any political rights at all. In these terms, democratization means any net shift toward citizenship, breadth of citizenship, equality of citizenship, binding consultation of citizens, and protection of citizens from arbitrary action by agents of government.

The Empirical Problem

What does our historical survey tell us about relations between democratization and social movements? Without far more extensive catalogs and chronologies of social movement claim making than are currently available, we have no hope of looking closely at point-by-point empirical relationships between democratization and social movements. We can, nevertheless, draw together threads from the earlier histories to think about the scale (number of simultaneous participants, localities, and/or actions) and scope (variety of programs, identities, sites, performances, and WUNC displays) involved in social movements. The nineteenth century showed us the French street demonstration coming into its own as authoritarian top-down controls weakened, while France in 1968 showed us French workers and students creating a temporary democratic opening on their own initiative. Similar partial stories in previous chapters suggest a broad sequence of this sort:

1. *little or no democratization:* no social movements
2. *incipient democratization:* campaigns, repertoires, or WUNC displays bearing partial resemblances to those of social movements, but no full-fledged combinations of campaigns, repertoires, and WUNC displays
3. *further democratization:* social movement combinations in limited sectors (for example students in Indonesia) without general availability of social movement means to other claimants
4. *extensive democratization:* widespread availability of social movement programs, repertoires, and WUNC displays across programs, identities, and localities
5. *incipient international democratization:* internationalization of social movement claim making

Figure 6.1 sums up this argument. It portrays the stages as overlapping ovals to emphasize that in any given regime at a particular point in time different political actors vary with regard to their involvement in different sorts of social movement activity. It also draws the "no social movements" oval very broadly to stress both that most historical regimes have lacked social movements and that historically some relatively democratic regimes have operated without social movements.

According to figure 6.1, at lower levels of democratization and through most of history no social movements form at all. Earlier chapters have recognized that, taken separately, claim-making campaigns, individual social movement performances such as the public meeting or the petition drive, and concerted public WUNC occurred in a wide variety of regimes long before the mid-eighteenth century. But they have also documented the initial *combination* of campaigns, repertoires, and WUNC displays in Great Britain and North America between the 1760s and the end of the Napoleonic Wars. The figure incorporates a distinction that has likewise served us helpfully in earlier chapters: between a) intermittent resemblances of particular claims, performances, or WUNC displays in the public politics of undemocratic regimes to similar claims, performances, or WUNC displays of regimes in which social movements regularly occur; b) combinations of the three in particular political mobilizations within regimes that have not institutionalized social movements; and c) full-scale availability of social movement campaigns, repertoires, and WUNC displays to a wide variety of claimants within a regime. Drawing on recent developments, the figure adds yet another level: d) the internationalization of social movement activity.

Overall, then, figure 6.1 argues that in the course of democratization resemblances generally precede combinations, particular combinations precede full availability of social movements, and availability within national regimes precedes in-

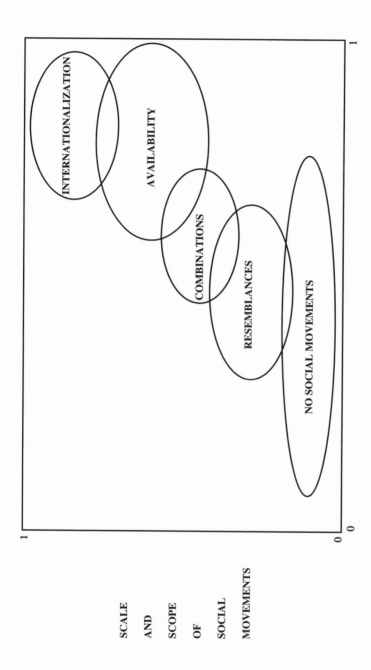

Figure 6.1 Scale and Scope of Social Movements at Different Degrees of Democratization

ternationalization. It also argues that availability and internationalization only take place within regimes having extensive democratic institutions and practices. In the absence of systematic evidence on the actual distribution of social movements across the world of the last two centuries, all stages of the argument take risks.

Stage 5 takes the greatest risks of all. The record of early-twenty-first-century social movements leaves open two possibilities that would blatantly contradict it. First, considering the political arena defined by international centers of power, it is not obvious that democratization is occurring internationally; categorically defined breadth, equality, consultation, and protection could actually be declining at the international scale as power shifts from states to international bodies and networks and as nationally grounded categories, breadth, equality, consultation, and protection thereby lose their impact. Second, as chapter 5 suggested, internationalization of power relations might in fact be reducing the efficacy of social movements at the local, regional, and national scales as it narrows the scope of effective social movement action to just those groups and networks that can organize large international collaborations. That eventuality would oblige us to interpret internationalization as a reversal of the long-term trends that for more than two centuries favored broad correspondence between social movements and democratization. Internationalization could be bringing dedemocratization.

What causes the strong but still incomplete correspondence between democratization and social movements? First, many of the same processes that cause democratization also independently promote social movements. Second, democratization as such further encourages people to form social movements. Third, under some conditions and in a more limited way social movements themselves promote democratization. Before examining those three causal paths, however, we must review what causes democratization in the first place.

Why Does Democratization Ever Occur?

To put the matter very schematically, in currently undemocratic regimes four social processes create favorable conditions for the establishment of political arrangements involving regular, categorical relations between subjects and governments, relatively broad and equal participation, binding consultation of political participants, and protection of political participants, especially members of vulnerable minorities, from arbitrary action by governmental agents. The four processes include:

- increases in the sheer numbers of people available for participation in public politics and/or in connections among those people, however those increases occur;
- equalization of resources and connections among those people, however that equalization occurs;

- insulation of public politics from existing social inequalities; and
- integration of interpersonal trust networks into public politics.

None of these constitutes democratization in itself, but all of them promote democratization, especially if they occur together. Let us consider each of the four in turn.

Increases in numbers and connections among potential political participants. When rulers form a tiny elite that governs through patronage, sale of state-controlled resources, and/or brute force, democracy has little chance to flourish. But circumstances such as defense against common enemies, calls for increased resources to support war or public works, demographic increase within the ruling class, expanding communications, and forceful demands for inclusion on the part of excluded parties push rulers to expand the circle of participants in public politics.

When that happens, ironically, the overall proportion of the subject population that is connected to and socially adjacent to the newly included (and therefore in a strengthened position to demand inclusion as well) usually increases. We have seen that sort of enlargement occurring with the British Reform Act of 1832, which brought merchants, smaller property owners, and masters into the governing coalition but excluded ordinary workers, many of whom had backed the Reform campaign. We have also seen how Chartism gained its edge from the fact that its coalition partners in the pro-Reform mobilization of 1830–1832 acquired power but then enacted legislation regulating the poor while denying workers political rights.

Equalization of resources and connections among potential political participants. If overall inequality between categories—male and female, religious affiliations, ethnic groups, and so on—diminishes for whatever reason, that equalization facilitates broad, equal involvement of category members in public politics as it discourages their unequal treatment by governmental agents. It thus boosts both protection and citizenship. Relevant resources and connections certainly include those provided by income, property, and kinship, but they also include literacy, access to communications media, and organizational memberships; when any of these equalize across the population at large, they promote democratic participation.

Equalization of resources and connections among potential political participants encourages both political competition and coalition formation. Together, competition and coalition formation promote establishment of categorically defined rights and obligations directly connecting citizens to agents of government in place of particular communal memberships and patron-client ties; legal establishment of electorates provides the most visible examples, but a similar enactment of legally equivalent categories commonly occurs in the licensing of associations, authorization of public meetings, policing of demonstrations, and registration of lobbyists.

The very articulation of rules for these activities produces categories rather than particularistic arrangements and thereby encourages collective seekers of rights to argue on the basis of their similarities to members of privileged categories rather than their valuable and distinctive properties. Women who struggled for political rights in Western countries during the nineteenth and twentieth centuries regularly pointed out that the rules and justifications backing male rights to vote and hold office provided no defensible rationale for excluding females from the same rights. For all the celebration of queer culture, gays and lesbians regularly insist on their political similarities to previously excluded minorities and demand rights that are already available to other categories of the population.

Competition and coalition formation also inhibit the pursuit of control over governmental activities, resources, and personnel by means other than those categorically defined rights and obligations; blatant use of personal connections or brute force becomes corruption. Eventually the sheer expansion and partial equalization of the British ruling classes made it advantageous for dissident members of the new elite to join forces with excluded people as a makeweight against the old landed classes.

Insulation of public politics from existing social inequalities. Democratization does not, however, depend on radical leveling of material conditions; the partial democracies of today's rich capitalist countries—all of which maintain extensive material inequalities—testify as much. Over the long run of democratization, indeed, erection of barriers to translation of existing inequalities by race, gender, ethnicity, religion, class, or locality into public politics has no doubt played a much larger part than material leveling. If barriers arise to the direct translation of persisting categorical inequalities into public politics (for example, through the institution of the secret ballot and the creation of coalition parties that cross lines of gender, race, or class), those barriers contribute to the creation of a relatively autonomous sphere of public politics within which categorically defined breadth, equality, binding consultation, and protection have at least a chance to increase. Although white male Americans fiercely excluded women and blacks from nineteenth-century public politics, adoption of a rigorously geographical system of representation, continuous movement of people to the frontier, and formation of patchwork political parties all blunted the direct translation of categorical differences within the white male population into public politics.

Despite residential segregation and despite gerrymandering, formation of heterogeneous political units and electoral districts similarly inhibits direct translation of categorical inequalities into public politics. We saw a primitive version of this representation effect in Great Britain, where the chiefly territorial allocation of parliamentary seats—by no means a democratic innovation back when barons and bishops forced the English king to hear their complaints, conditions, and demands—simultaneously gave voice to disfranchised British subjects and provided incentives for members of Parliament to seek expressions of popular support for dissident positions. As Parliament gained power relative to the Crown and great patrons during the eighteenth century (once again no triumph for democratization in its own terms), the insulating effects of territorial representation increased. Similarly, broadly shared jury duty, military service, school enrollment, and responsibility for public works need not originate in democratic practices but cumulatively tend to promote democratization by insulating public politics from existing social inequalities.

Trust networks and democratization. Trust networks figure more subtly, but no less potently, in democratization. As many democratic theorists have sensed, connections between interpersonal trust networks and public politics significantly affect democratization (Buchan, Croson, & Dawes 2002, Edwards, Foley, & Diani 2001, Landa 1994, Levi & Stoker 2000, Seligman 1997, Uslaner 2002, Warren 1999). Trust is the knowing exposure of valued future outcomes to the risk of malfeasance by others. Risk is threat multiplied by uncertainty. People frequently confront short-term risk without creating elaborate social structure; on their own they leap raging rivers, engage in unsafe sex, drive while drunk, or bet large sums of money. When it comes to the long-term risks of reproduction, cohabitation, investment, migration, or agricultural enterprise, however, people generally embed those risks in durable, substantial social organization. To that extent, they trust others—they make the reduction of threat and/or uncertainty contingent on the performance of other people they cannot entirely control. Such sets of relations to others constitute networks of trust.

When people commit themselves to risky, consequential long-term enterprises whose outcomes depend significantly on the performances of other persons, they ordinarily embed those enterprises in interpersonal networks whose participants have strong incentives to meet their own commitments and encourage others to meet theirs. Such networks often pool risks and provide aid to unfortunate members. They commonly operate well, if and when they do, because members share extensive information about each other and about their social environment, because third parties monitor transactions among pairs of members, and because exclusion from the network inflicts serious harm on members who fail to meet their commitments. Trade diasporas, rotating credit circles, skilled crafts, professions, lineages, patron-client chains, and religious sects often exhibit these characteristics. They couple easily with control over systems that generate inequality in work, community, and private life (Tilly 1998).

Through most of human history, participants in trust networks have guarded them jealously from governmental intervention. They have rightly feared that governmental agents would weaken them or divert them to less advantageous ends. Powerful participants who could not entirely escape governmental intervention have created partial immunities through such arrangements as indirect rule. Less powerful participants have characteristically adopted what James Scott calls weapons of the weak: concealment, foot-dragging, sabotage, and so on. Democratization, however, entails a double shift of trust. First, within the political arena citizens trust the organization of consultation and protection sufficiently to wait out short-term losses of advantage instead of turning immediately to nongovernmental means of regaining lost advantages. Second, citizens build into risky long-term enterprises the assumption that government will endure and meet its commitments. Both are extremely rare circumstances over the long historical run. Within any regime that is not currently democratic, their realization faces enormous obstacles.

In those rare cases where it actually occurs, integration of trust networks into public politics operates within any of three channels: 1) disintegration of previously effective insulated trust networks, as when regional patrons lose their capacity to pay, feed, or arm their clients; 2) formation of commitments directly binding governmental agents and citizens, as when governments establish welfare agencies and citizens begin to rely on those agencies for absorption of long-term risks; or 3) formation of similar commitments between major political actors and their citizen members or clienteles, as when legally recognized trade unions become administrators of workers' pension funds. We witnessed a dramatic instance of integration in the Switzerland of 1848 and thereafter, as the peace settlement of a civil war provided different segments of the Swiss population far greater access and redress with regard to the national government than they had ever exercised before.

In these terms, how should we explain the partial democratization that Great Britain (and then the United Kingdom) experienced after the 1760s? The four general causes of democratization—increases in numbers and connections among potential political participants, equalization of resources and connections among potential political participants, insulation of public politics from existing social inequalities, and integration of trust networks into public politics—all contributed to British democratization, but they contributed quite unequally. Expansion of British capitalism enormously increased the numbers of potential political participants as well as connections among them (Tilly 1995: chap. 2). On balance, despite sharpening material inequalities, the resources and connections provided by concentrated workplaces, urban growth, intensification of communications, and accelerated domestic trade produced some equalization in resources and connections among potential political participants. As compared with depending chiefly on local landlords, parish priests, small masters, and other patrons for political intervention, Parliament's increasing centrality in the British system of power partially insulated public politics from existing categorical inequalities. Rapid growth of a propertyless, wage-dependent, and urbanizing working class, finally, combined with huge expansions of tax payments and military service to undermine old local and segregated trust networks in favor of direct connections between British subjects and their national government.

The same checklist makes less mysterious that democratization has recently receded from its already low level in Kazakhstan: the flight of ethnic Russians from the post-Soviet country has depleted resources and connections, new inequalities have arisen between the (small) privileged segments of the national population and everyone else, President Nazarbayev and his allies have built the distinction between ethnic Kazakhs and others (not to mention the distinction between Nazarbayev's own clan and other Kazakhs) ever more sharply into public politics, and all but the privileged Kazakh elite have protected their trust networks more and more zealously from public politics. It would take a great reversal of all these processes for serious democratization to begin in Kazakhstan.

Processes That Promote Both Democratization and Social Movements

Some of the extensive historical overlap between democratization and social movements results from the fact that similar processes promote both of them. Recall the four main processes that promote democratization: 1) increases in the sheer numbers of people available for participation in public politics and/or in connections among those people; 2) equalization of resources and connections among those people; 3) insulation of public politics from existing social inequalities; and 4) integration of interpersonal trust networks into public politics. None of these qualifies as democratization in itself; none of them directly entails regular categorical relations, breadth, equality, binding consultation, or protection *within* public politics. But all of them also promote the formation of social movements.

Increases in numbers and connections expand the pool of people that could, in principle, join, support, or at least attend to a social movement campaign. They increase the likelihood that members of minority factions within the ruling class will seek allies outside the established range of powerful political actors. In Western history, dissident aristocrats and bourgeois alike recurrently sought to gain support outside their own circles; cautiously but consequentially, for example, Boston's property owners established alliances with Boston's property-poor workers against British royal power during the 1760s. Such reaching out provides opportunities for any organized group to gain credibility and power through displays of worthiness, unity, numbers, and commitment rather than through direct action or activation of patronage ties. Social movements facilitate just such displays, indeed center on them.

Equalization of resources and connections increases the likelihood that people and groups having particular interests or grievances will join with others from other social settings in common campaigns, social movement performances, and WUNC displays. Insulation of public politics from existing social inequalities facilitates the grouping of otherwise diverse participants in common claims with regard to programs, identities, and standing. (Indeed, it makes possible the dramatization of diversity as a social movement's claim to attention.) Finally, integration of interpersonal trust networks into public politics has a dual effect on social movements; it increases the stakes of potential participants in the outcomes of any new movement claims as it facilitates mobilization of already connected people.

Remember how that process works; concretely, it includes the following sorts of changes:

- creating publicly recognized associations, mutual aid societies, parties, unions, congregations, and communities, or seeking recognition for similar organizations that have existed underground;
- pursuing friendship, kinship, shared belief, security, and high-risk enterprises within such organizations;
- permitting family members to serve in national military and police forces;
- promoting careers of family members in public service, including government office;
- seeking (or at least tolerating) government registration of vital events such as births, deaths, and marriages, then using the registration to validate legal transactions;
- providing private information to public organizations and authorities through censuses, surveys, and applications for services;
- entrusting private contracts to governmental enforcement;
- using government-issued legal tender for interpersonal transactions and savings;
- purchasing government securities with funds (e.g., dowry) committed to maintenance of interpersonal ties; and
- relying on political actors and/or government agencies for vital services and long-term security.

Over the long historical run, such commitments of trust networks to public politics have rarely developed. Even in today's democratic countries, they have become common only during the last century or so. In addition to being consequential for individual lives and interpersonal relations, they greatly increase the stakes of network members in the proper conduct of public politics. They create new collective interests. In these ways, they promote social movement activity at the same time as they advance routine democratic functioning outside of social movements. Thus the same broad processes that promote democratization also promote formation and proliferation of social movements.

How Democratization Promotes Social Movements

With their specific forms of associations, public meetings, demonstrations, and the like, social movements emerged from particular histories as historical products of their times and places. They then spread as models to other times and places. Yet some features of social movements give them affinities with democracy in general. In addition to the common causes of democratization and social movements just reviewed, democratization in itself promotes formation and proliferation of social movements. It does so because each of its elements—regularity, breadth, equality, consultation, and protection—contributes to social movement activity. It also does so because it encourages the establishment of other institutions (e.g., political parties and labor unions) whose presence in turn usually facilitates social movement claim making. Let us take up each of these items in turn.

Formation of more regular and categorical relations between governments and subjects. To the extent that relations between governments and their subjects remain intermittent, mediated, coercive, and particular, incentives to join in collective, public claim making by means of social movement performances and WUNC displays remain minimal, indeed mostly negative. Through much of the Philippines, the previous chapter's survey suggests, people who dared to join in standard social movement claim making would threaten existing authorities, risk their lives, and condemn themselves to futility. Conversely, establishment of regular and categorical relations between governments and subjects—broadly speaking, of citizenship—in itself renders the making of rights-based claims feasible, visible, and attractive. In the Manila region, by contrast with outlying areas of the Philippines, at least a modicum of citizenship seems to have developed, facilitating social movement claim making.

Broadening of rights and obligations within public politics. We have long since noticed that firm rights to assemble, associate, and speak collectively, however they come into being, foster social movement activity. Similarly, broad obligations to vote, serve on juries, perform military service, pay taxes, deliberate on public services, and send children to school help create social connections and shared interests that promote participation in campaigns, social movement performances, and WUNC displays bringing together socially disparate participants.

Equalization of rights and obligations within public politics. To the extent that public politics inscribes social inequalities in the form of differential rights to participate, receive benefits, or enjoy state protection, movement coalitions crossing such boundaries or representing identities not already written into law face serious barriers to organizing and acting publicly. To the extent that such legal reflections of social inequalities disappear from public politics, conversely, barriers to cross-category coalitions and newly asserted identities weaken. During the twentieth century, Indian leaders such as Jawaharlal Nehru strove mightily, and with partial success, to exclude caste, religious, linguistic, and gender differences from inscription into public politics. They thus simultaneously defended India's precarious democratization and promoted social movements. To be sure, social movement activists sometimes seek legal inscription for their categories, as when representatives of indigenous peoples propose special rights for their constituents; when such claims succeed, they both diminish democracy and reduce opportunities for other social movements. Whether Hindu nationalists will overturn the democratic accomplishments of their more secular predecessors matters enormously for the futures of Indian democracy and Indian social movements.

Increase in binding consultation of subjects with regard to changes in governmental policy, resources, and personnel. Social movements benefit from consultation because social movement displays of worthiness, unity, numbers, and commitment gain weight from the possibility that movement activists or their constituents will actually acquire some say in governmental decision making. Most obviously, in systems where contested elections make a difference, mobilization and identification of supporters for a new social movement signal the presence of a constituency that an accommodating political party might be able to enlist in its own electorate.

Expansion of protections for subjects, especially members of vulnerable minorities, from arbitrary action by governmental agents. However protection and consultation expand, their combination provides new opportunities for the sorts of claim making in which social movements specialize. The installation of an intensely consultative regime in Switzerland after 1848 encouraged the proliferation of Swiss social movements. Social movements thrive on protection because associations, meetings, marches, demonstrations, petition drives, and related means of action pose enormous risks in the absence of governmental toleration and in the face of massive repression. Secure rights of assembly, association, and collective voice promote social movements, just as their abridgement threatens social movements. Remember how social movements disappeared with the rise of authoritarian regimes in Italy, Germany, Spain, and the Soviet Union.

Creation of complementary institutions. Democratization commonly fosters creation of crucial institutions that in their turn independently promote social movement mobilization. The most obvious and general of these are electoral campaigns, political parties, labor unions, other trade associations, nongovernmental organizations, lobbies, and governmental agencies committed to support of specific constituencies rather than the general public. Such institutions generally facilitate social movements by providing vehicles for their mobilization, by establishing allies that back social movement claims without participating directly in movement campaigns, by locating receptive friends within government, and/or by reinforcing legal precedents for social movement campaigns, performances, and WUNC displays.

The connections are neither necessary nor universal. One-party regimes, for example, frequently stamp out social movements, just as corporatist regimes often build labor unions directly into the governing structure. On the average, nevertheless, formation of complementary institutions in the course of democratization further facilitates social movement activity. In the United States, the influence clearly ran in both directions: social movements that broke with existing parties affected parties and other institutions as the operation of those institutions repeatedly provided support for social movements (Clemens 1997, Sanders 1999, Skocpol 1992).

The corollary also follows: when regimes dedemocratize, they offer less room to claims made in the social movement style. Italy under Mussolini, Germany under Hitler, and Spain under Franco all experienced sharp curtailment of what had been festivals of social movement activity under their previous regimes. To be more precise, these new authoritarian regimes selectively incorporated some performances from the social movement repertoire—notably the association, the march, the demonstration, and the mass meeting—but placed them so securely under central government control that they lost their meaning as autonomous assertions of WUNC. Noting that very process, political theorists of the generation following World War II mistakenly portrayed it as a transition from atomized mass society to authoritarianism. The first part (atomized mass society) was wrong, the second part (authoritarianism) right. In fact, Italy, Germany, and Spain made transitions from often undisciplined but burgeoning organized activity (some of it in standard social movement format) to highly coordinated central control.

When and How Social Movements Promote Democratization

A number of the same processes that promote democratization, then, also foster social movements, and vice versa. Democratization in itself further promotes social movements. That set of connections helps explain the affinity of social movements with democratization. It does not, however, answer the most difficult question with which we began: what about the *direct causal impact* of social movements on democracy and democratization? Precisely because of the broad covariation of democracy and social movements, reasoning from correlations will not resolve the problem. We have no choice but to close in on causal processes.

Which ones? In fact, my earlier survey catalogued the likely candidates: those processes that cause shifts from particularized and/or mediated to categorical and direct relations between citizens and government, broadening and equalization of relations among political actors, reduced penetration of social inequalities into public politics, and increasing integration of trust networks into public politics. The question now alters, however: which among our array of democracy-promoting processes do social movements themselves activate or reverse, under what conditions, and how? Remember that the great bulk of the social movements we have surveyed pursued particular interests rather than general programs of democratization. Remember also that a substantial minority organized around explicitly antidemocratic claims such as the abridgement of rights for members of particular racial, ethnic, or religious categories. It will therefore not suffice to look for social movements that explicitly demanded democracy and to ask when and how they made gains. We must ask under what conditions and how social movement claim making actually promoted expansion of democratic relations and practices.

Once relatively high-capacity governments began practicing direct rule by means including representative institutions, however narrow the representation, they set a powerful dialectic into motion: governments bargained with legislatures for authorization to gather resources for pursuit of governmental activities, bargained with groups of citizens for the actual delivery of those resources, sought the collaboration of major political actors in the levying of resources and the execution of programs, and established procedures for recognition of political actors. However grudgingly or unconsciously, they thereby created incentives and opportunities for new or previously unauthorized actors to assert their existence and for minority factions within legislatures to form coalitions with outside actors. Electoral logic provides the most obvious example of such effects: coordinated public displays of WUNC signal the existence of potential voting blocs that could collectively influence outcomes of future elections.

Increasingly, political entrepreneurs inside and outside of legislatures discovered that they could add weight to their proposals, complaints, and demands by organizing public displays of popular backing for those proposals, complaints, and demands. Our review of the Philippines in 2001 leaves unclear how large a part elite manipulation behind the scenes played in People Power II. At least in the Manila region, nevertheless, the Philippine adventure reveals both opponents and supporters of Joseph Estrada adding weight to their claims by means of dramatic public displays. Over the long run of social movements, to the extent that such displays verified the presence of worthy, united, numerous, and committed sets of supporters, they constituted at once threats to politics as usual and promises of new allies for beleaguered legislative minorities.

Without a general conscious design, the organization of performances in the form of public meetings, marches, voluntary associations, petition drives, and pamphleteering promoted additional effects:

- establishment of standard practices by which political activists formed and broadcast collective answers to the identity questions "Who are you?" and "Who are we?" and "Who are they?";
- development of problem-solving ties among activists in the very process of preparing and executing public performances;
- incorporation of existing organizations such as churches and mutual aid societies into these new forms of political activity; and
- development of procedures by which governmental agents responded differentially to performances and identity claims—negotiating boundaries between legitimate and illegitimate performances, recognizing some actors while refusing to recognize others, applying facilitation or repression, co-opting, channeling, infiltrating, or subverting various groups.

Together, these additional effects established social movements as regular participants in public politics. But they also created new social ties among activists, between activists and their constituencies, between activists and agents of government. Outside of any collective demands that activists made for democratization, the new social ties became crucial sites of democratization.

How so? The internal dynamics of social movements activated all three classes of democracy-promoting processes—processes that democratized public politics directly by broadening and equalizing collective political participation, processes that insulated public politics from existing social inequalities, and processes that reduced insulation of trust networks from major political actors. To the extent that social movement activism promoted establishment of recognized but autonomous collective political actors involving socially heterogeneous members and integrating their own distinctive trust networks, its democratizing effects increased. Conversely, to the extent that governments managed to destroy, deflect, disperse, ignore, or co-opt social movement coalitions and their trust networks, democratization suffered. After the profusion of French social movement activity during the 1930s, for instance, the German occupation of 1940–1944 rapidly closed down almost all visible social movements, which in turn contributed to the country's dedemocratization during those terrible years (Gildea 2002, Jackson 2001, Tartakowsky 1997).

In summary, proliferation of social movements promotes democratization chiefly in regimes that a) have created relatively effective direct rule through a central administration rather than governing through privileged intermediaries or communal segments, and b) have established at least a modicum of democratization, however that happened. The two conditions make it possible for the combination of campaigns, WUNC displays, and social movement performances to wield an impact on public politics, whereas their absence presents insuperable barriers to social movement effectiveness. In these circumstances, social movement strategies sometimes promote democratization directly by mobilizing effective claims on behalf of protected consultation. Despite the eventual dumping of working-class participants, Britain's social movement–based Reform mobilization of 1830–1832 did nudge the British regime toward greater categorically defined breadth, equality, binding consultation, and protection while establishing a precedent and model for subsequent prodemocracy mobilizations.

But, as our historical surveys have shown, such explicit, effective prodemocracy social movements rarely form; far more often, social movement participants make claims on behalf of more particular programs, identities, or standing, claims that in themselves have no necessary connection with democratization. Blocking construction of a highway, supporting or opposing abortion, forwarding the rights of indigenous people, and demanding better schools by social movement performances certainly take advantage of democratic liberties, but they do not necessarily advance democracy.

Cumulatively, nevertheless, several kinds of social movement campaigns contribute to democratization. That happens, on the average, when they:

- create coalitions that cross important categorical boundaries within public politics (example: visible members of the Filipino ruling class join with ordinary Manileños in opposition to Joseph Estrada);
- form a pool of brokers with skills in coalition-formation and boundary-crossing (example: church- and association-based nineteenth-century American activists bring together feminists, abolitionists, and supporters of temperance); and
- simultaneously a) establish connections within previously unmobilized and excluded categories of citizens, especially those embedded in segmented trust networks, and b) form alliances between those newly mobilized groups and existing political actors (example: Indian reformers recruit support from members of impoverished, stigmatized castes).

In short, social movements promote democratization when—either as explicit programs or as by-products of their action—they broaden the range of participants in public politics, equalize the weight of participants in public politics, erect barriers to the direct translation of categorical inequalities into public politics, and/or integrate previously segmented trust networks into public politics. Great Britain during the late 1820s and early 1830s looks like a place where social movements promoted democratization in most of these ways. Conversely, social movements promote dedemocratization when they narrow the range of participants in public politics, increase inequalities among participants in public politics, translate existing categorical inequalities more directly into public politics, and/or insulate trust networks from public politics. Alas, India during the early twenty-first century looks like a place where polarized, segmented Hindu and Muslim social movement activity might actually be dedemocratizing the national regime.

Taking such effects into account, we can hold out the hope that early-twenty-first-century mobilizations against world financial institutions will promote democratization at an international scale by drawing a wide range of new, previously marginalized groups into international public politics. We can hope that in such countries as Kazakhstan, Belarus, and China the standard democratizing processes—increases in the numbers and connections of people available for participation in public politics, equalization of resources and connections among those people, insulation of public politics from existing social inequalities, and integration of interpersonal trust networks into public politics—will eventually promote both democracy and social movements.

At a world scale, nevertheless, we can equally worry that highly selective access to NGOs and electronic communication will instead introduce fresh inequalities into international public politics and thus promote dedemocratization. To the extent that national governments lose the power to implement social movement programs, moreover, democracy will generally decline at the national level. Without a combination of vigilance and favorable developments over which democrats and activists themselves exercise only partial control, the futures of democracy and of social movements remain insecure.

7

FUTURES OF SOCIAL MOVEMENTS

At Homer, Alaska, Cook Inlet meets the Gulf of Alaska. According to its Chamber of Commerce, the town of four thousand people occupies a spectacular site on Kachemak Bay in sight of the Kenai Mountains. Once a coal-mining town, Homer now relies for its livelihood mainly on commercial fisheries—salmon and halibut in abundance—and tourists. With moose, bear, puffins, eagles, porpoises, and killer whales close at hand, it seems like the antithesis of my own New York City and well worth the visit.

Residents of Homer might be surprised to learn that their weekly routines owe something to the violent victories of a dissolute demagogue in London during the 1760s and to the anti-British agitation of a failed brewer in Boston about the same time. But by now we know that they do. John Wilkes, Samuel Adams, and their collaborators really started something. Citizens of Homer are still using a twenty-first-century version of that innovation of the eighteenth and nineteenth centuries. The online *Homer News* posted an intriguing story in April 2003.

> Monday has become the day for war supporters and peace activists to stage simultaneous demonstrations on the corner of Pioneer Avenue and Lake Street, prompting a barrage of honks and hollers—and the occasional profanity—from passing motorists. Saturday, meanwhile, has become the day that Anchor Point stakes its claim as the hub of patriotic rallying.

In nearby Anchor Point:

> Deanna Chesser said there were no peace activists present as roughly 90 people gathered to show their support for military action in Iraq and the efforts of the men and women in the US military. "And we don't have any Women in Black," said Chesser, referring to Homer's contingent of the global network that advocates peace and justice. The organizers of the Anchor Point rally are planning a repeat performance for noon on Saturday, with the addition of music and speak-

144

ers. Chesser, whose son Davin recently was deployed to Kuwait, said she expects an even bigger turnout.

Back in Homer:

> While those showing their support for the US-led war in Iraq have Anchor Point all to themselves on Saturdays, they have only begun joining the peace activists on the corner at Pioneer and Lake for the past several weeks. For weeks prior to that, passers-by out around noon on a Monday would see a subdued silent vigil taking place on the corner, which is also the site of Homer's Veteran's Memorial. The presence of protestors in front of the memorial stirred up resentment among some residents, prompting a call to begin a counter rally at the same time. "We want to take the corner back," said one flag-waving demonstrator. "Why don't you pray for our troops instead of for the Iraqis?" yelled a passing motorist, responding to the Women in Black assertion that their vigil is in observance of those lost in war.
>
> But Sharon Whytal said she believed the choice to stand near the Veteran's Memorial symbolizes a concern for all those who are lost in military conflict. "It's true that many of us are there because we're grieving for the loss of veterans," Whytal said, adding that having both groups share the site also provides a powerful symbol—freedom in action.
>
> While there had been reports of some unpleasant exchanges between the two groups, there was little sign of it on Monday as close to 100 people stood on the corner, split evenly. The group waving flags stood out front on the sidewalk, lined up at the curb waving flags and cheering as passing motorists honked and waved. Standing 15 yards behind them, a line of Women in Black joined by a number of men, also dressed in black, remained silent for the duration of their vigil. "I don't feel offended that there are two groups there expressing their minds," Whytal said, referring to a sign bearing a slogan popular at many protests around the country: "This is what democracy looks like." (*Homer News* 2003b; spacing and punctuation edited)

In Homer, the corner of Pioneer Avenue and Lake Street, where the two bands of around fifty people each stood fifteen yards apart, features not only the town's war memorial but also its police and fire departments. These activists stage their peaceful confrontations at one of Homer's central locations. Anchor Point, site of the solo prowar celebrations, lies sixteen miles west of Homer on the Sterling Highway, which leads up Kachemak Bay to Anchorage. Having only an elementary school at home, Anchor Point's adolescents bus down the Sterling Highway to Homer for their high school educations. Thus people from the two towns often interact. The same day that the *Homer News* reported Homer's dual displays of antiwar and prowar sentiment, it also ran a dispatch from Anchor Point. The second article described yellow ribbons tied to trees throughout the smaller town and invited people out for a new rally along the Sterling Highway. Participants, it said, should bring American flags and pictures of family members serving in the Iraq war (*Homer News* 2003c).

No North American who stayed alert to national and international news during the spring of 2003 should have any trouble decoding April's events in Homer and Anchor Point. Not only North Americans but also people across the world can easily recognize them as street demonstrations, a standard means of broadcasting support or opposition with regard to political issues. In this case, demonstration and counterdemonstration represented opposition to, and support for, U.S. military intervention in Iraq. On the same days when citizens of Anchor Point and Homer took to the street, hundreds of street demonstrations were occurring elsewhere in the world. Some of them likewise concerned the Iraq war, but most of them took up other locally urgent questions. In the early twenty-first century, the street demonstration looks like an all-purpose political tool—perhaps less effective in the short run than buying a legislator or mounting a military coup, but within democratic and semidemocratic regimes a significant alternative to elections, opinion polls, and letter writing as a way of voicing public positions.

Although the news from Homer and Anchor Point does not tell us so, we have seen that the twenty-first-century demonstration actually has two major variants. In the first variant, Homer style, participants gather in a symbolically potent public location, where through speech and action they display their collective attachment to a well-defined cause. In the second, they proceed through public thoroughfares offering similar displays of attachment. Often, of course, the two combine, as activists march to a favored rallying place, or as multiple columns converge from different places on a single symbolically powerful destination.

Occasionally, as in Homer, counterdemonstrators show up to advocate a contrary view and to challenge the demonstrators' claim to the spaces in question. Frequently, police or troops station themselves along the line of march or around the place of assembly. Sometimes police or troops bar demonstrators' access to important spaces, buildings, monuments, or persons. At times, they deliberately separate demonstrators from counterdemonstrators. As in Homer, passersby or spectators often signal their approval or disapproval of the cause that the demonstrators are supporting. Later, they may join the discussion in lunchtime arguments or letters to the editor. David Bitterman of Homer wrote his opinion to the *Homer News:*

> Driving in town recently, I noticed a group of women dressed in black standing along Pioneer Avenue near the fire station. I have been out of town awhile and did not know the story behind the women. When I asked my wife, she told me they were protesting war. I remarked that it was ironic that the military protects the right of people to protest against our country and the armed forces.

Bitterman described their son, an army specialist stationed in Germany, who had joined the army to protect his country after the 9/11 attacks. Bitterman argued that war was necessary for the defense of freedom:

Our nation's soldiers, sailors, airmen, Marines, and Coast Guardsmen are already in the field. They serve 24–7–365 to protect us from those who would harm us. Any action that weakens our armed forces personnel only serves to strengthen and embolden our enemies. Am I saying the Women in Black are unpatriotic? No, just uninformed. (*Homer News* 2003a)

Once his wife provided essential decoding, Mr. Bitterman clearly caught the demonstration's point. The symbolism and choreography of the street demonstration rival those of baseball and debutantes' balls. But its scorecard centers on contested public issues rather than league standing or social reputation.

As earlier chapters have shown, street demonstrations also have some identifiable kin: municipal parades, party conventions, mass meetings, inaugurals, commencements, religious revivals, and electoral rallies. Most citizens of democracies know the difference. Participants in such events sometimes bend them toward the forms and programs of demonstrations, for example by wearing ostentatious symbols or shouting slogans in support of a cause at a college commencement. Many of the same principles apply: the separation of participants from spectators, the presence of guards to contain the crowd, and so on. Considered as a whole, this array of gatherings exhibits 1) remarkable coherence, 2) systematic internal variation, and 3) type by type, impressive uniformity across places, programs, and participants.

Previous chapters linked street demonstrations firmly to a larger, evolving, two-century-old form of political struggle, the social movement. They documented the distinctive combination of campaigns, repertoire, and WUNC displays in a form of politics that existed nowhere before the mid-eighteenth century, yet became available for popular making of claims across much of the world during the next two centuries. They also documented the marvelous duality of social movements: quite general and recognizable in their broad outlines, yet impressively adaptable to local circumstances and idioms. That duality comes across in the news from Homer and Anchor Point.

As we approach the end of a book overflowing with historical facts, let us indulge a historical fantasy. Suppose that in April 2003 John Wilkes and Samuel Adams, transmuted intact from the 1760s, both traveled up the Gulf of Alaska to Cook Inlet, Homer, and Anchor Point. Suppose that they watched demonstrators in the two towns, and conferred to see if they could figure out what these twenty-first-century people were doing, and why.

Wilkes: I've never seen anything like it.

Adams: You can say that again.

Wilkes: But it's something like a church service . . .

Adams: Or a workmen's parade.

Wilkes: Where is the audience? Who are they talking to?

Adams: And where are the troops or constables?

Wilkes: Still one thing's familiar: they're arguing about a war.

Adams: You know, it reminds me of an election campaign, with people wearing candidates' colors, chanting slogans, gathering in central squares, and marching along major thoroughfares.

Wilkes: Except that it's so *civilized.* How do these people expect to make any difference?

Adams: Maybe we should ask them.

The fantastic encounter does not show Wilkes and Adams the full apparatus of social movements at work: the combination of multiple performances and WUNC displays in sustained, coordinated making of program, identity, and/or standing claims. Nor does it tell them about the many other activists outside of Homer and Anchor Point who are likewise joining social movements for and against the American invasion of Iraq, often employing news releases, petitions, and public meetings in addition to street demonstrations. But the imagined conversation does raise crucial questions about the present and future of social movements. Has the social movement lost its political effectiveness? Is the internationalization of power, politics, and social movement organization rendering amateur local, regional, or even national efforts obsolete? If the forms of social movements have changed so much over the last two centuries, what further changes might we expect to see during the twenty-first century?

How Can We Read the Future?

Most likely the right answer to all these questions is the old reliable: it depends. No doubt it depends on which countries, which issues, which claimants, and which objects of claims we have in mind; for the moment, the futures of all social movements in Zimbabwe and Kazakhstan, for example, look dim, while social movements still seem to be enjoying active lives in Canada and Costa Rica. As I write, movements protesting American military power are making little headway, while movements to curb the WTO's power are at least attracting energetic international support. More generally, we must distinguish among a number of possible future trajectories for social movements, on one side, and a number of different social movement scales, on the other. Figure 7.1 schematizes the distinctions.

The figure builds in two main dimensions, one directions of change from growth to decline, the other scales from local to global. The diagram's "global" scale represents the possibility voiced by today's advocates of transnational activism not merely that international actors and international targets will become routine in future social movements but that social movements will regularly coordinate popular claim making across the entire globe. Meanwhile, the diagram follows chapter 5 by insisting that despite some internationalization, local, regional, and national social movements continue to occur during the early twenty-first century.

Figure 7.1 flattens into two dimensions a series of likely further changes in social movements we have seen occurring from their earliest days: changes in cam-

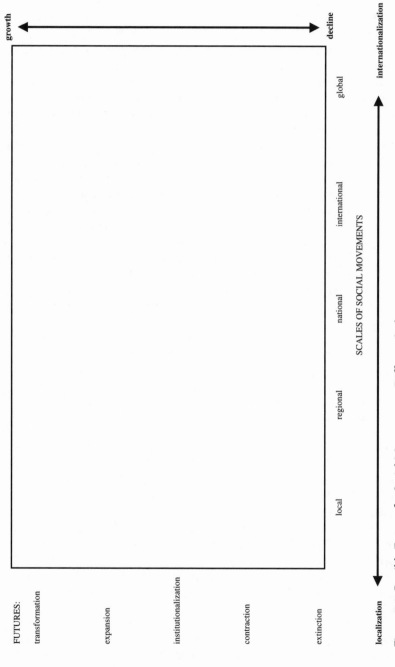

Figure 7.1 Possible Futures for Social Movements at Different Scales

paigns, repertoires, and WUNC displays. Surely the twenty-first century will bring new program, identity, and standing claims—new issues for campaigns—that the century's first few years leave almost unimaginable; suppose, for example, that animal rights activists mounted campaigns to gain citizenship rights for the great apes. Someone will almost certainly invent new social movement performances and thereby alter the general social movement repertoire; think about the possibility that activists in space capsules will broadcast their messages across all the world's airwaves. WUNC displays will evolve as well, perhaps by adopting technologies that will broadcast instantly how many people are voicing support or opposition for a given social movement claim—thus giving new expression to the N in WUNC. If social movements survive the twenty-first century, they will surely leave it much transformed with regard to campaigns, repertoires, and WUNC displays.

Despite neglecting such changes in social movement texture, the diagram implies a very wide range of hypothetical possibilities. We might, for example, imagine a future combination of extinction at the local level, institutionalization at the national level, and expansion plus dramatic transformation at the global level; that would conform to predictions by some enthusiastic analysts of electronic linkage in social movements. Or we could imagine that massive declines in state power will simultaneously activate linked regional and international movements, on the model of demands for indigenous rights or regional autonomy that seize power from states but also receive backing and guarantees from international organizations.

An overall shift to the right within the diagram would mean that local, regional, and perhaps even national social movements gave way to international and global movements: extensive internationalization. A general shift to the left— not much expected these days—would mean a decline of larger-scale movements in favor of a new localism. A net shift upward would signify general expansion and transformation of social movement activity. Vertical moves toward the middle would signal widespread institutionalization: the whole world involved in social movements at multiple scales, but with nongovernmental organizations, professional social movement entrepreneurs, and close relations to political authorities dominating the action. Below the midpoint, a general shift downward would represent decline or disappearance of social movements, likewise across the board. More plausible predictions would feature separate trajectories for social movements at different scales, for example expansion and transformation of international social movements at the same time as local social movements contracted and institutionalized.

We must, of course, ground any predictions on whatever knowledge we have gleaned from examining two centuries of social movement history. Remember the book's main arguments:

From their eighteenth-century origins onward, social movements have proceeded not as solo performances but as interactive campaigns. By now, this observation should have become self-evident. It matters, nevertheless, as a reminder that to predict future social movements involves thinking about changing relations among claimants, objects of claims, audiences, and authorities rather than simply extrapolating the most visible features of social movement performances. Remember the intricate interplay of movements, countermovements, authorities, publics, and external powers across the fast-changing state socialist world of 1989.

Social movements combine three kinds of claims: program, identity, and standing. Program claims involve stated support for or opposition to actual or proposed actions by the objects of movement claims. Identity claims consist of assertions that "we"—the claimants—constitute a unified force to be reckoned with. WUNC (worthiness, unity, numbers, and commitment) performances back up identity claims. Standing claims assert ties and similarities to other political actors, for example as excluded minorities, properly constituted citizens' groups, or loyal supporters of the regime. They sometimes concern the standing of *other* political actors, for example in calls for expulsion of immigrants or their exclusion from citizenship. The nineteenth-century United States showed us a dazzling (and sometimes depressing) array of program, identity, and standing claims with regard to which racial, ethnic, and gender categories deserved citizenship rights. Clearly, program, identity, and standing claims can evolve in partial independence from each other; standing claims, for example, depend sensitively on which political actors already have full standing, and which political procedures change an actor's standing. They thus depend on the rise or fall of democracy.

The relative salience of program, identity, and standing claims varies significantly among social movements, among claimants within movements, and among phases of movements. If institutionalization eclipsed identity and standing claims in favor of programs advocated or opposed by established specialists in social movement claim making, that eclipse would constitute a major change in twenty-first-century social movements. Professionalization of social movement organizations and entrepreneurs sometimes leads to new identity and standing claims; recent worldwide campaigns on behalf of indigenous people's rights illustrate that possibility. But on the whole, professionalization tips the balance away from identity and standing toward programs.

Democratization promotes the formation of social movements. Chapter 6 showed us that this apparently obvious statement hides a surprising degree of complexity. To single out the effects of democratization on social movements, we must separate them from common causes of democratization and social movements as well as from reciprocal influences of social movements on democratization. This done, however, we see that predicting the future of twenty-first-century social movements depends heavily on expectations concerning future democratization or dedemocratization. In the Philippines, for example, we must decide whether the Manila region's partial democracy or Mindanao's warlords mark the future path.

Social movements assert popular sovereignty. Over our two centuries of history, the argument holds up well. The rise and fall of social movements in France, for instance, neatly chart fluctuations in claims of popular sovereignty, so much so that France's authoritarian regimes took great care to suppress social movement campaigns, performances, and WUNC displays. Nevertheless, we have encountered two important qualifications to the general principle. First, professional social movement entrepreneurs and nongovernmental organizations sometimes represent themselves as speaking for "the people" without creating either deep grass roots or means for ordinary people to speak through them. Second, a minority of historical social movements have supported programs that, when realized, actually diminished popular sovereignty by implanting authoritarian leaders, charismatic cults, or programs of widespread exclusion. Any predictions concerning future social movements and their consequences will have to take into the account the possibility that these minority currents could become the majority.

As compared with locally grounded forms of popular politics, social movements depend heavily on political entrepreneurs for their scale, durability, and effectiveness. We have certainly seen political entrepreneurs repeatedly in the midst of social movements. From Great Britain's Reform mobilization of the 1830s to recent mobilizations against the WTO, entrepreneurs and their nongovernmental organizations have figured prominently in campaign after campaign. Indeed, the overall trend has increased the salience and influence of political entrepreneurs. The future depends in part on whether that trend will continue, and which sorts of entrepreneurs will flourish in social movements.

Once social movements establish themselves in one political setting, modeling, communication, and collaboration facilitate their adoption in other connected settings. This observation has taken on new meaning as our analysis has moved on. For connections of existing social movement settings with potential new settings always select radically from among all the new settings with which connections could, in principle, form. We have seen that selectivity most clearly in the connections facilitated by new communications media: generally lowering the cost of communications for people who have access to the system, but excluding others who lack that access. The same holds for interpersonal networks: expansion of social movement activity along existing networks excludes those who do not belong. Despite the engaging image of smart mobs, that play of inclusion and exclusion is likely to continue through the twenty-first century. As a consequence, some of our predictions will rest on estimates of who will connect with whom, and what segments of the world population those connections will exclude.

The forms, personnel, and claims of social movements vary and evolve historically. As our whimsical vignette of Wilkes and Adams in Homer, Alaska, suggests, social movement forms have undergone continuous mutation since the later eighteenth century and are mutating still. We have observed three distinguishable but interacting sources of change and variation in social movements: overall political environments, incremental change in campaigns, repertoires, and WUNC displays within social movements, and diffusion of social movement models among sites of activism. To anticipate the future, we must specify how each of the three will change, not to mention how they will interact. For clues, we should pay special attention to new sites of social movement action such as anti-WTO protests, asking who does what on behalf of which claims.

The social movement, as an invented institution, could disappear or mutate into some quite different form of politics. We still have no guarantee that the social movement as it has prevailed for two centuries will continue forever. We must take seriously the possibility that the twenty-first century will destroy social movements as vehicles of popular claim making because the conditions for their survival have dissolved or because new forms of claim making have supplanted them. One dream of digital democracy, after all, proposes continuous, electronically mediated opinion polling as a cheap, efficient substitute for associating, meeting, marching, petitioning, addressing mass media, and the rest of the social movement repertoire—a frightening prospect for lovers of social movements in something like their recognizable historical form.

Possible Futures

How can we apply these principles to the future? Figure 7.2 ransacks ideas and evidence in previous chapters to speculate about what could happen to social movements during the rest of the twenty-first century. It combines some of the more likely possibilities into four scenarios: internationalization, democratic decline, professionalization, and triumph. *Internationalization* entails a net shift away from local, regional, and national social movements toward international and global social movement activity. *Decline of democracy* would depress all sorts of social movements, especially at the large scale, but could leave pockets of local or regional social movement activity where some democratic institutions survived. *Professionalization* would most likely diminish the relative importance of local and regional social movements while shifting the energies of activists and organizers to national or, especially, international and global scales. *Triumph,* finally, describes the glorious dream of social movements everywhere, serving at all scales from local to global as a means for advancing popular claims. Let us draw on implications of previous chapters to identify circumstances that would cause each of the four scenarios as well as to reflect on likely consequences of each scenario for popular politics.

Internationalization. Many observers and activists of twenty-first-century social movements assume that internationalization is already sweeping the field and will continue to a point at which most social movements will operate internationally or even globally; they project that environmentalists, feminists, human rights advocates, and opponents of global capital will increasingly join forces across countries and continents. Under what conditions might we now expect internationalization to dominate the futures of social movements? Considering the evidence of previous chapters, these are the most likely candidates:

- continued growth and impact by international networks of power and of organizations implementing them: financial networks, trade connections, multinational corporations, international governmental and regulatory institutions, intercontinental criminal enterprises;

1. INTERNATIONALIZATION

2. DECLINE OF DEMOCRACY

3. PROFESSIONALIZATION

4. TRIUMPH

Figure 7.2 Alternative Scenarios for Future Social Movements

- vulnerability of those networks to shaming, subversion, boycotts, or governmental regulation;
- expansion of connections among widely dispersed populations whose welfare those international networks affect, especially adversely;
- proliferation of organizations, brokers, and political entrepreneurs specialized in connecting those populations and coordinating their action; and
- formation of at least a modicum of democracy at an international scale: relatively broad, equal, consultative, and protective relations between citizens and agents of international governmental institutions.

Predicting that extensive internationalization of social movements will occur during the twenty-first century depends on implicit predictions that most or all of these conditions will apply.

If the scenario of internationalization prevailed, we might reasonably expect some further consequences for popular politics in the short and medium runs. First, given the minimum requirements of large-scale social movements for information, time, contacts, and resources, the existing elite bias of social movement participation would increase; the lowering of communication costs through Internet and cellular telephone connections surely would not override the increased coordination costs for a very long time. Second, for this reason and because of uneven access to communication channels, inequality between sites of active movement participation and all others would sharpen; relatively speaking, excluded people would suffer even more acutely than today from lack of means to mount effective campaigns, performances, and WUNC displays. Third, brokers, entrepreneurs, and international organizations would become even more crucial to the effective voicing of claims by means of social movements. All these changes point to declines in democratic participation; they would both narrow the range of participants in social movements and make participation more unequal.

Democratic Decline. What if democracy declined, however, as a result of causes outside of the social movement sphere: weakening of barriers between categorical inequality and public politics, segregation of new or existing trust networks from public politics, and so on? Since democracy always operates in connection with particular centers of power, a lot would depend on whether the decline occurred at all scales or only, for example, at the national scale. A plausible version of this scenario would have large-scale democracy—national, international, and global—suffering more acutely than smaller-scale democracy, simply because it would take a political catastrophe to produce simultaneous dedemocratization across the world's thousands of local, regional, and national regimes. In contrast, escape of a small number of capitalists, military organizations, technologies, or scientific disciplines from collective constraint would immediately threaten such international democratic institutions as now exist. (Imagine rogue networks of bankers, soldiers, communications providers, or medical researchers, for example, who could decide which segments of the world population would—and would not—have access to their services.) Under most circumstances, democratic collapse at the large scale would still leave surviving democratic enclaves scattered across the world. We then might expect to find increasing differentiation of social movement practices across those surviving enclaves, as communication and collaboration among the world's social movements activists diminished and as local or regional activists adapted increasingly to their particular conditions.

Professionalization identifies another possibility. In our scenario, professionalization leads to institutionalization, hence to declining innovation in social movements. Committed populists often worry that social movement activists, already drawn disproportionately from prosperous, well-educated, well-connected segments of the population, will sell out the interests of truly disadvantaged people, establish comfortable relations with authorities, rely increasingly on support from the rich and powerful, and/or become social movement bureaucrats, more interested in forwarding their own organizations and careers than the welfare of their supposed constituencies.

As compared with the early nineteenth century, some professionalization and institutionalization of social movements have unquestionably occurred in relatively democratic regimes: creation of protective legal codes, formation of police forces specializing in contained protection of social movement activity, establishment of less lethal routines for police-demonstrator interaction, creation of reporting conventions for social movements in mass media, multiplication of organizations specializing in social movement campaigns, performances, and WUNC displays. These changes have, in turned, opened up full-time careers in social movement activism. Professionalization and institutionalization have proceeded hand in hand.

Up to the early twenty-first century, however, new issues, groups, tactics, and targets have repeatedly arisen at the edge of the established social movement sector. Many peripheral claimants failed, some quickly shifted to standard social movement practices, but a few brought their own innovations—sit-ins, occupations of public buildings, puppet shows, cartoonlike costumes, new uses of media—onto the public scene. Predicting general professionalization and institutionalization of social movements, then, implies that opportunities for genuinely new issues, groups, tactics, and targets will diminish significantly. That could occur, in principle, either through declining incentives for popular claim making or through closing out of claimants who are not already part of the social movement establishment. What if the more than nine-tenths of the world population that currently lacks Internet access had no chance to form or join social movements?

Triumph. What about across-the-board expansion of social movements at all scales from local to global? Such a surprising future would require democratization of the many world regions currently living under authoritarian regimes, warlords, or petty tyrannies. It would also require a more general division of government and of power such that local authorities still had the capacity to affect local lives and respond to local demands even if international authorities gained power within their own spheres. It would, finally, mean that local, regional, and national activist networks, organizations, and entrepreneurs continued to act in partial independence at their own scales instead of subordinating their programs to those of international or global scope. Conversely, if widespread dedemoc-ratization occurred at all scales across the world, if centers of power increased their own protections against popular pressure, and if linking networks, organizations, and brokers either disintegrated or fell under authorities' control, a general de-cline of social movements would follow.

In the domain of social movements, even if-then statements—if democrati-zation, then social movement expansion, if internationalization, then sharpening inequality, and so on—run enormous risks. Despite the ample documentation of previous chapters and generations of scholarly work, we have nothing like an if-then science of social movements. Flat predictions for the remainder of the twenty-first century involve even greater uncertainties. After all, they depend on a combi-nation of three sorts of reasoning: 1) extrapolation of existing trends into the future; 2) if-then statements about the proximate causes of change in social move-ments; and 3) speculations about changes in the causes of those causes. To predict that the modest internationalization of social movements since 1990 or so will swell into a great wave, for example, we must assume that we have actually read that trend correctly, that the expansion of connections among dispersed popula-tions affected by international power networks does, indeed, promote coordina-tion of social movement activity among those dispersed populations, and that whatever causes the expansion of connections to occur will continue to operate through the century's many remaining years.

In the face of all this uncertainty, can we place any bets on the likely preva-lence of one scenario or another? What combinations of internationalization, demo-cratic decline, professionalization, and/or triumph are more probable? Throwing all if-then prudence to the winds, let me state my own guesses about the twenty-first century:

Internationalization: slower, less extensive, and less complete than technology en-thusiasts say, but likely to continue for decades

Decline of democracy: a split decision, with some democratic decline (and there-fore some diminution in the prevalence and efficacy of social movements) in major existing democracies but substantial democratization (hence social movement expansion) in such currently undemocratic countries as China

Professionalization: another split decision, with professional social movement en-trepreneurs, nongovernmental organizations, and accommodations with au-thorities increasingly dominant in large-scale social movements but conse-quently abandoning those portions of local and regional claim making they cannot co-opt into international activism

Triumph: alas, exceedingly unlikely

I say "alas" because for all the reasons laid out in previous chapters, the triumph of social movements at all scales, despite all the dangers of movements that you or I would oppose, would benefit humanity. The broad availability of social movements signals the presence of democratic institutions and usually promotes their functioning. It provides a crucial channel for groups, categories, and issues that currently have no voice in a regime's routine politics to acquire visible places in public politics. We should scan future social movements carefully, in hope of refuting my pessimistic forecast.

REFERENCES

Ackerman, Peter, & Jack DuVall (2000): *A Force More Powerful: A Century of Nonviolent Conflict.* New York: Palgrave.

Alapuro, Risto (1988): *State and Revolution in Finland.* Berkeley: University of California Press.

Alexander, John K. (2002): *Samuel Adams: America's Revolutionary Politician.* Lanham, Md.: Rowman & Littlefield.

Aminzade, Ronald (1993): *Ballots and Barricades: Class Formation and Republican Politics in France, 1830–1871.* Princeton, N.J.: Princeton University Press.

Ananova (2001): multiple reports from Manila, Philippines, 19–22 January 2001. *www.ananova.com,* viewed 20 August 2003.

Anderson, Benedict (1998): *The Spectre of Comparisons: Nationalism, Southeast Asia, and the World.* London: Verso.

Anderson, Eugene N., & Pauline R. Anderson (1967): *Political Institutions and Social Change in Continental Europe in the Nineteenth Century.* Berkeley: University of California Press.

Andrey, Georges (1986): "La quête d'un État national." In Jean-Claude Fayez, ed., *Nouvelle Histoire de la Suisse et des Suisses.* Lausanne: Payot.

Anheier, Helmut K., Friedhelm Neidhardt, & Wolfgang Vortkamp (1998): "Movement Cycles and the Nazi Party: Activation of the Munich NSDAP, 1925–1930." *American Behavioral Scientist* 41: 1262–81.

Anheier, Helmut, & Thomas Ohlemacher (1996): "Aktivisten, Netzwerke und Bewegungservolg: Die 'Einzelmitglieder' der NSDAP, 1925–1930." *Kölner Zeitschrift für Soziologie und Sozialpsychologie* 48: 677–703.

Anheier, Helmut, & Nuno Themudo (2002): "Organisational Forms of Global Civil Society: Implications of Going Global." In Marlies Glasius, Mary Kaldor, & Helmut Anheier, eds., *Global Civil Society 2002.* Oxford: Oxford University Press.

d'Anjou, Leo (1996): *Social Movements and Cultural Change: The First Abolition Campaign Revisited.* New York: Aldine de Gruyter.

Archer, John E. (1990): *By a Flash and a Scare: Incendiarism, Animal Maiming, and Poaching in East Anglia 1815–1870.* Oxford: Clarendon Press.

Armstrong, W. W. (1989): "Labour I: Rural Population Growth, Systems of Employment, and Incomes." In Joan Thirsk, ed., *The Agrarian History of England and Wales. Vol. 6, 1750–1850.* Cambridge: Cambridge University Press.

Ash, Roberta (1972): *Social Movements in America.* Chicago: Markham.

Bagla, Pallava (2003): "Ayodhya Ruins Yield More Fuel for Ongoing Religious Fight." *Science* 301, 5 September, 1305.

Balbus, Isaac (1973): *The Dialectics of Legal Repression: Black Rebels before the American Criminal Courts.* New York: Russell Sage Foundation.

Ballbé, Manuel (1983): *Orden público y militarismo en la España constitucional (1812–1983).* Madrid: Alianza.

Barrington, Lowell (1995): "The Domestic and International Consequences of Citizenship in the Soviet Successor States." *Europe-Asia Studies* 47: 731–63.

Becker, Elizabeth (2003): "Hark! Voices from the Street Are Heard in the Trade Talks." *New York Times* 13 September, A6.

Beissinger, Mark (1993): "Demise of an Empire-State: Identity, Legitimacy, and the Deconstruction of Soviet Politics." In Crawford Young, ed., *The Rising Tide of Cultural Pluralism.* Madison: University of Wisconsin Press. (1998a): "Nationalist Violence and the State: Political Authority and Contentious Repertoires in the Former USSR." *Comparative Politics* 30: 401–33. (1998b): "Event Analysis in Transitional Societies: Protest Mobilization in the Former Soviet Union." In Dieter Rucht, Ruud Koopmans, & Friedhelm Neidhardt, eds., *Acts of Dissent: New Developments in the Study of Protest.* Berlin: Sigma. (2002): *Nationalist Mobilization and the Collapse of the Soviet State.* Cambridge: Cambridge University Press.

Belchem, John (1990): *Industrialization and the Working Class: The English Experience, 1750–1900.* Aldershot: Scolar.

Bennett, W. Lance (2003): "Communicating Global Activism." *Information, Communication & Society* 6: 143–68.

Bernstein, Thomas P., & Xiaobo Lü (2002): *Taxation without Representation in Contemporary Rural China.* Cambridge: Cambridge University Press.

Binder, Amy J. (2002): *Contentious Curricula: Afrocentrism and Creationism in American Public Schools.* Princeton, N.J.: Princeton University Press.

Birmingham, David (1993): *A Concise History of Portugal.* Cambridge: Cambridge University Press.

Birnbaum, Pierre (1993): *"La France aux Français": Histoire des haines nationalistes.* Paris: Seuil.

Black, Eugene C. (1969): ed., *British Politics in the Nineteenth Century.* New York: Walker and Company.

Blackstock, Allan (2000): "'The Invincible Mass': Loyal Crowds in Mid-Ulster, 1795–96." In Peter Jupp & Eoin Magennis, eds., *Crowds in Ireland c. 1720–1920.* London: Macmillan.

Bogolyubov, N. D., V. P. R'izhkova, B. C. Popov, & A. M. Dubinskii (1962): eds., *Istoria myezhdunarodnovo rabochevo I natsional'no-osvoboditel'novo dvizheniya.* 2 vols. Moscow: V'ishaya Partiinaya Shkola.

Boli, John, & George Thomas (1997): "World Culture in the World Polity: A Century of International Non-Governmental Organization." *American Sociological Review* 62: 171–90.

Böning, Holger (1998): *Der Traum von Freiheit und Gleichheit: Helvetische Revolution und Republik (1798–1803)—Die Schweiz auf dem Weg zur bürgerlichen Demokratie.* Zurich: Orell Füssli.

Bonjour, Edgar (1948): *Die Gründung des schweizerischen Bundesstaates.* Basel: Benno Schwabe.

Bonjour, Edgar, H. S. Offler, & G. R. Potter (1952): *A Short History of Switzerland.* Oxford: Clarendon.

Bose, Sugata, and Ayesha Jalal (1998): *Modern South Asia: History, Culture, Political Economy.* London: Routledge.

Botz, Gerhard (1976): *Gewalt in der Politik: Attentäte, Zusammenstösse, Putschversuche, Unruhen in Österreich 1918 bis 1934.* Munich: Wilhelm Fink. (1987): *Krisenzonen einer Demokratie: Gewalt, Streik und Konfliktunderdrückung in Österreich seit 1918.* Frankfurt: Campus Verlag.

Bourges, Hervé (1968): ed., *La Révolte étudiante: Les animateurs parlent.* Paris: Seuil.

te Brake, Wayne (1989): *Regents and Rebels: The Revolutionary World of the Eighteenth Century Dutch City.* Oxford: Blackwell. (1990): "How Much in How Little? Dutch Revolution in Comparative Perspective." *Tijdschrift voor Sociale Geschiedenis* 16: 349–63. (1998): *Shaping History: Ordinary People in European Politics 1500–1700.* Berkeley: University of California Press.

Brass, Paul R. (1994): *The Politics of India since Independence.* Cambridge: Cambridge University Press. The New Cambridge History of India, IV–1, rev. ed.

Brewer, John (1976): *Party Ideology and Popular Politics at the Accession of George III.* Cambridge: Cambridge University Press. (1989): *The Sinews of Power: War, Money and the English State, 1688–1783.* New York: Knopf.

Bright, Charles, & Susan Harding (1984): eds., *Statemaking and Social Movements.* Ann Arbor: University of Michigan Press.

Brinkley, Alan (1983): *Voices of Protest: Huey Long, Father Coughlin, and the Great Depression.* New York: Vintage.

Broeker, Galen (1970): *Rural Disorder and Police Reform in Ireland, 1812–36.* London: Routledge & Kegan Paul.

Brown, Richard Maxwell (1975): *Strain of Violence: Historical Studies of American Violence and Vigilitantism.* New York: Oxford University Press.

Bruneteaux, Patrick (1993): "Le désordre de la répression en France 1871–1921: Des conscrits aux gendarmes mobiles." *Genèses* 12: 30–46.

Brustein, William (1998): ed., "Nazism as a Social Phenomenon." Special issue of *American Behavioral Scientist* 41: 1189–362.

Bryan, Dominic (2000): *Orange Parades: The Politics of Ritual, Tradition and Control.* London: Pluto Press.

Buchan, Nancy R., Rachel T. A. Croson, & Robyn M. Dawes (2002): "Swift Neighbors and Persistent Strangers: A Cross-Cultural Investigation of Trust and Reciprocity in Social Exchange." *American Journal of Sociology* 108: 168–206.

Bucher, Erwin (1966): *Die Geschichte des Sonderbundskrieges.* Zurich: Berichthaus.

Buechler, Steven M. (1990): *Women's Movements in the United States: Woman Suffrage, Equal Rights, and Beyond.* New Brunswick: Rutgers University Press. (2000): *Social Movements in Advanced Capitalism: The Political Economy and Cultural Construction of Social Activism.* New York: Oxford University Press.

Burke, Edmund III (1988): ed., *Global Crises and Social Movements: Artisans, Peasants, Populists, and the World Economy.* Boulder, Colo.: Westview.

Calhoun, Craig (1995): "'New Social Movements' of the Early Nineteenth Century." In Mark Traugott, ed., *Repertoires and Cycles of Collective Action.* Durham, N.C.: Duke University Press.

Capitani, François de (1986): "Vie et mort de l'Ancien Régime." In Jean-Claude Fayez, ed., *Nouvelle Histoire de la Suisse et des Suisses.* Lausanne: Payot.

Caramani, Daniele (2003): *The Formation of National Electorates and Party Systems in Europe.* Cambridge: Cambridge University Press.

Carter, Neal Allan (2003): "Political Identity, Territory, and Institutional Change: The Case of Belgium." *Mobilization* 8: 205–20.

Castells, Manuel (1983): *The City and the Grassroots: A Cross-Cultural Theory of Urban Social Movements.* Berkeley: University of California Press.

Chabot, Sean (2000): "Transnational Diffusion and the African-American Reinvention of the Gandhian Repertoire." *Mobilization* 5: 201–16.

Chabot, Sean, & Jan Willem Duyvendak (2002): "Globalization and Transnational Diffusion between Social Movements: Reconceptualizing the Dissemination of the Gandhian Repertoire and the 'Coming out' Routine." *Theory and Society* 31: 697–740.

Chandhoke, Neera (2002): "The Limits of Global Civil Society." In Marlies Glasius, Mary Kaldor, & Helmut Anheier, eds., *Global Civil Society 2002.* Oxford: Oxford University Press.

Chaturvedi, Jayati, and Gyaneshwar Chaturvedi (1996): "*Dharma Yudh*: Communal Violence, Riots, and Public Space in Ayodhya and Agra City: 1990 and 1992." In Paul R. Brass., ed., *Riots and Pogroms.* New York: New York University Press.

Church, Roy A. (1966): *Economic and Social Change in a Midland Town: Victorian Nottingham 1815–1900.* New York: Augustus Kelley.

Clark, S. D. (1959): *Movements of Social Protest in Canada, 1640–1840.* Toronto: University of Toronto Press.

Clark, Samuel D., J. Paul Grayson, & Linda M. Grayson (1975): ed., *Prophecy and Protest: Social Movements in Twentieth-Century Canada.* Toronto: Gage.

Clemens, Elisabeth S. (1997): *The People's Lobby: Organizational Innovation and the Rise of Interest Group Politics in the United States, 1890–1925.* Chicago: University of Chicago Press.

Cohen, Jean (1985): "Strategy or Identity: New Theoretical Paradigms and Contemporary Social Movements." *Social Research* 52: 663–716.

Cohen, Jean L., & Andrew Arato (1992): *Civil Society and Political Theory.* Cambridge: MIT Press.

Collier, David, & Steven Levitsky (1997): "Democracy with Adjectives: Conceptual Innovation in Comparative Research." *World Politics* 49: 430–51.

Collier, Ruth Berins (1999): *Paths toward Democracy: The Working Class and Elites in Western Europe and South America.* New York: Cambridge University Press.

Cronin, James E., & Jonathan Schneer (1982): eds., *Social Conflict and the Political Order in Modern Britain.* London: Croom Helm.

CSCE [Commission on Security and Cooperation in Europe] (1998): *Political Reform and Human Rights in Uzbekistan, Kyrgyzstan and Kazakhstan.* Washington, D.C.: CSCE.

Davis, David Brion (1987): "Capitalism, Abolitionism, and Hegemony." In Barbara Solow & Stanley Engerman, eds., *British Capitalism and Caribbean Slavery: The Legacy of Eric Williams.* Cambridge: Cambridge University Press.

Davis, Gerald F., Doug McAdam, W. Richard Scott, & Mayer Zald (2004): eds., *Social Movements and Organizational Theory.* Cambridge: Cambridge University Press.

Davis, Gerald F., & Tracy A. Thompson (1994): "A Social Movement Perspective on Corporate Control." *Administrative Science Quarterly* 39: 141–73.

Deibert, Ronald J. (2000): "International Plug 'n' Play? Citizen Activism, the Internet, and Global Public Policy." *International Studies Perspectives* 1: 255–72.

Dekker, Rudolf (1982): *Holland in beroering: Oproeren in de 17de en 18de eeuw.* Baarn:

Amboeken. (1987): "Women in Revolt: Popular Protest and Its Social Basis in Holland in the Seventeenth and Eighteenth Centuries." *Theory and Society* 16: 337–62.

Deneckere, Gita (1997): *Sire, het volk mort: Sociaal protest in België (1831–1918)*. Antwerp, Amsab.

Deutsch, Karl (1976): *Die Schweiz als ein paradigmatischer Fall politischer Integration*. Bern: Haupt.

Diani, Mario (2003): "Introduction: Social Movements, Contentious Actions, and Social Networks: 'From Metaphor to Substance'?" In Mario Diani & Doug McAdam, eds., *Social Movements and Networks: Relational Approaches to Collective Action*. Oxford: Oxford University Press.

DiMaggio, Paul, Eszter Hargittai, W. Russell Neuman, & John P. Robinson (2001): "Social Implications of the Internet." *Annual Review of Sociology* 27: 307–36.

Dobbin, Murray (1999): "Building a Social Movement in Canada." *Canadian Dimension* 33, December, online version, pp. 6, 8.

Dolléans, Édouard, & Michel Crozier (1950): *Mouvements ouvrier et socialiste: Chronologie et bibliographie: Angleterre, France, Allemagne, États-Unis (1750–1918)*. Paris: Éditions Ouvrières.

Dowe, Dieter (1970): *Aktion und Organisation: Arbeiterbewegung, sozialistische und kommunistische Bewegung in der preussischen Rheinprovinz 1820–1852*. Hannover: Verlag für Literatur und Zeitgeschehen.

Drescher, Seymour (1982): "Public Opinion and the Destruction of British Colonial Slavery." In James Walvin, ed., *Slavery and British Society, 1776–1946*. Baton Rouge: Louisiana State University Press. (1986): *Capitalism and Antislavery: British Mobilization in Comparative Perspective*. London: Macmillan. (1994): "Whose Abolition? Popular Pressure and the Ending of the British Slave Trade." *Past and Present* 143: 136–66.

Drobizheva, Leokadia, Rose Gottemoeller, Catherine McArdle Kelleher, & Lee Walker (1996): eds., *Ethnic Conflict in the Post-Soviet World: Case Studies and Analysis*. Armonk, N.Y.: M. E. Sharpe.

Dumont, Georges-Henri (2002): *Le miracle belge de 1848*. Brussels: Le Cri.

Duyvendak, Jan Willem (1994): *Le poids du politique: Nouveaux mouvements sociaux en France*. Paris: L'Harmattan.

Duyvendak, Jan Willem, Hein-Anton van der Heijden, Ruud Koopmans, & Luuk Wijmans (1992): eds., *Tussen Verbeelding en Macht: 25 jaar nieuwe social bewegingen in Nederland*. Amsterdam: Sua.

Earl, Jennifer, Sarah A. Soule, & John D. McCarthy (2003): "Protest under Fire? Explaining the Policing of Protest." *American Sociological Review* 68: 581–606.

Economist (2003a): "The Perils of Recycling: Excise Hate from One Place, and It Pops up in Another." 30 August: 22. (2003b): "Shut Up, Unless You Fawn." 20 September: 46. (2003c): "In the Name of the Father." 4 October: 41.

Edelman, Marc (2001): "Social Movements: Changing Paradigms and Forms of Politics." *Annual Review of Anthropology* 30: 285–317.

Edwards, Bob, Michael W. Foley, & Mario Diani (2001): eds., *Beyond Tocqueville: Civil Society and the Social Capital Debate in Comparative Perspective*. Hanover, N.H.: University Press of New England.

Ekiert, Grzegorz, & Jan Kubik (1999): *Rebellious Civil Society: Popular Protest and Democratic Consolidation in Poland, 1989–1993*. Ann Arbor: University of Michigan Press.

Eltis, David (1993): "Europeans and the Rise and Fall of African Slavery in the Americas: An Interpretation." *American Historical Review* 98: 1399–423.

164   *References*

Emsley, Clive (1983): *Policing and Its Context, 1750–1870.* London: Macmillan.

Emsley, Clive, & Barbara Weinberger (1991): eds., *Policing in Western Europe: Politics, Professionalism, and Public Order, 1850–1940.* New York: Greenwood.

Epstein, James A. (1994): *Radical Expression: Political Language, Ritual, and Symbol in England, 1790–1850.* New York: Oxford University Press.

Farrell, Sean (2000): *Rituals and Riots: Sectarian Violence and Political Culture in Ulster, 1784–1886.* Lexington: University Press of Kentucky.

Favre, Pierre (1990): ed., *La Manifestation.* Paris: Presses de la Fondation Nationale des Sciences Politiques.

Fendrich, James Max (2003): "The Forgotten Movement: The Vietnam Antiwar Movement." *Sociological Inquiry* 73: 338–58.

Fillieule, Olivier (1997a): *Stratégies de la rue: Les manifestations en France.* Paris: Presses de la Fondation Nationale des Sciences Politiques. (1997b): "Maintien de l'ordre." Special issue of *Cahiers de la Sécurité Intérieure.*

Fredrickson, George M. (1997): *The Comparative Imagination: On the History of Racism, Nationalism, and Social Movements.* Berkeley: University of California Press.

Frey, Bruno, & Alois Stutzer (2002): *Happiness and Economics: How the Economy and Institutions Affect Well-Being.* Princeton, N.J.: Princeton University Press.

Gaillard, Jeanne (1971): *Communes de Province, Commune de Paris 1870–1871.* Paris: Flammarion.

Gamson, William A. (1990): *The Strategy of Social Protest,* 2d ed. Belmont, Calif.: Wadsworth.

Gans, Herbert J. (2003): *Democracy and the News.* Oxford: Oxford University Press.

Geddes, Barbara (1999): "What Do We Know about Democratization after Twenty Years?" *Annual Review of Political Science* 2: 115–44.

Gildea, Robert (2002): *Marianne in Chains: In Search of the German Occupation 1940–45.* London: Macmillan.

Gilje, Paul A. (1987): *The Road to Mobocracy: Popular Disorder in New York City, 1763–1834.* Chapel Hill: University of North Carolina Press. (1996): *Rioting in America.* Bloomington: Indiana University Press.

Gilliard, Charles (1955): *A History of Switzerland.* London: George Allen & Unwin.

Gitlin, Todd (1980): *The Whole World Is Watching: Mass Media in the Making and Unmaking of the New Left.* Berkeley: University of California Press.

Giugni, Marco G., Doug McAdam, & Charles Tilly (1998): eds., *From Contention to Democracy.* Lanham, Md.: Rowman & Littlefield.

Glasius, Marlies, Mary Kaldor, & Helmut Anheier (2002): eds., *Global Civil Society 2002.* Oxford: Oxford University Press.

Glen, Robert (1984): *Urban Workers in the Early Industrial Revolution.* London: Croom Helm.

Glenn, John K., III (2001): *Framing Democracy: Civil Society and Civic Movements in Eastern Europe.* Stanford, Calif.: Stanford University Press.

Goldstein, Robert J. (1983): *Political Repression in Nineteenth-Century Europe.* London: Croom Helm. (2000): ed., *The War for the Public Mind: Political Censorship in Nineteenth-Century Europe.* Westport, Conn.: Praeger. (2001): *Political Repression in Modern America from 1870 to 1976.* Urbana: University of Illinois Press.

Goldstone, Jack A. (2003): "Introduction: Bridging Institutionalized and Noninstitutionalized Politics." In Jack A. Goldstone, ed., *States, Parties, and Social Movements.* Cambridge: Cambridge University Press.

González Calleja, Eduardo (1998): *La Razón de la Fuerza: Orden público, subversion y violencia política en la España de la Restauración (1875–1917).* Madrid: Consejo Superior de Investigaciones Científicas. (1999): *El Máuser y el Sufragio: Ordén público, subversión y violencia política en la crisis de la Restauración.* Madrid: Consejo Superior de Investigaciones Científicas.

Goodway, David (1982): *London Chartism 1838–1848.* Cambridge: Cambridge University Press.

Gossman, Lionel (2000): *Basel in the Age of Burkhardt: A Study in Unseasonable Ideas.* Chicago: University of Chicago Press.

Granjon, Fabien (2002): "Les répertoires d'action télémathiques du néo-militantisme." *Le Mouvement Social* 200: 11–32.

Greenberg, Louis (1971): *Sisters of Liberty: Paris, Marseille, Lyon and the Reaction to the Centralized State.* Cambridge, Mass.: Harvard University Press.

Grimsted, David (1998): *American Mobbing, 1828–1861: Toward Civil War.* New York: Oxford University Press.

Gurr, Ted Robert (2000): *Peoples Versus States: Minorities at Risk in the New Century.* Washington, D.C.: United States Institute of Peace Press.

Gusfield, Joseph R. (1966): *Symbolic Crusade: Status Politics and the American Temperance Movement.* Urbana: University of Illinois Press.

Gwertzman, Bernard, & Michael T. Kaufman (1991): eds., *The Collapse of Communism,* rev. ed. New York: Times Books.

Hanagan, Michael (1998): "Irish Transnational Social Movements, Deterritorialized Migrants, and the State System: The Last One Hundred and Forty Years." *Mobilization* 13: 107–26. (2002): "Irish Transnational Social Movements, Migrants, and the State System." In Jackie Smith & Hank Johnston, eds., *Globalization and Resistance: Transnational Dimensions of Social Movements.* Lanham, Md.: Rowman & Littlefield.

Harare Daily News (2002): "Civil Society Needs to Build a Social Movement" (editorial). Copied from online version 23 June 2003.

Haythornthwaite, Caroline, & Barry Wellman (2002): "The Internet in Everyday Life: An Introduction." in Caroline Haythornthwaite & Barry Wellman, eds., *The Internet in Everyday Life.* Malden, Mass.: Blackwell.

Heberle, Rudolf (1951): *Social Movements: An Introduction to Political Sociology.* New York: Appleton-Century-Crofts.

Hertzberg, Hendrik (2003): "Radio Daze." *The New Yorker,* August 11: 23–24.

Hinde, Wendy (1992): *Catholic Emancipation: A Shake to Men's Minds.* Oxford: Blackwell.

Hobsbawm, E. J. (1975): *The Age of Capital, 1848–1875.* London: Weidenfeld & Nicolson. (1988): *The Age of Imperialism.* New York: Pantheon. (1994): *The Age of Extremes: A History of the World, 1914–1991.* New York: Pantheon.

Hocke, Peter (2002): *Massenmedien und lokaler Protest: Eine empirische Fallstudie zur Medienselektivität in einer westdeutschen Begwegungshochberg.* Wiesbaden: Westdeutscher Verlag.

Hoerder, Dirk (1977): *Crowd Action in Revolutionary Massachusetts, 1765–1780.* New York: Academic Press.

Hoffmann, Stefan-Ludwig (2003): "Democracy and Associations in the Long Nineteenth Century: Toward a Transnational Perspective." *Journal of Modern History* 75: 269–99.

Homer News (2003a): "Support for Soldiers." HomerNews.com, 13 March. (2003b): "War Prompts Street Demonstrations." HomerNews.com, 3 April. (2003c): "Pro-Troops Demonstrators to Rally Again This Week." HomerNews.com, 3 April.

Honacker, Karin van (1994): *Lokaal Verzet en Oproer in de 17de en 18de Eeuw: Collectieve Acties tegen het centraal gezag in Brussel, Antwerpen en Leuven.* Heule: UGA. (2000): "Résistance locale et émeutes dans les chef-villes brabançonnes aux XVIIe et XVIIIe siècles." *Revue d'Histoire Moderne et Contemporaine* 47: 37–68.

Huggins, Martha Knisely (1985): *From Slavery to Vagrancy in Brazil.* New Brunswick: Rutgers University Press. (1998): *Policing: The United States and Latin America.* Durham, N.C.: Duke University Press.

Human Rights Watch (1999): *Kazakhstan: Human Rights Developments. www.hrw.org/ hrw/worldreport99/europe/kazakstan.* (2000): *World Report 2000.* New York: Human Rights Watch.

Hunt, Lynn (1978): *Revolution and Urban Politics in Provincial France: Troyes and Reims, 1786–1790.* Stanford, Calif.: Stanford University Press. (1984): *Politics, Culture, and Class in the French Revolution.* Berkeley: University of California Press.

Husung, Hans-Gerhard (1983): *Protest und Repression im Vormärz: Norddeutschland zwischen Restauration und Revolution.* Göttingen: Vandenhoeck & Ruprecht.

Ibarra, Pedro (2003): ed., *Social Movements and Democracy.* New York: Palgrave Macmillan.

Ibarra, Pedro, & Benjamín Tejerina (1998): eds., *Los movimientos sociales: Transformaciones políticas y cambio cultural.* Madrid: Trotta.

Imig, Doug, & Sidney Tarrow (2001): "Mapping the Europeanization of Contention: Evidence from a Quantitative Data Analysis." In Doug Imig & Sidney Tarrow, eds., *Contentious Europeans: Protest and Politics in an Emerging Polity.* Lanham, Md.: Rowman & Littlefield.

Inkeles, Alex (1991): ed., *On Measuring Democracy, Its Consequences and Concomitants.* New Brunswick: Transaction.

International Viewpoint (1997): "Building a European Social Movement." 6 November, copied from online version 23 June 2003.

Jackson, Julian (2001): *France: The Dark Years, 1940–1944.* Oxford: Oxford University Press.

Jameson, J. Franklin (1956): *The American Revolution Considered as a Social Movement.* Boston: Beacon. First published in 1926.

Jarman, Neil (1997): *Material Conflicts: Parades and Visual Displays in Northern Ireland.* Oxford: Berg.

Jessen, Ralph (1994): "Polizei, Wohlfahrt und die Anfänge des modernen Sozialstaats in Preussen während des Kaiserreichs." *Geschichte und Gesellschaft* 20: 157–80.

Johnson, Gordon (1996): *Cultural Atlas of India.* New York: Facts on File.

Jones, Peter (2003): *Liberty and Locality in Revolutionary France: Six Villages Compared, 1760–1820.* Cambridge: Cambridge University Press.

Kaiser, Robert J. (1994): *The Geography of Nationalism in Russia and the USSR.* Princeton, N.J.: Princeton University Press.

Kakar, Sudhir (1996): *The Colors of Violence: Cultural Identities, Religion, and Conflict.* Chicago: University of Chicago Press.

Kaplan, Temma (1992): *Red City, Blue Period: Social Movements in Picasso's Barcelona.* Berkeley: University of California Press.

Karatnycky, Adrian (2000): ed., *Freedom in the World: The Annual Survey of Political Rights and Civil Liberties.* Piscataway, N.J.: Transaction.

Kaufman, Jason (2002): *For the Common Good? American Civic Life and the Golden Age of Fraternity.* New York: Oxford University Press.

Kazakhstan (2003): "The Constitution of the Republic of Kazakhstan." www.president.kz/ articles/stat.

Keck, Margaret, & Kathryn Sikkink (1998): *Activists beyond Borders: Advocacy Networks in International Politics.* Ithaca, N.Y.: Cornell University Press. (2000): "Historical Precursors to Modern Transnational Social Movements and Networks." In John A. Guidry, Michael D. Kennedy, & Mayer N. Zald, eds., *Globalizations and Social Movements: Culture, Power, and the Transnational Public Sphere.* Ann Arbor: University of Michigan Press.

Khazanov, Anatoly M. (1995): *After the USSR: Ethnicity, Nationalism, and Politics in the Commonwealth of Independent States.* Madison: University of Wisconsin Press.

Kinealy, Christine (2003): "Les marches orangistes en Irlande du Nord: Histoire d'un droit." *Le Mouvement Social* 202: 165–82.

Klausen, Kurt Klaudi, & Flemming Mikkelsen (1988): *Konflikter, Kollektive Aktioner og Protestbevaegelser i Danmark.* Copenhagen: Samfunds Fagsnyt.

Kohn, Hans (1956): *Nationalism and Liberty: The Swiss Example.* London: George Allen & Unwin.

Koopmans, Ruud (2004): "Movements and Media: Selection Processes and Evolutionary Dynamics in the Public Sphere." *Theory and Society,* forthcoming.

Koshar, Rudy (1986): *Social Life, Local Politics, and Nazism: Marburg, 1880–1935.* Chapel Hill: University of North Carolina Press.

Kriesi, Hanspeter, Ruud Koopmans, Jan Willem Duyvendak, & Marco Giugni (1995): *New Social Movements in Western Europe: A Comparative Analysis.* Minneapolis: University of Minnesota Press.

Kriesi, Hanspeter, René Levy, Gilbert Ganguillet, & Heinz Zwicky (1981): *Politische Aktivierung in der Schweiz, 1945–1978.* Diessenhofen: Verlag Rüegger.

Kuczynski, Jürgen (1967a): *Darstellung der Lage der Arbeiter in Frankreich von 1789 bis 1848.* Berlin: Akademie Verlag. (1967b): *Darstellung der Lage der Arbeiter in Frankreich seit 1848.* Berlin: Akademie Verlag.

Laitin, David (1998): *Identity in Formation: The Russian-Speaking Populations in the Near Abroad.* Ithaca, N.Y.: Cornell University Press. (1999): "The Cultural Elements of Ethnically Mixed States: Nationality Re-formation in the Soviet Successor States." In George Steinmetz, ed., *State/Culture: State Formation after the Cultural Turn.* Ithaca, N.Y.: Cornell University Press.

Landa, Janet Tai (1994): *Trust, Ethnicity, and Identity: Beyond the New Institutional Economics of Ethnic Trading Networks, Contract Law, and Gift-Exchange.* Ann Arbor: University of Michigan Press.

Le Monde (2001): *Bilan du Monde.* Paris: Le Monde.

Lepetit, Bernard (1982): "Fonction administrative et armature urbaine: Remarques sur la distribution des chefs-lieux de subdélégation en France à l'Ancien Régime." In Institut d'Histoire Economique et Sociale de l'Université de Paris I, *Recherches et Travaux* 2: 19–34. (1988): *Les villes dans la France moderne (1740–1840).* Paris: Albin Michel.

Levi, Margaret, & Laura Stoker (2000): "Political Trust and Trustworthiness." *Annual Review of Political Science* 3: 475–508.

Liang, Hsi-Huey (1992): *The Rise of Modern Police and the European State System from Metternich to the Second World War.* Cambridge: Cambridge University Press.

Lida, Clara E. (1972): *Anarquismo y Revolución en la España del XIX.* Madrid: Siglo XXI.

Lijphart, Arend (1999): *Patterns of Democracy: Government Forms and Performance in Thirty-Six Countries.* New Haven, Conn.: Yale University Press.

Lindenberger, Thomas (1995): *Strassenpolitik: Zur Sozialgeschichte der öffentlichen Ordnung in Berlin 1900 bis 1914.* Bonn: Dietz.

López-Alves, Fernando (2000): *State Formation and Democracy in Latin America, 1810–1900.* Durham, N.C.: Duke University Press.

Lüdtke, Alf (1989): *Police and State in Prussia, 1815–1850.* Cambridge: Cambridge University Press. (1992): *"Sicherheit" und "Wohlfahrt": Polizei, Gesellschaft und Herrschaft im 19. und 20. Jahrhundert.* Frankfurt: Suhrkamp.

Lundqvist, Sven (1977): *Folkrörelserna i det svenska samhället, 1850–1920.* Stockholm: Almqvist & Wiksell.

Madan, T. N. (1997): "Religion, Ethnicity, and Nationalism in India." In Martin E. Marty and R. Scott Appleby, eds., *Religion, Ethnicity, and Self-Identity: Nations in Turmoil.* Hanover, N.H.: University Press of New England/Salzburg Seminar.

Maier, Pauline (1972): *From Resistance to Revolution: Colonial Radicals and the Development of American Opposition to Britain, 1765–1776.* New York: Vintage.

Mamdani, Mahmood, & Ernest Wamba-dia-Wamba (1995): eds., *African Studies in Social Movements and Democracy.* Dakar: CODESRIA.

Mann, Michael (1988): *States, War and Capitalism: Studies in Political Sociology.* Oxford: Blackwell.

Margadant, Ted (1992): *Urban Rivalries in the French Revolution.* Princeton, N.J.: Princeton University Press.

Markoff, John (1996a): *The Abolition of Feudalism: Peasants, Lords, and Legislators in the French Revolution.* University Park: Pennsylvania State University Press. (1996b): *Waves of Democracy: Social Movements and Political Change.* Thousand Oaks, Calif.: Pine Grove Press.

Marx, Karl, & Frederick Engels (1958): *Selected Works.* 2 vols. Moscow: Foreign Languages Publishing House.

McAdam, Doug, Sidney Tarrow, and Charles Tilly (2001): *Dynamics of Contention.* Cambridge: Cambridge University Press.

McCammon, Holly J., & Karen E. Campbell (2002): "Allies on the Road to Victory: Coalition Formation between the Suffragists and the Women's Christian Temperance Union." *Mobilization* 7: 231–52.

McCarthy, John D., Clark McPhail, & Jackie Smith (1996): "Images of Protest: Estimating Selection Bias in Media Coverage of Washington Demonstrations 1982 and 1991." *American Sociological Review* 61: 478–99.

McFaul, Michael (1997): "Russia's Rough Ride." In Larry Diamond, Marc F. Plattner, Yun-han Chu, & Hung-mao Tien, eds., *Consolidating the Third Wave Democracies: Regional Challenges.* Baltimore: Johns Hopkins University Press.

McKivigan, John R., & Stanley Harrold (1999): eds., *Antislavery Violence: Sectional, Racial, and Cultural Conflict in Antebellum America.* Knoxville: University of Tennessee Press.

McPhee, Peter (1988): "Les formes d'intervention populaire en Roussillon: L'exemple de Collioure, 1789–1815." In *Centre d'Histoire Contemporaine du Languedoc Méditerranéen et du Roussillon: Les pratiques politiques en province à l'époque de la Révolution française.* Montpellier: Publications de la Recherche, Université de Montpellier.

Mendle, Michael (2001): ed., *The Putney Debates of 1647: The Army, the Levellers, and the English State.* Cambridge: Cambridge University Press.

Meyer, David S., & Sidney Tarrow (1998): eds., *The Social Movement Society: Contentious Politics for a New Century.* Lanham, Md.: Rowman & Littlefield.

Mihalisko, Kathleen J. (1997): "Belarus: Retreat to Authoritarianism." In Karen Dawisha

& Bruce Parrott, eds., *Democratic Changes and Authoritarian Reactions in Russia, Ukraine, Belarus, and Moldova.* Cambridge: Cambridge University Press.

Mikkelsen, Flemming (1986): ed., *Protest og Oprør.* Aarhus: Modtryk.

Miller, Judith, & Steve Levine (1999): "To Appease U.S., Kazakh Acts on MIG Sales." *New York Times* (12 September): A6.

Mirala, Petri (2000): "'A Large Mob, Calling Themselves Freemasons': Masonic Parades in Ulster." In Peter Jupp & Eoin Magennis, eds., *Crowds in Ireland, c. 1720–1920.* London: Macmillan.

Monjardet, Dominique (1996): *Ce que fait la police: Sociologie de la force publique.* Paris: La Découverte.

Montgomery, David (1993): *Citizen Worke: The Experience of Workers in the United States with Democracy and the Free Market during the Nineteenth Century.* Cambridge: Cambridge University Press.

Morgan, Edmund S. (1988): *Inventing the People: The Rise of Popular Sovereignty in England and America.* New York: Norton.

Morison, Samuel Eliot (1965): *Oxford History of the American People.* New York: Oxford University Press.

Munger, Frank (1979): "Measuring Repression of Popular Protest by English Justices of the Peace in the Industrial Revolution." *Historical Methods* 12: 76–83. (1981): "Suppression of Popular Gatherings in England, 1800–1830." *American Journal of Legal History* 25: 111–40.

Mustafa, Sabir (2002): "Diarrhoea Control Becomes a Social Movement in Bangladesh." *www.rehydrate.org/darrhoea /control_in_bangladesh.htm,* copied 23 June 2003.

Nabholz, Hans, Leonhard von Muralt, Richard Feller, & Edgar Bonjour (1938): *Geschichte der Schweiz.* 2 vols. Zurich: Schultheiss & Co.

Nahaylo, Bohdan, & Victor Swoboda (1990): *Soviet Disunion: A History of the Nationalities Problem in the USSR.* New York: Free Press

Nelson, Joan M., Charles Tilly, & Lee Walker (1998): eds., *Transforming Post-Communist Political Economies.* Washington, D.C.: National Academy Press.

Nicolas, Jean (1985): ed., *Mouvements populaires et conscience sociale, XVIe–XIXe siècles.* Paris: Maloine.

O'Ferrall, Fergus (1985): *Catholic Emancipation: Daniel O'Connell and the Birth of Irish Democracy 1820–30.* Dublin: Gill & Macmillan.

Öhngren, Bo (1974): *Folk i rörelse: Samhällsutveckling, flyttningsmonster och folkrörelser i Eskilstuna 1870–1900.* Uppsala: Almqvist & Wicksell.

Olcott, Martha Brill (1997): "Democratization and the Growth of Political Participation in Kazakhstan." In Karen Dawisha & Bruce Parrott, eds., *Conflict, Cleavage, and Change in Central Asia and the Caucasus.* Democratization and Authoritarianism in Postcommunist Societies: 4. Cambridge: Cambridge University Press.

Oliver, Pamela E., & Gregory M. Maney (2000): "Political Processes and Local Newspaper Coverage of Protest Events: From Selection Bias to Triadic Interactions." *American Journal of Sociology* 106: 463–505.

Oliver, Pamela E., & Daniel J. Myers (1999): "How Events Enter the Public Sphere: Conflict, Location, and Sponsorship in Local Newspaper Coverage of Public Events." *American Journal of Sociology* 105: 38–87.

Ozouf-Marignier, Marie-Vic (1986): "De l'universalisme constituant aux intérêts locaux: Le débat sur la formation des départements en France (1789–1790)." *Annales: Economies, Sociétés, Civilisations* 41: 1193–214.

Paige, Jeffery M. (1997): *Coffee and Power: Revolution and the Rise of Democracy in Central America*. Cambridge, Mass.: Harvard University Press.

Palmer, Stanley H. (1988): *Police and Protest in England and Ireland 1780–1850*. Cambridge: Cambridge University Press.

Paxton, Robert O. (1995): "Leçon sur les fascismes." *Vingtième Siècle* 45: 3–13.

Pérez-Stable, Marifeli (1993): *The Cuban Revolution: Origins, Course, and Legacy*. New York: Oxford University Press.

Perry, Elizabeth J. (2002): *Challenging the Mandate of Heaven: Social Protest and State Power in China*. Armonk, N.Y.: M. E. Sharpe.

Pettifor, Ann (2001): "Why Jubilee 2000 Made an Impact." In Helmut Anheier, Marlies Glasius, & Mary Kaldor, eds., *Global Civil Society 2001*. Oxford: Oxford University Press.

Philippine Star (2001): multiple articles, 17–23 January 2001. *www.philstar.com*, viewed 20 August 2003.

Pigenet, Michel, & Danielle Tartakowsky (2003): eds., "Les marches." *Le mouvement social* 202, January–March.

Porta, Donatella della (1995): *Social Movements, Political Violence, and the State: A Comparative Analysis of Italy and Germany*. Cambridge: Cambridge University Press.

Porta, Donatella della, & Herbert Reiter (1998): eds., *Policing Protest: The Control of Mass Demonstrations in Western Democracies*. Minneapolis: University of Minnesota Press.

Price, Richard (1986): *Labour in British Society: An Interpretive History*. London: Croom Helm.

Prothero, Iowerth (1979): *Artisans and Politics in Early Nineteenth-Century London: John Gast and His Times*. Folkestone: Dawson. (1997): *Radical Artisans in England and France, 1830–1970*. Cambridge: Cambridge University Press.

Przeworski, Adam, Michael Alvarez, José Antonio Cheibub, & Fernando Limongi (2000): *Democracy and Development: Political Institutions and Well-Being in the World, 1950–1990*. Cambridge: Cambridge University Press.

Radio Free Europe (1999): "Kazakhstan: President Meets Challenge of Growing Discontent." www.rferl.org/nca/features/1999/07/F.RU.990701133005.

Rafael, Vicente (2003): "The Cell Phone and the Crowd: Messianic Politics in the Contemporary Philippines." *Public Culture* 15: 399–425.

Ray, Raka, & A. C. Korteweg (1999): "Women's Movements in the Third World: Identity, Mobilization, and Autonomy." *Annual Review of Sociology* 25: 47–71.

Remak, Joachim (1993): *A Very Civil War: The Swiss Sonderbund War of 1847*. Boulder: Westview.

Rheingold, Howard (2003): *Smart Mobs: The Next Social Revolution*. New York: Perseus.

Riles, Annelise (2000): *The Network Inside Out*. Ann Arbor: University of Michigan Press.

Robert, Vincent (1996): *Les chemins de la manifestation, 1848–1914*. Lyon: Presses Universitaires de Lyon.

Rock, David (1987): *Argentina 1516–1987*. Berkeley: University of California Press.

Rucht, Dieter (2003): "Media Strategies and Media Resonance in Transnational Protest Campaigns." Unpublished paper presented to conference on Transnational Processes and Social Movements, Bellagio, Italy.

Rude, Fernand (1969): *L'Insurrection lyonnaise de novembre 1831: Le mouvement ouvrier à Lyon de 1827–1832*. Paris: Anthropos.

Rudé, George (1962): *Wilkes and Liberty*. Oxford: Clarendon Press. (1971): *Hanoverian London, 1714–1808*. London: Secker & Warburg.

Ryan, Mary P. (1997): *Civic Wars: Democracy and Public Life in the American City during the Nineteenth Century.* Berkeley: University of California Press.

Sabato, Hilda (2001): *The Many and the Few: Political Participation in Republican Buenos Aires.* Stanford, Calif.: Stanford University Press.

Sanders, Elizabeth (1999): *Roots of Reform: Farmers, Workers, and the American State 1877–1917.* Chicago: University of Chicago Press.

Sassen, Saskia (2002): "Toward a Sociology of Information Technology." *Current Sociology* 50: 29–52.

Scalmer, Sean (2002a): *Dissent Events: Protest, the Media and the Political Gimmick in Australia.* Sydney: University of New South Wales Press. (2002b): "The Labor of Diffusion: The Peace Pledge Union and the Adaptation of the Gandhian Repertoire." *Mobilization* 7: 269–85.

Schama, Simon (1977): *Patriots and Liberators: Revolution in the Netherlands 1780–1813.* London: Collins.

Schultz, Patrick (1982): *La décentralisation administrative dans le département du Nord (1790–1793).* Lille: Presses Universitaires de Lille.

Scott, James C. (1985): *Weapons of the Weak.* New Haven, Conn.: Yale University Press.

Seip, Jens Arup (1974, 1981): *Utsikt over Norges Historie.* 2 vols. Oslo: Gylendal Norsk Forlag.

Seligman, Adam (1997): *The Problem of Trust.* Princeton, N.J.: Princeton University Press.

Service, Robert F. (2003): "'Combat Biology' on the Klamath." *Science* 300, 4 April, 36–39.

SIPRI [Stockholm International Peace Research Institute] (2001): *SIPRI Yearbook 2001: Armaments, Disarmament and International Security.* Oxford: Oxford University Press.

Skidmore, Thomas E., & Peter H. Smith (1984): *Modern Latin America.* New York: Oxford University Press.

Skocpol, Theda (1992): *Protecting Soldiers and Mothers: The Political Origins of Social Policy in the United States.* Cambridge, Mass.: Harvard University Press. (1999): "How Americans Became Civic." In Theda Skocpol & Morris P. Fiorina, eds., *Civic Engagement in American Democracy.* Washington, D.C.: Brookings Institution Press & New York: Russell Sage Foundation.

Smith, Adam (1910): *The Wealth of Nations.* 2 vols. London: Dent. First published in 1776.

Smith, Graham, Vivien Law, Andrew Wilson, Annette Bohr, & Edward Allworth (1998): *Nation-Building in the Post-Soviet Borderlands: The Politics of National Identity.* Cambridge: Cambridge University Press.

Smith, Jackie (1997): "Characteristics of the Modern Transnational Social Movement Sector." In Jackie Smith, Charles Chatfield, & Ron Pagnucco, eds., *Transnational Social Movements and Global Politics: Solidarity Beyond the State.* Syracuse: Syracuse University Press. (2002): "Globalizing Resistance: The Battle of Seattle and the Future of Social Movements." In Jackie Smith & Hank Johnston, eds., *Globalization and Resistance: Transnational Dimensions of Social Movements.* Lanham, Md.: Rowman & Littlefield. (2003): "Exploring Connections between Global Integration and Political Mobilization." *Journal of World Systems Research,* forthcoming.

Stein, Lorenz von (1959): *Geschichte der sozialen Bewegung in Frankreich von 1789 bis auf unsere Tage.* Hiledesheim: Georg Olms.

Steinberg, Jonathan (1996): *Why Switzerland?* 2d ed. Cambridge: Cambridge University Press.

Stenius, Henrik (1987): *Frivilligt, Jämlikt, Samfällt: Föreningsväsendets utveckling I Finland fram till 1900–talets början med speciell hänsyn till massorganisationsprincipens genombrott*. Helsinki: Svenska Litteratursällskapet I Finland.

Storch, Robert D. (1976): "The Policeman as Domestic Missionary: Urban Discipline and Popular Culture in Northern England, 1850–1880." *Journal of Social History* 9: 481–509.

Stutzer, Alois, & Bruno Frey (2002): "What Can Economists Learn from Happiness Research?" *Journal of Economic Literature* 40: 402–35.

Suny, Ronald Grigor (1993): *The Revenge of the Past: Nationalism, Revolution, and the Collapse of the Soviet Union*. Stanford, Calif.: Stanford University Press. (1995): "Ambiguous Categories: States, Empires, and Nations." *Post-Soviet Affairs* 11: 185–96.

Suri, Jeremy (2003): *Power and Protest: Global Revolution and the Rise of Détente*. Cambridge, Mass.: Harvard University Press.

Tambiah, Stanley J. (1996): *Leveling Crowds: Ethnonationalist Conflicts and Collective Violence in South Asia*. Berkeley: University of California Press.

Tarrow, Sidney (1989): *Democracy and Disorder: Protest and Politics in Italy 1965–1975*. Oxford: Clarendon Press. (1996): "Movimenti politici e sociali." *Enciclopedia delle Scienze Sociali*, vol. 6: 97–114. (1998): *Power in Movement*, 2d ed. Cambridge: Cambridge University Press. (2002): "From Lumping to Splitting: Specifying Globalization and Resistance." In Jackie Smith & Hank Johnston, eds., *Globalization and Resistance: Transnational Dimensions of Social Movements*. Lanham, Md.: Rowman & Littlefield. (2003): "The New Transnational Contention: Social Movements and Institutions in Complex Internationalism." Working Paper 2003.1, Transnational Contention Project, Cornell University.

Tartakowsky, Danielle (1997): *Les Manifestations de rue en France, 1918–1968*. Paris: Publications de la Sorbonne. (1999): *Nous irons chanter sur vos tombes: Le Père-Lachaise, XIXe–XXe siècle*. Paris: Aubier.

Temperley, Howard (1981): "The Ideology of Antislavery." In David Eltis & James Walvin, eds., *The Abolition of the Atlantic Slave Trade: Origins and Effects in Europe, Africa, and the Americas*. Madison: University of Wisconsin Press.

Thompson, Dorothy (1984): *The Chartists: Popular Politics in the Industrial Revolution*. New York: Pantheon.

Thompson, E. P. (1972): "Rough Music: Le Charivari anglais." *Annales; Economies Sociétés, Civilisations* 27: 285–312. (1991): *Customs in Common*. London: Merlin Press.

Thompson, Ginger (2003): "Protesters Swarm the Streets at W.T.O. Forum in Cancún." *New York Times*, online edition, 14 September.

Tilly, Charles (1962): "Rivalités de bourgs et conflits de partis dans les Mauges." *Revue du Bas-Poitou et des Provinces de l'Ouest*, no. 4 (July–August): 3–15. (1983): "Speaking Your Mind without Elections, Surveys, or Social Movements." *Public Opinion Quarterly* 47: 461–78. (1984): "Demographic Origins of the European Proletariat." In David Levine, ed., *Proletarianization and Family Life*. Orlando, Fla.: Academic Press. (1986): *The Contentious French*. Cambridge, Mass.: Harvard University Press. (1995): *Popular Contention in Great Britain, 1758–1834*. Cambridge, Mass.: Harvard University Press. (1997): "Parliamentarization of Popular Contention in Great Britain, 1758–1834." *Theory and Society* 26: 245–73. (1998): *Durable Inequality*. Berkeley: University of California Press. (1999): "Conclusion: Why Worry about Citizenship?" In Michael Hanagan & Charles Tilly, eds., *Extending Citizenship, Reconfiguring States*. Lanham, Md.: Rowman & Littlefield. (2001a): "Mechanisms in Political Processes."

Annual Review of Political Science 4: 21–41. (2001b): "Historical Analysis of Political Processes." In Jonathan H. Turner, ed., *Handbook of Sociological Theory.* New York: Kluwer/Plenum. (2002a): *Stories, Identities, and Political Change.* Lanham, Md.: Rowman & Littlefield. (2002b): "Event Catalogs as Theories." *Sociological Theory* 20: 248–54 (2003): *The Politics of Collective Violence.* Cambridge: Cambridge University Press. (2004): *Contention and Democracy in Europe, 1650–2000.* Cambridge: Cambridge University Press.

Tilly, Charles, Louise Tilly, & Richard Tilly (1975): *The Rebellious Century, 1830–1930.* Cambridge: Harvard University Press.

Tilly, Charles, & Lesley Wood (2003): "Contentious Connections in Great Britain, 1828–1834." In Mario Diani & Doug McAdam, eds., *Social Movements and Networks: Relational Approaches to Collective Action.* New York: Oxford University Press.

Tilly, Richard (1980): *Kapital, Staat und sozialer Protest in der deutschen Industrialisierung.* Göttingen: Vandenhoeck & Ruprecht.

Time Asia (2001): "People Power Redux." *www.tim.com/time/asia/magazine/2001/0129.* Copied from online version 14 August 2003.

Titarenko, Larissa, John D. McCarthy, Clark McPhail, & Boguslaw Augustyn (2001): "The Interaction of State Repression, Protest Form and Protest Sponsor Strength during the Transition from Communism in Minsk, Belarus, 1990–1995." *Mobilization* 6: 129–50.

Tocqueville, Alexis de (1983): *Correspondance d'Alexis de Tocqueville et de Francisque de Corcelle.* Paris: Gallimard. Oeuvres Complètes, t. XV.

Torpey, John (2000): *The Invention of the Passport: Surveillance, Citizenship and the State.* Cambridge: Cambridge University Press.

Touraine, Alain (1968): *Le Mouvement de Mai ou le Communisme Utopique.* Paris: Seuil.

Touraine, Alain, François Dubet, Michel Wieviorka, & Jan Strzelecki (1982): *Solidarité: Analyse d'un mouvement social: Pologne 1980–1981.* Paris: Fayard.

Trechsel, Alexander (2000): *Feuerwerk Volksrechte: Die Volksabstimmungen in den scheizerischen Kantonen 1970–1996.* Basel: Helbing & Lichtenhahn.

Trif, Maria, & Doug Imig (2003): "Demanding to Be Heard: Social Movements and the European Public Sphere." Working Paper 2003–06, Cornell University Workshop on Transnational Contention.

UNDP [United Nations Development Program] (2001): *Human Development Report 2001: Making New Technologies Work for Human Development.* Oxford: Oxford University Press. (2002): *Human Development Report 2002: Deepening Democracy in a Fragmented World.* Oxford: Oxford University Press.

United Nations (1995): *Kazakhstan: The Challenge of Transition: Human Development Report 1995. www.undp.org/undp/rbec/nhdr/Kazakhstan.*

U.S. Department of State (2002): "Bureau of Democracy, Human Rights, and Labor." *Country Reports on Human Rights Practices: Republic of Kazakhstan.* Washington, D.C.: U.S. Department of State.

Uslaner, Eric M. (2002): *The Moral Foundations of Trust.* Cambridge: Cambridge University Press.

van der Veer, Peter (1996): "Riots and Rituals: The Construction of Violence and Public Space in Hindu Nationalism." In Paul R. Brass., ed., *Riots and Pogroms.* New York: New York University Press.

Vanhanen, Tatu (2000): "A New Dataset for Measuring Democracy, 1810–1998." *Journal of Peace Research* 37: 251–65.

Vernon, James (1993): *Politics and the People: A Study in English Political Culture c. 1815–1867.* Cambridge: Cambridge University Press.

Wåhlin, Vagn (1986): "Opposition og statsmagt." In Flemming Mikkelsen, ed., *Protest og Oprør: Kollektive aktioner i Danmark 1700–1985.* Aarhus: Modtryk.

Walton, John, & David Seddon (1994): *Free Markets and Food Riots: The Politics of Global Adjustment.* Oxford: Blackwell.

Walvin, James (1980): "The Rise of British Popular Sentiment for Abolition, 1787–1832." In Christine Bolt and Seymour Drescher, eds., *Anti-Slavery, Religion, and Reform: Essays in Memory of Roger Anstey.* Folkestone: Dawson/Archon. (1981): "The Public Campaign in England against Slavery, 1787–1834." In David Eltis and James Walvin, eds., *The Abolition of Atlantic Slave Trade: Origins and Effects in Europe, Africa, and the Americas.* Madison: University of Wisconsin Press.

Ward, J. T. (1973): *Chartism.* London: B. T. Batsford.

Warren, Mark E. (1999): ed., *Democracy and Trust.* Cambridge: Cambridge University Press.

Wellman, Barry (2000): "Changing Connectivity: A Future History of Y2.03K." *Sociological Research Online* 4, no. 4. (2001a): "Physical Place and CyberPlace: The Rise of Personalized Networking." *International Journal of Urban and Regional Research* 25: 227–52. (2001b): "Does the Internet Increase, Decrease, or Supplement Social Capital? Social Networks, Participation, and Community Commitment." *American Behavioral Scientist* 45: 437–56.

Westhues, Kenneth (1975): "Inter-Generational Conflict in the Sixties." In Samuel D. Clark, J. Paul Grayson, & Linda M. Grayson, eds., *Prophecy and Protest: Social Movements in Twentieth-Century Canada.* Toronto: Gage.

Wignaraja, Ponna (1993): ed., *New Social Movements in the South: Empowering the People.* Atlantic Highlands, N.J.: Zed Books.

Williams, Robin M., Jr. (2003): *The Wars Within: Peoples and States in Conflict.* Ithaca, N.Y.: Cornell University Press.

Wilson, Alex (1970): "Chartism." In J. T. Ward, ed., *Popular Movements c. 1830–1850.* London: Macmillan.

Wilson, Frederick T. (1969): *Federal Aid in Domestic Disturbances 1787–1903.* New York: Arno Press & *New York Times.*

Wimmer, Andreas (2002): *Nationalist Exclusion and Ethnic Conflict: Shadows of Modernity.* Cambridge: Cambridge University Press.

Wirtz, Rainer (1981): *'Widersetzlichkeiten, Excesse, Crawalle, Tumulte und Skandale": Soziale Bewegung und gewalthafter sozialer Protest in Baden 1815–1848.* Frankfurt: Ullstein.

Woloch, Isser (1970): *Jacobin Legacy: The Democratic Movement under the Directory.* Princeton, N.J.: Princeton University Press. (1994): *The New Regime: Transformations of the French Civic Order, 1789–1820s.* New York: Norton.

Wood, Lesley J. (2003): "Breaking the Bank and Taking to the Streets—How Protesters Target Neoliberalism." *Journal of World Systems Research,* forthcoming.

Wyrsch, Paul (1983): *Der Kanton Schwyz äusseres Land 1831–1833.* Lachen: Gutenberg. Schwyzer Hefte, Band 28.

Young, Michael P. (2002): "Confessional Protest: The Religious Birth of U.S. National Social Movements." *American Sociological Review* 67: 660–88.

Zaleski, Eugène (1956): *Mouvements ouvriers et socialistes (Chronologie et bibliographie): La Russie, t. I: 1725–1907.* Paris: Éditions Ouvrières.

Zelizer, Viviana A. (1999): "Multiple Markets: Multiple Cultures." In Neil J. Smelser &

Jeffrey C. Alexander, eds., *Diversity and Its Discontents: Cultural Conflict and Common Ground in Contemporary American Society.* Princeton, N.J.: Princeton University Press. (2004): "Circuits within Capitalism." In Victor Nee & Richard Swedberg, eds., *The Economic Sociology of Capitalism.* Princeton, N.J.: Princeton University Press.

Zhao, Dingxin (2001): *The Power of Tiananmen: State-Society Relations and the 1989 Beijing Student Movement.* Chicago: University of Chicago Press.

Zolberg, Aristide (1978): "Belgium." In Raymond Grew, ed., *Crises of Political Development in Europe and the United States.* Princeton, N.J.: Princeton University Press.

PUBLICATIONS ON SOCIAL MOVEMENTS BY CHARLES TILLY, 1977–2004

1977 "Getting It Together in Burgundy, 1675–1975." *Theory and Society* 4: 479–504.

"Collective Action in England and America, 1765–1775." In Richard Maxwell Brown & Don Fehrenbacher, eds., *Tradition, Conflict, and Modernization: Perspectives on the American Revolution.* New York: Academic Press.

1978 *From Mobilization to Revolution.* Reading, Mass.: Addison-Wesley.

1979 "Repertoires of Contention in America and Britain." In Mayer N. Zald & John D. McCarthy, eds., *The Dynamics of Social Movements.* Cambridge, Mass.: Winthrop.

1981 "The Web of Contention in Eighteenth-Century Cities." In Louise A. Tilly & Charles Tilly, eds., *Class Conflict and Collective Action.* Beverly Hills: Sage.

1982 "Britain Creates the Social Movement." In James Cronin & Jonathan Schneer, eds., *Social Conflict and the Political Order in Modern Britain.* London: Croom Helm.

"Charivaris, Repertoires, and Urban Politics." In John Merriman, ed., *French Cities in the Nineteenth Century.* London: Hutchinson.

1983 "Speaking Your Mind without Elections, Surveys, or Social Movements." *Public Opinion Quarterly* 47: 461–78.

1984 "Social Movements and National Politics." In Charles Bright & Susan Harding, eds., *Statemaking and Social Movements. Essays in History and Theory.* Ann Arbor: University of Michigan Press.

"Les origines du répertoire de l'action collective contemporaine en France et en Grande Bretagne." *Vingtième Siècle* 4: 89–108.

1985 "De Londres (1768) à Paris (1788)." In Jean Nicolas, ed., *Mouvements populaires et conscience sociale: XVIe–XIXe siècles*. Paris: Maloine.

The Contentious French. Cambridge, Mass.: Belknap Press of Harvard University Press.

1988 "Social Movements, Old and New." In Louis Kriesberg, Bronislaw Misztal, & Janusz Mucha, eds., *Social Movements as a Factor of Change in the Contemporary World*. Greenwich, Conn.: JAI Press. Research in Social Movements, Conflicts and Change, vol. 10.

1992 "Réclamer Viva Voce." *Cultures et Conflits* 5: 109–26.

1993 "Contentious Repertoires in Great Britain, 1758–1834." *Social Science History* 17: 253–80. Also in Mark Traugott, ed., *Repertoires and Cycles of Collective Action*. Durham:, N.C.: Duke University Press, 1995.

1994 "Social Movements as Historically Specific Clusters of Political Performances." *Berkeley Journal of Sociology* 38 (1993–94): 1–30.

1995 *Popular Contention in Great Britain, 1758–1834*. Cambridge, Mass.: Harvard University Press.

1997 "Parliamentarization of Popular Contention in Great Britain, 1758–1834." *Theory and Society* 26: 245–73.

1998 "Social Movements and (All Sorts of) Other Political Interactions—Local, National, and International—Including Identities. Several Divagations from a Common Path, Beginning with British Struggles over Catholic Emancipation, 1780–1829, and Ending with Contemporary Nationalism." *Theory and Society* 27: 453–80.

1999 "From Interactions to Outcomes in Social Movements." In Marco Giugni, Doug McAdam, & Charles Tilly, eds., *How Social Movements Matter*. Minneapolis: University of Minnesota Press.

(with Doug McAdam & Sidney Tarrow) *Dynamics of Contention*. Cambridge: Cambridge University Press.

Stories, Identities, and Political Change. Lanham, Md.: Rowman & Littlefield.

2003 "When Do (and Don't) Social Movements Promote Democratization?" In Pedro Ibarra, ed., *Social Movements and Democracy*. New York: Palgrave.

(with Lesley Wood) "Contentious Connections in Great Britain, 1828–1834." In Mario Diani & Doug McAdam, eds., *Social Movements and Networks: Relational Approaches to Collective Action*. New York: Oxford University Press.

"Agendas for Students of Social Movements." In Jack A. Goldstone, ed., *States, Parties, and Social Movements*. Cambridge: Cambridge University Press.

The Politics of Collective Violence. Cambridge: Cambridge University Press.

"Political Identities in Changing Polities." *Social Research* 70: 1301–15.

2004 "WUNC." In Jeffrey T. Schnapp & Matthew Tiews, eds., *Crowds.* Stanford, Calif.: Stanford University Press.

Contention and Democracy in Europe, 1650–2000. Cambridge: Cambridge University Press.

INDEX